The 60's

The Hits and the Trivia

by

Ted Yates

CG Publishing Inc

We acknowledge the financial support of the Government of Canada through the Book Publishing Industry Development Program for our publishing activities.
Published by Collector's Guide Publishing Inc., Box 62034, Burlington, Ontario, Canada, L7R 4K2
Printed and bound in Canada
The 60's The Hits and the Trivia / Ted Yates © 2010 CG Publishing Inc/Ted Yates ISBN 9781-926592-18-3

The 60's

The Hits and the Trivia

by

Ted Yates

Acknowledgements

First of all, I would like to thank my family and friends. I would like to thank my love Alyson for understanding my love for music and commitment to complete this book, despite the long hours during many evenings and weekends, which I spent working on this labor of love.

I would like to thank my mother Patricia for encouraging me through the years and allowing me to play the 60's music as loud as I wanted, downstairs in the Rec room during my teen years.

My sons Ted Jr. and James will hopefully enjoy this music of another era and will appreciate what the 60's gave us musically. My brother Mike and sisters Pat and Jackie were there when we grew up as one happy family growing up on Moberly Avenue in Toronto with the hits of the 60's playing on our radios and record players.

I would like to acknowledge my friends who share the love of the music of the 60's including Sheldon Frymerman, Burt Thombs, Roger Ashby, Peter Murray, Jeff Paul, Nevin Grant, Douglas Roy, Don Hetherington, Jack Peets , Peter Grodde, Phil Warnell, Wolf Schimanski and the many others including all the great people I work with every day at Astral Media Radio in Hamilton.

Thank you to all the great singers, songwriters and producers of the hits of the most exciting decade in pop music, the 60's. Please search and purchase your favorite hits of the 60's now that you'll know what you're looking for. Thanks to all the Record Companies/labels including Capitol, Atlantic, London, Atco, Laurie, MGM, Epic, RCA, Fantasy, Bang, Decca, Uni, Motown, Apple, Columbia, Dot, Electra, Philips, Polydor, Mercury, Dunhill, Monument, Pye, ABC, Date, United Artists, Kama Sutra, Roulette, Stax, A & M, Deram, Fontana, Buddah, Reprise, Liberty, Parrot, Smash, Soul City, Kapp, Imperial, Cadet, Sceptor and all the others.

I would like to thank Robert Godwin of CG Publishing for all his advice and answers to my many questions and to Ric Connors who is great at what he does with marketing and promotion.

Also, thanks to everyone who buys this book.

Contents

Page Chart For Lists By Year

Charts	1969	1968	1967	1966	1965	1964	1963	1962	1961	1960
Top 16 Albums	30	68	93	120	145	179	204	228	260	284
Top Country Hits	31	69	94	121	146	180	205	229	261	285
Top One Hit Wonders	32	70	95	122	147	181	206	230	262	286
Top Lost 45's	33	71	96	123	148	182	207	231	263	287
Top Soul & R&B Hits	34	72	97	124	149	183	208	232	264	288
Top Rock Hits	35	73	98	125	150	-	-	-	-	-
Top Dance Hits	-	-	-	-	-	184	209	233	265	289

INTRODUCTION By Ted Yates

I was 16 when I got hooked on the hits of the 60's. Growing up in Toronto, it was the late summer of '66 when I realized just how much I loved the music. Summer of 1966 hits like 'Summer in the City', 'The Pied Piper', 'Red Rubber Ball' and 'Bus Stop' sounded so great to me. I started buying the new hits on 45 rpm records. I remember the first record I bought was 'Get Away' by Georgie Fame. It was not a big hit, but it sure caught my ears as a wonderful sound. Singles were 66 cents back then and I started buying them with my allowance, and any other money I got from doing chores. When I got a part time job at a grocery store, I started buying upwards of 16 singles a week!

It was also in the summer of 1966 that I got hooked on radio, and the desire to do it as a career. At the age of 16, while visiting the Canadian National Exhibition in Toronto I saw 1050 Chum Radio broadcasting from a trailer just inside the main entrance. After watching the D.J. announcing the songs, I decided that I wanted to do that for a living. With the help of Chum DJ Roger Ashby several years later, my wish came true when I landed my first job in radio in 1973. Today, I'm still doing what I loved to do when I was 16...playing the hits of the 60's. The big difference now, is that I'm doing it on Canada's Number One Oldies station, Oldies 1150 CKOC where I am Morning Show Host, Music Director and Program Director.

You will notice throughout this book that the lists are either 'Top 160', 'Top 116' or 'Top 16'. Why the number 16? First of all, I use the 16 for a couple of reasons. First of all, because this book is all about the 60's, I chose to use the '6'. Secondly, 16 is around the age we are having the time of our lives. For me personally, it was when I realized my true love for the music. It's the age in our lives when music plays an important part as we develop our personal tastes and favorites. We have more free time to enjoy music and generally speaking, we have fewer responsibilities. It's a time in life that is carefree. We connect the music with the good times we are enjoying and sharing with others. The emotional attachment with the music we grew up with, will usually last a lifetime. In a world where the only constant is change, (and it's not always for the better) its nice to know that you can return to the comfort zone whenever you wish. As you read through this book, you will see many great songs you remember, and some you almost forgot about. It's a great source to find and rediscover the songs you'll want to acquire again

The 60's... bring it on...it's all here in one book and it's yours for a lifetime!

This book is all about the music of the 60's, the most exciting decade in the history of popular music! The music from the 60's lives on today everywhere we go. We hear it regularly in movies, TV Shows, commercials, shopping areas and of course, on the radio where we heard it first.

Why is the 60's the most exciting decade in the history of pop music? We had it all.

There were so many new and innovative sounds spanning the decade. We had Beatlemania, Motown, Surf, Hard Rock, Girl Groups, Bubblegum music, Novelty hits, psychedelic sounds, instrumentals, Folk Music, Rock and Roll and Elvis Presley too!

The 60's were like 3 decades in one because of all the musical changes and attitudes.

The early 60's (1960 – 1963) brought us the fun and innocent dance hits like The Twist, The Locomotion, The Swim, The Limbo and many others that got us up on the dance floor back then. It was a time of the hits by the 'Bobby' singers, Vee, Vinton, Rydell, Darin and others. During the early 60's, the Motown sound began and the stage was set for some of the greatest soul hits of the decade. Girl groups like The Shirelles, The Ronettes, The Crystals and The Chiffons flourished in the early 60's. Harmonizing acts like the Beach Boys, Four Seasons and The Tokens had their first hits during the early 60's. The sound of the early 60's was like a decade on its own.

Things changed in early 1964 when the Beatles arrived on the scene. In 1964, Beatlemania created excitement not seen since Elvis Presley came on the scene in 1956. The Beatles brought a new sound and a new look as they spearheaded The British Music Invasion with new acts like The Rolling Stones, Gerry & The Pacemakers, The Animals, Dave Clark Five, Herman's Hermits and many other notable acts. In the period 1964 to 1966, Motown's Supremes, had one number one hit after another and acts like The Temptations, The Four Tops, Marvin Gaye, Stevie Wonder, Martha and The Vandellas among others were all part of the Motown Sound. The Beach Boys were kings of surf and car tunes , while Roy Orbison was on top with Pretty Woman. There was so much more variety back then on our AM radio stations playing all the Top 40 hits of the day. In the 60's, you would see Dean Martin on the same chart as The Beatles, The Supremes, Elvis, Ray Charles and even Roger Miller. Death rock songs like 'Last Kiss' and 'Leader Of The Pack' were rarely absent from the charts during the mid 60's. Music also became more progressive during the mid- sixties with acts like The Yardbirds, The Kinks and The Who.

The period 1967 through 1969 expanded on what hard, heavy and psychedelic music started in the mid-60's with the arrival of Jimi Hendrix, Jefferson Airplane, Deep Purple and The Doors. Flower Power grew in the late 60's with popular hits by Donovan, The Strawberry Alarm Clock and Scott McKenzie's anthem song 'San Francisco' which suggested we wear flowers in our hair. It was such a groovy time.

I have compiled the 60's lists from various sources and influences. The ranking of the 60's lists is based on a combination of chart success on Billboard Pop Charts, RPM (Canada) charts and U.K. charts. The ranking of the 60's hit lists is also influenced by the hits appeal, sales and exposure (sometimes in later years) on radio airplay, films, TV shows and various other media outlets.

Inside this book, you will see that musically the 60's were the most exciting decade in pop music history because we had it all…. And it's yours again!

♫ 60'S! THE HITS &TRIVIA ♫

♫ 1969 in review with the TOP 160 HITS , plus trivia and fascinating facts for all the hits plus a listing of the Top 16 Albums, Country Hits, Soul/R & B, One Hit Wonders, Lost 45's, Rock hits and much more!

♫ 16 'Whatever Became Of' Singers from the 60's

♫ 1968 in review with the TOP 160 HITS , plus trivia and fascinating facts for all the hits plus a listing of the Top 16 Albums, Country Hits, Soul/R & B, One Hit Wonders, Lost 45's, Rock hits and much more!

♫ THE TOP 116 60's Hits by American Artists

♫ 1967 in review with the TOP 160 HITS , plus trivia and fascinating facts for all the hits plus a listing of the Top 16 Albums, Country Hits, Soul/R & B, One Hit Wonders, Lost 45's and much more!

♫ THE TOP 116 60's Hits by British Artists

♫ 1966 in review with the TOP 160 HITS , plus trivia and fascinating facts for all the hits plus a listing of the Top 16 Albums, Country Hits, Soul/R & B, One Hit Wonders, Lost 45's, Rock hits and much more!

♫ THE TOP 116 60's Hits by Canadian Artists

♫ 1965 in review with the TOP 160 HITS , plus trivia and fascinating facts for all the hits plus a listing of the Top 16 Albums, Country Hits, Soul/R & B, One Hit Wonders, Lost 45's, Rock hits and much more!

♫ 16 60's LISTS OF TOP 16 Hits of the decade, Top Artists, Albums, Novelty hits, plus a dozen more Top 16's!

♫ 1964 in review with the TOP 160 HITS , plus trivia and fascinating facts for all the hits plus a listing of the Top 16 Albums, Country Hits, Soul/R & B, One Hit Wonders, Lost 45's, Rock hits and much more!

♫ Find out what was Number one in the 60's on the day today's stars were born!

♫ 1963 in review with the TOP 160 HITS , plus trivia and fascinating facts for all the hits plus a listing of the Top 16 Albums, Country Hits, Soul/R & B, One Hit Wonders, Lost 45's, Dance and party hits and much more!

♫ TOP 60 Remakes of 60's hits in the same decade

♫ 1962 in review with the TOP 160 HITS , plus trivia and fascinating facts for all the hits plus a listing of the Top 16 Albums, Country Hits, Soul/R & B, One Hit Wonders, Lost 45's, Dance and party hits and much more!

♫ TOP 16 Summer in the 60's hits from each summer 1960 through 1969

♫ 1961 in review with the TOP 160 HITS , plus trivia and fascinating facts for all the hits plus a listing of the Top 16 Albums, Country Hits, Soul/R & B, One

Hit Wonders, Lost 45's, Dance and party hits and much more!

♫ Had they lived, how old would these music stars be today?

♫1960 in review with the TOP 160 HITS , plus trivia and fascinating facts for all the hits plus a listing of the Top 16 Albums, Country Hits, Soul/R & B, One Hit Wonders, Lost 45's, Dance and party hits and much more!

♫ **PLUS! Bonus CD! featuring 16 Interviews by the Author with 60's music artists including Del Shannon, Paul Anka, Bo Diddley, Bobby Vinton and more, including an important question answered by Ringo Starr!**

♫ 60'S! ...1969 HITS INSIDE! Find out... ♫

♫ What fictitious group had a multi-million seller in 1969?

♫ This one hit wonder act was produced by the legendary Jimi Hendrix. Any idea who it was?

♫ Graham Nash was turned down by his former group the Hollies to record this song, so instead, it became the first hit for Crosby, Stills & Nash.

♫ Before they were known as Badfinger, this group had a hit under another group name on The Beatles Apple Record Label.

♫ The biggest selling Motown hit of the decade was number one in 1969 by this murdered Motown singer.

♫ There were four top ten hits from this Rock Musical in 1969, including the number one song of the year! Find out what they were!

♫ A few weeks after leaving the Rolling Stones, Brian Jones was found dead in his swimming pool while this hit was number one on the charts.

FIND OUT THAT…and MUCH MORE…INSIDE…1969!

1. **Aquarius/Let the Sunshine In** by the 5th Dimension was a medley of two songs from the rock musical 'Hair'. It was the number one song of the entire year. Five songs from the rock musical 'Hair', written by Rado, Ragni and McDermott charted in 1969.

2. **I Heard It Through The Grapevine** by Marvin Gaye was the biggest selling Motown hit of the 60's. It was number one for almost 2 months. Gladys Knight and The Pips reached number two with the original version two years earlier in 1967.

3. **In The Year 2525** by one hit wonder duo Zager and Evans was a song about the future written 6 years earlier in 1963. It became the biggest one hit wonder act of the 60's.

4. **Get Back** by The Beatles was recorded on Apple Records rooftop along with its 'B' side, '**Don't Let Me Down'**. Billy Preston played keyboards on both recordings. Alan Parsons engineered the Beatles rooftop concert, atop the roof of their 'Apple' building in London.

5. **Sugar Sugar** by The Archies featured Ron Dante on lead vocals. This multi-million seller was written by Andy Kim and Jeff Barry. Among those in the studio at the time of recording were Andy Kim, Toni Wine and Ray Stevens, who helped with the hand clapping.

6. **Honky Tonk Women** by The Rolling Stones was number one at the time Brian Jones was found dead in his swimming pool in the summer of '69, shortly after leaving the group. The 'B' side of this 45 was the superb 'You Can't Always Get What You Want'.

7. **Dizzy** was Tommy Roe's biggest hit , topping the charts for four consecutive weeks. The song was co-written by Freddy Weller who also had a career as a member of Paul Revere & the Raiders, as well as a country singer.

8. **Crimson & Clover** by Tommy James & The Shondells was a progressive psychedelic hit produced by Meco Menardo, best known for his 'Star Wars' instrumental hit in the late 70's.

9. **Na Na Hey Hey Kiss Him Goodbye** was a number one hit by Steam, a One Hit Wonder studio group from N.Y.C. who got their name from something a group member noticed coming out of a manhole cover while exiting the recording studio in the early morning hours after completing this hit. This song was originally intended to be the 'B' side of the single.

10. **Someday We'll Be Together** was the farewell song for Diana Ross as a member of the Supremes. This number one hit was co-written by Johnny Bristol who also was featured vocally on this recording. It was the final number one hit of the decade.

11. **Everyday People** by Sly & the Family Stone was best known for the line 'different strokes for different folks'. It was their biggest number one hit. The 'B' side 'Sing A Simple Song' was also notable.

12. **Wedding Bell Blues** by the 5th Dimension was number one the year group members Marilyn McCoo and Billy Davis Jr. were married. 'Will you marry me Bill' was part of the lyrics delivered by Marilyn McCoo, who sang lead on this number one hit.

13. **Suspicious Minds** was Elvis Presley's last official number one hit. It was written by Mark James, who also wrote the 1969 hit song 'Hooked on a Feeling'.

14. **I Can't Get Next To You** was a number one hit for The Temptations which featured all group members taking turns on lead vocals.

15. **Something/Come Together** were from The Beatles Abbey Road album. 'Something' was George Harrison's first 'A' side as a writer. He also sang lead on this hit. The 'B' side was 'Come Together, written by John Lennon, who also sang lead vocals.

16. **Leavin' on a Jet Plane** was folk trio Peter, Paul & Mary's only number one hit. It was written by a then-unknown John Denver.

17. **Proud Mary** was the signature hit for Creedence Clearwater Revival, who surprisingly, never had an official # 1 hit, although they had 5 hits peak at #2.

18. **Spinning Wheel** by Blood, Sweat & Tears was written by lead singer David Clayton-Thomas from Toronto. It was the 2nd of 3 big hits for B,S & T in 1969.

19. **Crystal Blue Persuasion** by Tommy James & The Shondells was one of three 1969 hits with religious overtones recorded by this successful late 60's music act and one of 5 they charted in 1969 alone.

20. **Bad Moon Rising** was one of 7 songs charted by Creedence Clearwater Revival in 1969 alone. The 'B' side of this 45 was **'Lodi'**. 1969 was the first year of all original hits written by lead singer, producer, and guitarist John Fogarty.

21. **A Boy Named Sue** by Johnny Cash was recorded 'live' at San Quentin Prison. It was written by former playboy cartoonist Shel Silverstein.

22. **Theme from Romeo & Juliet** by Henry Mancini was the theme from the film which starred Olivia Hussey as Juliet.

23. **Hair** was the title song from the rock musical as performed by the family act The Cowsills, from Rhode Island. All songs from 'Hair' were written by James Rado, Jerome Ragni and Galt McDermott.

24. **Jean** by Oliver was from the movie 'The Prime Of Miss Jean Brodie' starring Maggie Smith. This song was written by Rod McKuen. It was the second of two hits for Oliver in his exclusive year on the charts. 'Good Morning Starshine' was his first 1969 hit.

25. **You've Made Me So Very Happy** was the first hit for Blood, Sweat & Tears. This song was co-written by Brenda Holloway who recorded it originally in 1967.

26. **Sweet Caroline** by singer/songwriter Neil Diamond was inspired by Caroline Kennedy, daughter of former U.S. President John F. Kennedy. This summer of '69 hit became one of Neil Diamond's most popular. He performed it at the Grammy Awards in February of 2009.

27. **Take A Letter Maria** was the biggest hit for R. B. Greaves, the nephew of singer Sam Cooke. He was born Ronald Bertram A. Greaves.

28. **It's Your Thing** was the biggest hit of the 60's by The Isley Brothers, an R & B trio from Cincinnati. The Isley Brothers added younger brother Ernie to their lineup on this spring 1969 hit. They followed it with the similar sounding, but less successful 'I Turned You On' which also used the line 'sock it to me' in the song.

29. **Love Can Make You Happy** was a beautiful ballad by Mercy, a one hit wonder vocal group based in Florida. This song was recorded on both the Columbia and Warner Brothers record labels.

30. **Build Me up Buttercup** was the most successful hit by The Foundations, a British based multi-cultural group. Their hits were co-written

by Tony Macauley who wrote hits for others including 'Love Grows (Where My Rosemary Goes) for Edison Lighthouse and Smile A Little Smile For Me for the Flying Machine.

31. **And When I Die** by Blood, Sweat & Tears, featuring David Clayton-Thomas, was the third of three consecutive 1969 hits to peak at number 2 on the charts. This thought-provoking song was written by Laura Nyro.

32. **These Eyes** by the Guess Who was the breakthrough hit by this super group from Canada featuring Burton Cummings and Randy Bachman.

33. **In the Ghetto** was a social comment hit by Elvis Presley written by Scott 'Mac' Davis. Mac Davis would write no less than three popular hits for the King. The others included 'Don't Cry Daddy' and 'A Little Less Conversation'.

34. **Hot Fun in The Summertime** by Sly & The Family Stone was a more mellow style than their usual psychedelic soul/funk sound. Leader Sylvester (Sly Stone) Stewart was the former producer of 60's group The Beau Brummels, known for their hits 'Laugh Laugh' and 'Just A Little.'

35. **Grazing In The Grass** was an energetic, upbeat hit for the L.A - based Friends Of Distinction. This was a vocal remake of the Hugh Masekela instrumental from 1968.The Friends of Distinction were discovered by Pro Football player Jim Brown.

36. **Green River** was one of five C.C.R. hits which peaked at #2. 'Commotion' was the 'B' side of this popular 45 featuring guitarist/songwriter/producer John Fogarty on lead vocals.

37. **Worst That Could Happen** by The Brooklyn Bridge featured Johnny Maestro on powerful lead vocals. 10 years earlier he was the lead voice of the Crests on '16 Candles'

38. **Touch Me** was a big hit by The Doors which features 'stronger than dirt' as the last line. This was taken from a popular Ajax TV commercial from then. The beat of this song was inspired by the 50's classic 'Tequila'.

39. **I'm Gonna Make You Love Me** was a teaming of two of Motown's top acts, The Supremes and The Temptations for one great song. It was originally a hit for Madeline Bell in 1968.

40. **Fortunate Son/Down on The Corner** was a double-sided hit single by Creedence Clearwater Revival from their album 'Willy & The Poorboys'. All of their hits were recorded on the 'Fantasy' record label.

41. **Traces** was the third of four notable hits by this late 60's group known as The Classics 4, featuring lead singer Dennis Yost, who died in December 2008.

42. **Little Woman** was the first hit for teen idol Bobby Sherman who starred in TV's 'Here Comes the Brides' in 1969. He was a regular on the TV show Shindig during the mid 60's.

43. **Put A Little Love In Your Heart** was the most successful hit for Jackie DeShannon, who later wrote 'Bette Davis Eyes' for Kim Carnes.

44. **Time of The Season** by The British group The Zombies reached the top ten two years after their breakup in 1967. This song went on to become their biggest hit, selling two million copies.

45. **Soulful Strut** was a top ten instrumental hit by Young-Holt Unlimited. The group consisted of two thirds of the Ramsey Lewis Trio.

46. **My Cherie Amour** was one of almost 30 top ten hits achieved by Motown's Stevie Wonder. This was a perfect summer song in '69.

47. **Get Together** by The Youngbloods featured Jesse Colin Young on this hit originally released two years earlier in 1967.

48. **Hooked on a Feeling** by B.J. Thomas was written by Mark James, who also wrote the number one 1969 hit Suspicious Minds for Elvis Presley.

49. **This Magic Moment** by Jay & The Americans featured the powerful voice of Jay Black on lead vocals. This was a remake of the 1960 Drifters hit.

50. **Good Morning Starshine** was one of five charted 1969 hits from the rock musical 'Hair'. This was one of Oliver's two big hits in 1969, his only year on the charts. Oliver's real name was William Oliver Swofford.

51. **What Does It Take (To Win Your Love)** was by Motown sax act Jr. Walker (Autry Dewalt) & The All-Stars. This hit was co-written and produced by Johnny Bristol who also sang harmony on this and other Motown hits of the 60's.

52. **Galveston** by Glen Campbell was popular the year he co-starred with John Wayne in the movie 'True Grit'. Like many of his hits, 'Galveston' was also written by Jimmy Webb.

53. **Only the Strong Survive** was the highest charted hit for Mississippi born soul singer Jerry Butler whose nickname was 'The Iceman'.

54. **Too Busy Thinkin' Bout My Baby** by Motown's Marvin Gaye was the second of three major hits he achieved in 1969.

55. **One** was the first top ten hit for 3 Dog Night. It was written by Harry Nilsson who had a hit of his own in 1969 with 'Everybody's Talkin'.

56. **Hawaii Five-0** by the instrumental group the Ventures was the theme of the TV series which starred Jack Lord and James MacArthur.

57. **Oh Happy Day** was a hit for the gospel group The Edwin Hawkins Singers who backed up Melanie the following year on 'Lay Down' (Candles In The Rain).

58. **Smile a Little Smile for Me** by The Flying Machine was the only North American hit for this British studio group which recorded on the popular Pye record label in Canada and England and on Congress in the United States.

59. **Indian Giver** was another top ten bubblegum hit by The 1910 Fruitgum Company produced by Jerry Kasenetz and Jeff Katz for the Buddah record label. They also produced other bubblegum groups at the time, including the Ohio Express.

60. **Holly Holy** was Neil Diamond's follow up to 'Sweet Caroline' making it his 3rd notable hit of '69. His first of the year was 'Brother Love's Traveling Salvation Show'.

61. **I'll Never Fall In Love Again** was a powerful ballad by Tom Jones which originally charted in 1967, but didn't become a top ten hit until 1969.

62. **Baby its You** by Smith featured Gayle McCormack belting out this song, which was a remake of the Shirelles 1962 hit. This great recording was produced by Del Shannon.

63. **Easy to Be Hard** by 3 Dog Night was a song from the Rock Musical 'Hair' and it was one of five hits from the Broadway soundtrack and movie that year.

64. **Can I Change My Mind** was a Top Ten hit on the pop charts and a number one hit on the R & B charts for Chicago-based Tyrone Davis who died in 2005.

65. **Twenty Five Miles** was the biggest 60's hit for Edwin Starr, whose real name was Charles Hatcher. He died in 2003.

66. **Ruby, Don't Take Your Love to Town** was the first pop country hit for Kenny Rogers & The First Edition. It was written by Mel Tillis, father of Pam Tillis.

67. **Everybody's Talkin'** was a top ten hit for Nilsson from the 'Midnight Cowboy' movie which starred Dustin Hoffman and Jon Voight.

68. **Baby I Love You** was one of two Ronettes' hits recycled by Andy Kim. The other was 'Be My Baby'. Jeff Barry produced this and dozens of other big hits during the 60's.

18

69. **Lay Lady Lay** by Bob Dylan featured a softer, deeper singing voice from his 'Nashville Skyline' album. Nashville studio musicians on this recording included Charlie Daniels and Pete Drake. The song was originally intended to be included in the movie 'Midnight Cowboy', but wasn't submitted by the deadline.

70. **Time Is Tight** was a great instrumental by Booker T. & the MG's heavy on organ, guitar and drums. It was featured in the film 'Uptight' starring Ruby Dee.

71. **Gitarzan** was a fun novelty original by Ray Stevens, who did the voices of Gitarzan, the monkey and Jane. It climbed into the top ten in the spring of '69.

72. **I Started a Joke** by The Bee Gees featured Robin Gibb on lead vocals. That year he also left the group briefly to go solo.

73. **Laughing/Undun** was a double-side hit single by The Guess Who featuring Burton Cummings on lead vocals. The 'B' side 'Undun', written by Randy Bachman' didn't become a hit until 3 months after its 'A' side 'Laughing' was popular.

74. **Yester Me, Yester You, Yesterday** was a top ten hit for Stevie Wonder the year before he married singer Syreeta.

75. **Ballad of John & Yoko** by the Beatles featured only John Lennon and Paul McCartney on the recording. George Harrison was on vacation and Ringo Starr was filming 'The Magic' Christian'. It was from the year both John & Yoko and Paul & Linda got married.

76. **Color Him Father** by The Winstons was a story song by this one hit wonder soul septet from Washington.

77. **Israelites** by Desmond Dekkar and The Aces was an early reggae hit by this singer from Kingston, Jamaica whose real name was Desmond Dacres.

78. **Sweet Cherry Wine** was the first of three religious hits in 1969 recorded by Tommy James & The Shondells. The other two were 'Crystal Blue Persuasion' and 'Ball Of Fire'. All of their 60's hits were recorded on the Roulette record label

79. **Backfield in Motion** was an R & B hit by Mississippi cousins Mel Hardin and Tim McPherson, better known as 'Mel & Tim'.

80. **Polk Salad Annie** by Louisiana swamp rock singer Tony Joe White was later recorded by Elvis. Tony Joe White also wrote Brook Benton's million seller Rainy Night in Georgia. Billy Swan was the producer of 'Polk Salad Annie', a top ten hit during the summer of '69.

81. **The Boxer** was a hit for the most successful duo of the 60's, Simon & Garfunkel. This was their only charted hit of 1969, although the 'B' side of the single 'Baby Driver' was a minor hit. They were inducted into the Rock & Roll Hall of Fame in 1990.

82. **Cloud Nine** was the first Temptations hit with their new psychedelic soul sound. Motown Funk Brothers Session man Dennis Coffey introduced the 'wah wah' guitar on this hit produced by Norman Whitfield.

83. **You Showed Me** by The Turtles was their final official top ten hit and was written by Jim McGuinn and Gene Clark of the Byrds.

84. **Tracy** by The Cuff Links was actually Ron Dante's (lead singer on Sugar Sugar by The Archies) voice overdubbed several times to make it sound like an entire vocal group. His voice was the only one featured on this top ten hit.

85. **Atlantis/To Susan On The West Coast Waiting** was a double-side hit by Donovan. 'Atlantis' was a song with spoken word about the lost Continent. 'To Susan on the West Coast Waiting' was a song about a relationship while the soldier was off fighting in the war in Vietnam.

86. **That's The Way Love Is** by Marvin Gaye was the third of three 1969 hits by this popular Motown singer from Washington, D.C.

87. **Son of a Preacher Man** was a top ten 1969 hit by Dusty Springfield, whose real name was Mary O'Brien. This hit was later revived in the film 'Pulp Fiction'.

88. **No Time** was The Guess Who's final hit of the 60's. It was followed by their biggest hit of all time, 'American Woman'.

89. **This Girl Is a Woman now** was a powerful ballad and the final top ten hit for late 60's exclusive group, Gary Puckett & The Union Gap.

90. **Hang 'Em High** by the instrumental group Booker T. & the MG's was the theme for the 1968 spagetti western which starred Clint Eastwood.

91. **I'm Gonna Make You Mine** was a bright, upbeat hit with great harmony from falsetto-voiced Lou Christie, whose real name is Lugee Sacco. Backup singers on this recording included Ellie Greenwich and Linda Scott of 'I've Told Every Little Star' fame.

92. **One Tin Soldier** by Canadian quintet Original Caste was written by Potter and Lambert who wrote other hits like 'Don't Pull Your Love' and 'Two Divided By Love'. It was Coven's version of this song which was featured in the movie 'Billy Jack'.

93. **Oh What a Night** by the vocal soul group The Dells was a remake of their own hit from the 50's with a great spoken word intro by bass singer Chuck Barksdale.

94. **More Today than Yesterday** was the only hit for Spiral Starecase, a one hit wonder group from Sacramento, California featuring lead singer/ songwriter Pat Upton.

95. **Games People Play** by Joe South was the Grammy Award Winning Song of the Year in 1969. It was Joe South's biggest hit as a singer, although he had many hits as a songwriter.

96. **Rock Me** by Steppenwolf was the third of three top ten hits for this L.A. band headed by Canadian John Kay.

97. **Who's Making Love** was the biggest 60's hit for Johnny Taylor, an Arkansas- born Soul singer who recorded on the 'Stax' record label.

98. **I'm Livin' In Shame** was The Supremes' follow up to Love Child and was another social comment hit co-written by singer/songwriter R. Dean Taylor.

99. **Which Way You Going Billy** was the first and biggest hit for Canadian couple Terry and Susan Jacks, better known as The Poppy Family.

100. **Gimme Gimme Good Lovin'** was the only hit for Crazy Elephant, a one hit wonder bubblegum group associated with the Ohio Express.

101. **When I Die** was the only hit for Canadian group Motherlode fronted by Steve Kennedy. In the U.S. they recorded on the Buddah record label.

102. **Ramblin' Gamblin' Man** was the first major hit for the Bob Seger System. A then-unknown future Eagles singer/guitarist/writer Glenn Frey was one of the musicians featured on this early 1969 hit.

103. **Suite: Judy Blue Eyes** by Crosby, Stills and Nash was written by Steve Stills for Judy Collins. They performed this song at Woodstock with Neil Young, who joined the band after they recorded this 1969 hit.

104. **Good ol Rock And Roll** was a medley of some classic 50's songs by one hit wonder group Cat Mother & The All-Night Newsboys from New York City. The group was produced by the legendary Jimi Hendrix.

105. **Hot Smoke & Sasafrass** was a psychedelic hit by one hit wonder Bubble Puppy from Houston, Texas.

106. **Going up The Country** by Canned Heat featured Alan Wilson on lead vocals. He died of a drug overdose at the age of 27 the following year, in 1970.

107. **So Good Together** was Andy Kim's follow up to 'Baby I Love You' and once again a production of Jeff Barry, who co-wrote many hits with his wife Ellie Greenwich during this decade.

108. **Cherry Hill Park** was Billy Joe Royal's final top ten hit and the only one not written by Joe South.

109. **May I** was the first of 3 1969 hits by Bill Deal & the Rhondells. 'May I' was written by Maurice Williams, the writer of 'Little Darlin' and 'Stay' which he took to number one.

110. **My Pledge of Love** was a catchy soul song from The Joe Jeffrey Group, a one hit wonder R & B act from Buffalo, New York.

111. **Don't Cry Daddy** was one of two 1969 Elvis Presley hits written by Mac Davis. The social comment hit 'In the Ghetto' was the other Top ten hit.

112. **Run Away Child, Running Wild** by The Temptations was a social comment hit featuring their new 'psychedelic-sounding' style which began with their hit 'Cloud Nine'.

113. **Something In the Air** was the only notable hit by British group Thunderclap Newman produced by The Who's Pete Townsend. This hit was featured in the 'Magic Christian' soundtrack. A then-16 year old guitarist Jimmy McCulloch, later joined Paul McCartney's Wings, but died of a drug overdose in 1979.

114. **Marakesh Express** was the first hit for Crosby, Stills & Nash before Neil Young joined. Graham Nash wrote this song when he was a member of The Hollies, but they turned it down.

115. **Everyday with You Girl** was the 4th and final hit for this Florida group The Classics Four, featuring Dennis Yost on lead vocals. Their 3 other notable hits 'Spooky', 'Stormy' and 'Traces' all had one word titles.

116. **Give Peace a Chance** by John Lennon's Plastic Ono Band was recorded at a bed-in for peace in a Montreal Hotel room. Participants on the session included Timothy Leary, Murray The K and Tommy Smothers of the Smothers Brothers.

117. **Up on Cripple Creek** by the Band, was written by J. Robbie Robertson and featured drummer Levon Helm on lead vocals.

118. **Mendocino** opened with the lead singer Doug Sahm introducing the name of this Texas group, Sir Douglas Quintet. Their biggest hit of the 60's was She's About A Mover from 1965.

119. **I Can Hear Music** by The Beach Boys featured Carl Wilson on lead vocals on this remake of a minor hit by the Ronettes from 1966.

120. **Goodbye** by Mary Hopkin was produced and written by Paul McCartney and recorded on the Beatles 'Apple' record label.

121. **I'd Wait a Million Years** by The Grassroots was another goodtime hit featuring Rob Grill on lead vocals. All of their big hits were recorded on the RCA/Dunhill label.

122. **Things I'd like To Say** was a soft melodic ballad by Chicago's New Colony Six.

123. **You Gave Me a Mountain** was a powerful song written by Marty Robbins by 'Rawhide' singer, Frankie Laine, who died at the age of 93 in 2007. Elvis Presley also recorded this song on an album.

124. **The Chokin' Kind** by soul singer Joe Simon was written by country singer Harland Howard. This hit reached number one on the R & B charts.

125. **Eli's Coming** was the third of three Top ten hits by 3 Dog Night in 1969, their first year on the charts. Eli's Coming was also one of three big 1969 hits written by Laura Nyro. The other two were 'And When I Die' and 'Wedding Bell Blues'.

126. **If I Can Dream** was the first of four hits for Elvis Presley in 1969, his comeback year.

127. **Pinball Wizard** by The Who was the hit that launched their rock opera 'Tommy', written by Pete Townsend.

128. **Yesterday When I was Young** was the biggest pop hit for country singer Roy Clark. He was starring in the popular 'Hee Haw' TV Show back then.

129. **Morning Girl** was a hit for a symphonic-sounding assemblage of musicians known as Neon Philharmonic under the direction of leader and composer Tupper Saussy. The lead singer was Don Gant.

130. **Nothing but A Heartache** was a powerful production by The Flirtations, a one hit wonder girl group featuring The Pearce Sisters from South Carolina.

131. **Is That All There Is** was a comeback hit for 40's/50's singer Peggy Lee. This unique hit was written and produced by the famous songwriting team of Leiber & Stoller and arranged and conducted by a then-unknown Randy Newman. This hit won Peggy Lee a Grammy Award for best female pop vocal performance.

132. **My Whole World Ended (The Moment You Left Me)** was a solo hit for David Ruffin, a former lead singer of The Temptations and brother of Motown singer Jimmy Ruffin.

133. **Heaven Knows** by The Grassroots was one of 5 hits this San Francisco group charted in 1969.

134. **Keem-O-Sabe** was an instrumental hit by one hit wonder Electric Indian which featured many musicians who were later known as M.F.S.B.and had a major hit with T.S.O.P. This hit was produced by Len Barry of '1 2 3' 'fame.

135. **Choice of Colors** by The Impressions was a social comment hit written by lead singer Curtis Mayfield.

136. **J'Taime** by Jane Birkin and Serge Gainsborough was banned from radio airplay in Britain for being too suggestive, but still managed to reach number one in the U.K.

137. **Brother Love's Travelling Salvation Show** by Neil Diamond opens with the line 'Hot August Night', also the title of his 1969 album. This song features the memorable line "pack up the babies and grab the old ladies".

138. **What Kind Of Fool Do You Think I Am** was the third and final hit for Bill Deal & the Rhondells from 1969, their only year on the charts. This was a remake of the Tams 1964 hit.

139. **The Weight** was the first notable hit for The Band, the former backup group for Bob Dylan. They formed in Woodstock, New York. This recording was from their "Music from Big Pink" album.

140. **Lo Mucho Que Te Quera** was one of the surprise hits of 1969 by a Mexican-American duo from Texas known as Rene & Rene. Their names were Rene Ornelas and Rene Herrera.

141. **Soul Deep** by The Box Tops was the final hit for this Memphis group which disbanded in 1970.

142. **My Way** by Frank Sinatra was co-written by Paul Anka, who also wrote The Tonight Show theme.

143. **Mind, Body & Soul** was a powerful recording by Flaming Ember, a blue-eyed soul group from Detroit who recorded on The Buddah record Label. Their biggest hit was 1970's Westbound # 9.

144. **Medicine Man** was the only hit for The Buchanan Brothers, who were actually writers/producers Cashman, Pistilli and West. They previously wrote

'Sunday Will Never Be the Same' for Spanky & Our Gang. Terry Cashman and Tommy West later went on to produce all of the hits of Jim Croce.

145. **The Letter** by The Arbors (two brothers from Ann Arbor, Michigan) was a unique remake of the 1967 hit by The Box Tops. In 1970 Joe Cocker made it a hit again when he brought his version into the top ten .

146. **Workin' on A Groovy Thing** by The 5th Dimension was written by Neil Sedaka and was one of four hits they achieved in 1969 alone.

147. **But You Know I Love You** by Kenny Rogers and The First Edition was a popular ballad for this former New Christy Minstrels member.

148. **Sugar on Sunday** by The Clique was written by Tommy James and was the only top 40 hit for this Texas quintet.

149. **Will You Be Staying After Sunday** was the most successful hit for this harmony vocal group which were similar in style to that of Spanky & Our Gang.

150. **Sorry Suzanne** was the first hit by The Hollies to feature new member Terry Sylvester, who replaced Graham Nash. This song was co-written by Tony MacAuley who was responsible for many British hits including 'Build Me Up Buttercup', 'Love Grows', 'Smile A Little Smile For Me' and over a dozen others.

151. **Along Came Jones** featured Ray Stevens doing all the character voices in this remake of The Coasters hit from 1959.

152. **I Got a Line on You** was a hit for L.A band Spirit featuring Jay Ferguson and the late Randy California.

153. **Black Pearl** by Sonny Charles & The Checkmates was one of the final hits produced by Phil Spector before he became a retired recluse.Phil Spector was convicted of second degree murder in April of 2009.

154. **Maybe Tomorrow** was a hit on the Beatles Apple Label by The Iveys. They changed their name to Badfinger the following year.

155. **I've Been Hurt** was the second of three 1969 hits by Bill Deal & The Rhondells, an 8-piece band from New York City.

156. **Hurt So Bad** by The Lettermen was a harmonizing remake of Little Anthony & The Imperials hit from 1965.

157. **In the Bad, Bad Old Days** was a moderate hit for the British multi-cultural group The Foundations. It was their follow up to their biggest hit 'Build Me Up Buttercup'.

158. **What's The Use of Breaking Up** was the final top 20 hit for soul singer Jerry Butler. Most of his late 60's hits were written by the songwriting team of Gamble & Huff.

159. **Goodnight My Love** was Paul Anka's remake of a hit made popular in 1956 by Jesse Belvin.

160. **Make Believe** was a great production by one hit wonder New York studio group Wind, featuring Tony Orlando on lead vocals.

More hits of 1969

Playgirl was the only hit for Thee Prophets, a pop rock quartet from Milwaukee.

Without Love (There Is Nothing) by Tom Jones was a ballad, not unlike the hit it followed, 'I'll Never Fall In Love Again'. He was born Thomas Jones Woodward in Pontyprid, South Wales. All of his 60's hits were produced by Peter Sullivan.

The Thought of Loving You was a moderate and regional hit for the Crystal Mansion, an eight man group which featured Johnny Caswell on lead vocals.

Apricot Brandy was a high energy rock instrumental by Rhinoceros, a Los Angeles-based rock group headed by Canadian John Finley. Electra records producer Paul Rothchild recruited this group to the label. John Finley later wrote 'Let Me Serenade You' for 3 Dog Night.

You, I by the Rugbys had some great guitar riffs and was very progressive for its time. This was their only hit.

Witchi Tai To was a very unusual sounding chanting hit by the two man band known as 'Everything Is Everything'.

Stand by Your Man was Tammy Wynette's signature hit. Her man at the time was Country star George Jones whom she married in 1969. She stood by her man until they divorced in 1975.

Groovy Grubworm was an instrumental hit for Country guitarist Harlow Wilcox. Although this was his only hit, he was a popular guitar session player.

It's Getting Better was the most successful of three solo hits by Mama Cass the year after the Mamas & Papas split up. This bright and bouncy hit was written by Barry Mann and Cynthia Weil.

Cupid by Johnny Nash was a reggae-flavored remake of the Sam Cooke classic. The song became a hit later for both Tony Orlando and Dawn and the Spinners.

To Know You Is to Love You was Bobby Vinton's remake of the Teddy Bears original with the title changed from 'To Know Him Is To Love Him', created by Phil Spector.

Heather Honey was one of four hit singles achieved by Tommy Roe in 1969. This was Tommy's follow up to his biggest hit 'Dizzy'.

Let Me was an energetic hit by Paul Revere and The Raiders featuring Mark Lindsay on lead vocals. There's a great false ending on this hit with Lindsay coming back with a screaming 'na na na na na' before getting back into the chorus. Mark Lindsay also co-wrote and produced most of their hits from 1968 to 1969.

Birthday was a cover of the Beatles song by one hit wonder group Underground Sunshine. This group consisted of 2 members from Wisconsin and a couple from Germany.

Sweet Cream Ladies (Forward March) was a hit for The Box Tops featuring a teenaged Alex Chilton on lead vocals. This song had an interesting and memorable use of horns.

A Ray of Hope was the first of four moderately successful singles for The Rascals in 1969, their final year on the charts. Like 'People Got To Be Free', this was also a social comment hit by the blue-eyed soul group from New York City.

Carry Me Back was an upbeat, piano-driven hit by the Rascals, featuring the soulful voice of Felix Cavaliere upfront.

That's The Way God Planned It was Billy Preston's first solo hit in the year he played keyboards on the Beatles hit 'Get Back'. This catchy, inspirational hit was produced by George Harrison and recorded on the Beatles' 'Apple' record label.

Jack And Jill was a pop bubblegum hit for Tommy Roe, co-written with Country singer Freddy Weller, who also assisted in composing 'Dizzy' and some of his other late 60's hits.

No, Not Much was the Vogues final top 40 hit and was very similar in style to their mellow tunes like 'My Special Angel', and 'Turn Around, Look at Me'

Stay And Love Me All Summer was a hook-laden minor hit for Brian Hyland in the summer of '69. This singer from Queens, New York previously gave us the summer hits 'Itsy Bitsy Teenie Weenie Yellow Polka Dot Bikini' and 'Sealed With A Kiss'. His next hit, 'Gypsy Woman' in 1970, was his final top 40 hit.

In A Moment was the only top 40 hit for the Intrigues, a soul trio from Philadelphia.

Midnight Cowboy by instrumentalists Ferrante And Teicher featured the 'Water Sound' guitar of Vincent Bell. This was the title tune of the movie which starred Jon Voight and Dustin Hoffman.

Everybody Knows Matilda was a fun story song by American one hit wonder Duke Baxter. Although it was a minor hit in most parts of North America, it was a bigger hit in others, including Toronto, Ontario, Canada.

Mr. **Sun Mr**. **Moon** was a hit for Portland, Oregon's Paul Revere and the Raiders featuring Mark Lindsay, the pony-tailed lead singer who frequently appeared on the cover of the teen magazines back then.

Heaven by the Rascals was an inspirational hit which barely made the top 40. It was their 11th top 40 hit, which included 3 number ones.

Condition Red by one hit wonder female trio the Goodees was a novelty hit similar to 'Leader of The Pack'. This was the first hit to use the new siren sound on an ambulance.

Special Delivery was the final top 40 hit by the 1910 Fruitgum Company, best known for the bubblegum hits 'Simon Says' and '1,2,3 Redlight'. Like the very similar sounding Ohio Express, they also recorded on the Buddah record label and had hits at the same time.

The River Is Wide by the Grassroots was a remake of a song popular two years earlier by the Forum. The Grassroots charted five hits in 1969 with 'I'd Wait A Million Years' being the biggest.

Lovin' Things was another 1969 goodtime hit by the Grassroots featuring Rob Grill on lead vocals. All of their hits were recorded on the Dunhill label in the U.S.

Friend, Lover, Woman, Wife by O.C. Smith was written by Mac Davis. This positive hit highlighted the powerful voice of the singer who also gave us 'Little Green Apples' the year before.

See was perhaps the most progressive hit by the Rascals and certainly not their typical style. This fast paced hit was heavy on guitars and keyboards with great production all the way around. Unfortunately it was a commercial flop.

Get It from The Bottom was an energetic soul hit by the one hit wonder act the Steelers, an R & B vocal quintet from Chicago.

Jingle Jangle was the fictitious group the Archies' follow up to 'Sugar Sugar', a multi-million seller in '69. While Ron Dante sang lead on 'Sugar Sugar', it was Toni Wine who supplied the female lead on 'Jingle Jangle'. Songwriter Jeff Barry supplied the bass voice on 'Jingle Jangle'. Both of the Archies hits of 1969 were written by Jeff Barry and Andy Kim.

Reconsider Me was a hit for New Orleans soul singer Johnny Adams. He was also known as 'the tan canary' for the amazing range of his singing voice.

Abergavenny by Shannon was a goodtime hit from the summer of '69. 'Shannon' was actually British singer Marty Wilde.

Stand/I Want to Take You Higher was a double sided hit single by Sly & The Family Stone. The 'B' side of this 45 became more popular after they performed it at Woodstock in the summer of that year.

Going in Circles was The Friends of Distinction's follow up to their top ten hit 'Grazing In The Grass' from the spring of '69. They would have one more hit, 'Love or Let Me Be Lonely' in 1970 before fading into obscurity.

Moody Woman was one of three top 40 hits for Jerry Butler in 1969. Songwriters Gamble and Huff wrote many of his hits during this time period.

Twilight Woman was a moderate hit for Canadian group The 49th Parallel. They later changed their name to Painter, then Hammersmith.

Happy Heart was a hit for Andy Williams written by James Last and Jackie Rae. Andy had his own variety show in prime time when this was a hit.

1. Hair Soundtrack - Original Cast
2. Abbey Road - Beatles
3. The Beatles (White Album) - Beatles
4. Blood, Sweat & Tears - Blood, Sweat & Tears
5. Green River - C.C.R.
6. Johnny Cash At San Quentin - Johnny Cash
7. Blind Faith - Blind Faith
8. TCB - Supremes & Temptations
9. Let It Bleed - Rolling Stones
10. Through The Past Darkly Vol.1 - Rolling Stones
11. Best Of Cream - Cream
12. Goodbye - Cream
13. Greatest Hits Vol. 1 - Association
14. Ball - Iron Butterfly
15. Galveston - Glen Campbell
16. Greatest Hits - Donovan

TOP 16 COUNTRY HITS OF 1969

1. Daddy Sang Bass - Johnny Cash
2. A Boy Named Sue - Johnny Cash
3. Okie From Muskogee - Merle Haggard
4. Galveston - Glen Campbell
5. Running Bear - Sonny James
6. Since I Met You Baby - Sonny James
7. Afraid Of Losing You Again - Charley Pride
8. Only The Lonely - Sonny James
9. Who's Gonna Mow Your Grass - Buck Owens
10. Until My Dreams Come True - Jack Greene
11. The Ways To Love A Woman - Tammy Wynette
12. Johnny B. Goode - Buck Owens
13. Statue Of A Fool - Jack Greene
14. Singing My Song - Tammy Wynette
15. My Life (Throw It Away If I Want To) - Bill Anderson
16. Hungry Eyes - Merle Haggard

TOP 16 ONE HIT WONDERS OF 1969

1. Zager & Evans - In The Year 2525
2. Steam - Na Na Hey Hey Kiss Him Goodbye
3. Mercy - Love Can Make You Happy
4. Smith - Baby Its You
5. Flying Machine - Smile A Little Smile For Me
6. Desmond Dekker - Israelites
7. The Winstons - Color Him Father
8. Tony Joe White - Polk Salad Annie
9. Cuff Links - Tracy
10. Spiral Starecase - More Today Than Yesterday
11. Crazy Elephant - Gimme Gimme Good Lovin'
12. Joe Jeffrey Group - My Pledge Of Love
13. Bubble Puppy - Hot Smoke & Sasafrass
14. Electric Indian - Keem-O-Sabe
15. Cat Mother & The All-Night Newsboys - Good Ol' Rock 'n Roll
16. Buchanan Brothers - Medicine Man

16 GREAT 'LOST 45's' OF 1969

1. Let Me - Paul Revere & The Raiders
2. Abergavenny - Shannon
3. That's The Way God Planned It - Billy Preston
4. Playgirl - Thee Prophets
5. Lovin' Things - Grassroots
6. A Ray Of Hope - The Rascals
7. Everybody Knows Matilda - Duke Baxter
8. Sweet Cream Ladies - Box Tops
9. Reconsider Me - Johnny Adams
10. Stay & Love Me All Summer - Brian Hyland
11. Mr. Sun, Mr. Moon - Paul Revere & The Raiders
12. Carry Me Back - The Rascals
13. Witchi Tai To - Everything Is Everything
14. Heather Honey - Tommy Roe
15. Evil Woman, Don't Play Your Games With Me - Crow
16. Did You See Her Eyes - The Illusion

1. I Heard It Through The Grapevine - Marvin Gaye
2. Everyday People - Sly & The Family Stone
3. I Can't Get Next To You - Temptations
4. It's Your Thing - Isley Brothers
5. Too Busy Thinkin' 'Bout My Baby - Marvin Gaye
6. Baby I'm For Real - The Originals
7. I'm Gonna Make You Love Me - Supremes & Temptations
8. Share Your Love With Me - Aretha Franklin
9. Can I Change My Mind - Tyrone Davis
10. The Chokin' Kind - Joe Simon
11. What Does It Take (To Win Your Love) - Jr. Walker & All-Stars
12. Only The Strong Survive - Jerry Butler
13. Hot Fun In The Summertime - Sly & The Family Stone
14. Twenty Five Miles - Edwin Starr
15. Run Away Child, Running Wild - Temptations
16. Mother Popcorn - James Brown

TOP 16 ROCK/HARD ROCK HITS OF 1969

1. Honky Tonk Women - Rolling Stones
2. Ballad Of John & Yoko - Beatles
3. Rock Me - Steppenwolf
4. Fortunate Son - C.C.R.
5. Hot Smoke & Sasafrass - Bubble Puppy
6. Good Times, Bad Times - Led Zeppelin
7. Ramblin' Gamblin' Man - Bob Seger System
8. Give Peace A Chance - John Lennon/Plastic Ono Band
9. Evil Woman, Don't Play Your Games - Crow
10. Bad Moon Rising - C.C.R.
11. You Can't Always Get What You Want - Rolling Stones
12. Apricot Brandy - Rhinoceros
13. Kick Out The Jams - MC5
14. Green River - C.C.R.
15. Crossroads - Cream
16. Goo Goo Barabajagal - Donovan

16 WHATEVER BECAME OF SINGERS FROM THE 60'S!

60's WHATEVER BECAME OF... Bobby Sherman

Remember Bobby Sherman, the California-born pop teen idol of the late 60's and early 70's? He first became famous as a house singer on the music television show 'Shindig', which ran in prime time from 1964 to 1966. A few years later he resurfaced as Jeremy Bolt in the series 'Here Comes The Brides', and that's when his career really took off. Bobby Sherman launched his string of hits in 1969 with 'Little Woman', followed by 'La La La (If I Had You), 'Easy Come, Easy Go' and 'Julie Do Ya Love Me'. After the spotlight faded and his face on the front cover of the Teen Magazines disappeared, Bobby Sherman found a new calling. After guest starring in several episodes of the TV Show 'Emergency', he took an interest in paramedics. He left the public spotlight and volunteered with the Los Angeles Police Department, and worked with paramedic, CPR, and first aid classes. He is now a San Bernardino County Deputy Sheriff. Through the years, Bobby Sherman has been given several awards for his humanitarian efforts. His official website is Bobbysherman.com.

60's WHATEVER BECAME OF ... Jerry Butler

Remember Jerry Butler, one of the great R & B singers of the 60's? Chicago crooner Jerry Butler began his vocal career in 1958 when he and another young singer, Curtis Mayfield, formed the Impressions. Butler penned the group's first gold single, 'For Your Precious Love' and later launched a solo career that included such hits as 'He Will Break Your Heart', "Hey Western Union Man' and 'Only The Strong Survive'. He also had a big hit with a duet with Betty Everett with the ballad 'Let It Be Me'. Today, the three-time Grammy Award nominee and Rock And Roll Hall Of Famer enjoys a different kind of fame as a Cook County Commissioner in Chicago. Butler is also an American politician. He serves as a Commissioner for Cook County, Illinois, having first been elected in 1985. As a member of this 17-member County Board, he chairs the Health and Hospitals Committee, and serves as Vice-Chair of the Construction Committee. One of 17 officials, he helps approve the budget for the second-largest county in the U.S. Butler still performs most weekends at supper clubs, concerts and music festivals. Jerry Butler, the Ice Man keeps busy and active and is a strong survivor of the 60's.

60's WHATEVER BECAME OF... Bobby Goldsboro

Ever wondered whatever became of Bobby Goldsboro? He had almost a dozen hits in his heyday, including 'Little Things', 'See The Funny Little Clown', 'Watching Scotty Grow' and his biggest hit of all, 'Honey', a multi-week number one hit in 1968. Florida-born Bobby Goldsboro started his music career playing guitar for Roy Orbison and touring with the Big O. In the early 70's, he hosted a syndicated television variety series, 'The Bobby Goldsboro Show'. Although he retired from full-time performing in the 80's, he continued to be active. In the 90's, he scored the soundtrack to the CBS sitcom 'Evening Shade', and in '95, he launched the children's TV series 'The Swamp Creature Of Lost Lagoon'. Now, Bobby Goldsboro is a professional artist. He paints nature settings and sells his artwork on his website Bobbygoldsboro.com for a few thousand dollars each. From music to painting, he's an artist of a different kind now.

60's WHATEVER BECAME OF...Patty Duke

Remember when Patty Duke was on TV, movies and on the radio with hit songs? Patty Duke was one of the top stars of the 60's. At 16, Patty Duke became the youngest person at the time to win an Academy Award. She won the Best Supporting Actress Oscar for her role playing Helen Keller in 'The

Miracle Worker'. She went on to star in her own series, 'The Patty Duke Show' in which she played both main characters, identical cousins. Patty Duke also had a couple of mid-60's hit songs. But, despite her success, Patty Duke later revealed that she was deeply unhappy during her teenage years. She had problems with substance abuse, and later, many failed relationships and marriages, and mental issues including being diagnosed with bipolar disorder in 1982. These days Patty Duke prefers to be called 'Anna', her real first name. Now in her early 60's, life is getting better for the former child star. Anna has authored two books and in December of 2007 was awarded an Honorary Doctorate from the University of North Florida for her work in advancing awareness of mental health issues. In October of 2008 she received a 'Woman Of The Year' Award by Operation Hope. Her TV film 'Love Finds A Home' icame out in 2009 and she is working on other TV projects. Things are looking up these days for 'Anna', better known as Patty Duke. Her official website is at www.officialpattyduke.com.

60's WHATEVER BECAME OF...Shelley Fabares & Paul Petersen

Remember when Shelley Fabares and Paul Petersen had hit records back in the early 60's? Both were starring in the popular Donna Reed Show at the time. Shelley played Donna Reed's daughter and oldest child, Mary Stone from 1958 to 1963. She also had a number one hit with 'Johnny Angel' before leaving the show for a career in movies. She starred in 3 Elvis movies including 'Girl Happy'. She was happy to marry Record Producer Lou Adler in 1964, but separated two years later. They didn't divorce until 1980. In the 90's, Shelley starred in the long-running sitcom 'Coach'. She's now with Mash actor Mike Farrell, whom she married on New Year's Eve in 1984. In 2000, she received a life-saving liver transplant after being diagnosed with hepititus. In 2007, she joined her husband on a promotional book tour for his autobiography. Her TV brother, the three times married, Paul Petersen played Jeff Stone from the time he was twelve until he was twenty. He also had a few hit records in the early 60's including 'My Dad' and 'She Can't Find Her Keys'. Although he had various roles in TV and movies, his success was limited and he returned to University to obtain a degree in literature which helped him write sixteen Adventure novels. In 1990, he founded the child-actor support group "A Minor Consideration' and at last report is a board member of the Donna Reed Foundation. His official website is Paulpetersen.com.

60's WHATEVER BECAME OF...Bob Lind

Remember Bob Lind, the singer of the song 'Elusive Butterfly'? Baltimore born singer/songwriter Bob Lind had a big hit in the spring of 1966 with a song he wrote titled 'Elusive Butterfly'. The spotlight was shining on this promising new singer as he performed it on various popular TV shows of the day. Fans were waiting for the next hit...but it never happened. Many thought he would become the next Bob Dylan. That was just a wish. Although he's regarded as a One Hit Wonder, over 200 artists including The Four Tops, Petula Clark, Aretha Franklin and Eric Clapton have covered songs written by Bob Lind. He retired from the music business in 1969 to pursue other interests. In recent years he lives in Florida and makes a living as a writer. He became a writer for many years for the tabloid 'Weekly World News' until it folded a few years ago. He is also the author of five novels. Recently, he got back into the music business and began performing again, when he's not busy with his almost fulltime passion, writing books and newspaper articles. His official website is Boblind.com.

60's WHATEVER BECAME OF...Hayley Mills

Remember British child actor and singer Hayley Mills? She's best known as starring in several Walt Disney films during the early 60's and also having a few hit singles from those movies. Academy and Golden Globe winning Hayley Mills was born in London, England, the younger daughter of actor Sir John Mills and playwright Mary Hayley Bell. Hayley was 12 when she was discovered by J. Lee Thompson, who was initially looking for a boy to play the lead role in 'Tiger Bay'. Walt Disney's wife, Lillian Disney, saw her performance and suggested that Mills be given the lead role in 'Pollyanna'. She made four additional films for Disney including 'The Parent Trap', which cast Hayley Mills as twins Sharon and Susan. Alongside her film career, she's had hits with 'Let's Get Together' and 'Johnny Jingo'. After her contract with Disney expired in 1966, she starred in 'The Trouble With Angels' opposite Rosalind Russell. She then went home to England to star in 'The Family Way'. During Filming, a 20 year old Hayley Mills met 53 year old Director Roy Boulting, whom she married in 1971. Many did not approve of the marriage because he was 33 years older. Hayley Mills is divorced with two sons and since 2007 has had a prominent role in the ITV African Vet Drama, 'Wild At Heart'. Her official website is Hayleymills.com.

60's WHATEVER BECAME OF... Frankie Avalon

Remember Frankie Avalon, the star of the Beach Party movies and singer of hits like 'Bobby Sox To Stockings', 'Why' and his number one hit 'Venus'? Philadelphia born Frankie Avalon is best known on the big screen for his early 60's Beach Party movies, including 'Beach Blanket Bingo' 'Bikini Beach', 'Muscle Beach Party' and of course the original 'Beach Party' in which Annette Funicello co-starred. He also had dramatic roles in the films 'The Alamo' with John Wayne and 'Voyage To The Bottom Of the Sea' with Barbara Eden. Back in 1963, a 23 year old Frankie Avalon married Kathryn Diebel, a former beauty pageant winner, despite his agent warning him that the marriage would spoil his teen idol mystique. Still together since 1963, they have eight children and 10 grandchildren. Frankie Avalon continues to perform, sometimes with Bobby Rydell and Fabian as 'The Golden Boys Of Bandstand'. He not only starred in the rock musical 'Grease', but invested in the long running stage show, which made him a millionaire. Today, he also has the company 'Frankie Avalon Products' that sells a line of health supplements products. He lives in the Los Angeles area and is happy spending time his wife and his one big happy family when he's not on the road touring. His official website is Frankieavalon.com.

60's WHATEVER BECAME OF... James Darren

Remember James Darren, the guy who played 'Moondoggy' in the 'Gidget' movies back in the early 60's? He was a popular actor and singer having hits with 'Goodbye Cruel World', 'Her Royal Majesty' and a couple of other notable pop hits during the early 60's. After the fun in the sun tan faded, the Beach guy turned to Sci-fi with the popular television series 'The Time Tunnel' in which he starred as impulsive scientist and adventurer Tony Newman from '66 to '67. In the 80's, James Darren resurfaced on TV as Officer James Corrigan on the police drama 'T.J.Hooker', alongside Heather Locklear and William Shatner. Darren also worked as a Director on many television action-based series including 'The A-Team', 'Hunter' as well as dramas such as 'Beverly Hills 90210' and 'Melrose Place'. James Darren was later re-discovered by a whole new generation through his appearances on 'Star Trek:Deep Space Nine' in the role of holographic crooner and advice-giver Vic Fontaine. He's been married twice, has 3 children and in his 70's, continues to tour, singing to adoring fans. His official website is Jamesdarren.com.

60's WHATEVER BECAME OF ... Herb Alpert

Remember Herb Alpert of the Tijuana Brass, the top instrumental act of the 60's? They had hits with 'A Taste Of Honey', 'Tijuana Taxi', 'The Lonely Bull' and many others. Herb Alpert is also famous for being a recording industry executive, - he was the 'A' of 'A & M' Records, a label he and business partner Jerry Moss founded and eventually sold. Herb Alpert was born in Los Angeles and began taking trumpet lessons at the age of eight. In the early 60's during a visit to Tijuana, Mexico, he happened to hear a mariachi band while attending a bullfight. Following the experience, he recalled that he was inspired to find a way to musically express what he felt while watching the wild responses of the crowd, and hearing the brass musicians introducing each new event. He then created the Tijuana Brass. Herb Alpert's musical accomplishments are huge as both the leader of the Tijuana Brass and co-owner of A & M Record label. Alpert and Moss both agreed in 1987 to sell A & M records for a reported $55 million. These days, Herb Alpert, now in his 70's, continues to play his trumpet, but also devotes time to his second career as an abstract painter and sculptor with shows around the U.S. He is also a very generous man. He and his wife Lani Hall donated $30 million to the University Of California in 2007 and another $24 million to CalArts for its music cirricula. Herb Alpert and his wife Lani Hall, lead singer on the hits of Sergio Mendes and Brazil '66 play concerts in selected cities from time to time. His official website is herbalpert.com

60's WHATEVER BECAME OF... Brenda Lee

Remember Brenda Lee, Little Miss Dynamite, one of the most successful singers of the 60's? A matter of fact, in the 60's, she had more charted hits than any other female vocalist of the decade. The little singer with the big voice from Georgia had her first major hit when she was just 15 years old with 'Sweet Nothin's'. That was followed by number one hits 'I'm Sorry' and 'I Want To Be Wanted' along with many others. In the 70's, she was immortalized in Golden Earring's song 'Radar Love' with the line 'Brenda Lee is coming on strong'. She met her husband Ronnie Shacklett at a Jackie Wilson concert and were married in 1963. They've been together ever since! Brenda Lee and her husband live in Nashville, and have two daughters and three grandchildren. In 2002, Brenda Lee released her 'Little Miss Dynamite' autobiography and was inducted into the Rock And Roll Hall Of Fame that year. The little lady with the big heart has done charity work for over a dozen organizations and continues to tour and perform to sell-out audiences around the world. In 2009, Brenda Lee received a Lifetime Achievement Grammy Award. She's still coming on strong and actively performing. Her official website is Brendalee.com

60's WHATEVER BECAME OF... Davy Jones of the Monkees

Remember when Davy Jones was one of the most popular members of The Monkees and had one hit single after another? Davy Jones was the top teen idol pin-up and teen magazine cover boy of the zany and popular 60's group, The Monkees. They began their string of hits in '66 when their TV series debuted with 'Last Train To Clarksville' and 'I'm A Believer'. Davy Jones was the Monkee who sang lead on 'Daydream Believer', 'A Little Bit Me, A Little Bit You' and their final Top 10 hit, 'Valleri'. After the breakup of the Monkees in 1968, Davy Jones kept busy singing and acting on stage. Manchester, England born Davy Jones loves theatre and has not only performed in 'Oliver', but productions of 'The Boyfriend', Harry Nilsson's 'The Point' and appeared as Jesus in 'Godspell', which played in London's West End. He also rides and trains his beloved racehorses to be winners. In 1996, he won his first race in England on his prized horse, 'Digpast'. Davy Jones is also a regular on the charity sports circuit. His proudest effort for charity was a successful completion of the London Marathon in 3 hours, 40 minutes. Davy Jones is also an accomplished writer and humorous storyteller. His talents extend to short stories, poetry, and photography. He recently completed the second edition of his autobiography, 'Davy Jones': Daydream Believer' which updates his life and career to the present. His official website is Davyjones.net.

60's WHATEVER BECAME OF... Lulu

Remember Lulu, the singer of the number one 1967 hit 'To Sir With Love'? She was born in Scotland as Marie McDonald McLaughlin Lawrie, but became better known as Lulu when she started her singing career in the early 60's. When she was only 15 years old in 1964, Lulu belted out her first U.K. hit, - a remake of the Isley Brothers, 'Shout'. She became best known in North America when her hit 'To Sir With Love' became a million seller from the movie in which she appeared with Sidney Poitier. In 1969, she married Maurice Gibb of the Bee Gees. That marriage lasted until 1973. In 1977, she married her former hairdresser and they stayed together for 20 years until divorcing in 1997. Although Lulu hasn't had any hit records in awhile, in 1993, she had her first smash hit as a songwriter with the Grammy nominated 'I Don't Wanna Fight', recorded by Tina Turner. Lulu continues to keep busy. She's performed on stage many times, including on the London stage in Andrew Lloyd Webber's 'Song And Dance' and the National Theatre's musical 'Guys And Dolls'. In 2007, Lulu was a mentor and guest performer on American Idol. In early 2009, Lulu began a four week stint as an advisor/coach on the NBC Show 'Eurovision: Your Country Needs You, helping to choose the singer to represent the UK at the 2009 Eurovision Song contest in May. Her official website is Luluofficial.co.uk.

60's WHATEVER BECAME OF... Donovan

Whatever became of Donovan, the Scottish singer/songwriter and guitarist who had a respectable string of hits during the late 60's? He gave us 'Sunshine Superman', 'Mellow Yellow', 'Hurdy Gurdy Man' and other hits which featured his unique, eclectic and distinctive style that blended folk, jazz, pop and psychedelia. Donovan was rarely absent from the pop charts in the late 60's. He influenced many, including John Lennon and Paul McCartney. After 1969, he left the music industry for a time. Donovan has four children, including two from his first relationship that have become profession actors, Donovan Leitch Jr. and Ione Sky. In 2005 Donovan's autobiography 'The Hurdy Gurdy Man' was published and in 2007 he toured the UK with film Director David Lynch, who was presenting a discussion on Transcendental Meditation. Donovan has a new DVD Documentary 'Sunshine Superman' about his life and songs and tours in 2009 promoting his album 'Ritual Groove'. In early 2009 Donovan was presented with the top national award for cultural achievement in Cannes France. The award took place at the prestigious Midem Music fair at the Majestic Hotel in Cannes.His official website is Donovan.ie.

60's WHATEVER BECAME OF... Cliff Richard

Remember Cliff Richard, Britain's answer to Elvis Presley? He was born Harry Rodger Webb in British India on October 14th 1940. Cliff Richard starred in many teen films in the early 60's and had many hits including 'Summer Holiday', 'It's All In The Game' and 'The Young Ones'. He has sold more than 260 million records worldwide. Cliff Richard has always been more popular in Britain and Canada, than in the United States. As a matter of fact, his first hit in the U.S. didn't arrive until 1976 with 'Devil Woman'. In 1995, Cliff Richard became the very first rock star to be knighted. In 2008, Sir Cliff Richard, in his 50th year in music, released an 8 CD Box Set. One of his hits in the 60's was 'Bachelor Boy', and he is a lifelong bachelor. He was apparently considered marriage, but it never happened. He currently lives with a former Roman Catholic priest, John McElynn, whom he met in 2001 while doing charity work. This friendship has added to long-standing rumors that he is gay, a claim that he denies. Cliff Richard is an entrepreneur who owns a luxurious hotel in Britain and a winery in Portugal. He is one of Britain's richest music stars, with a fortune estimated at well over 80 million dollars. He also gives over half a million dollars a year to charity. These days Cliff Richard is doing well, and also does well for others. His official website is Cliffrichard.org.

60's **WHATEVER BECAME OF...** Michael Nesmith

Ever wonder whatever became of Michael Nesmith, The Monkee who wore the toque? After spending a couple of years in the U.S. Air Force, Michael Nesmith became fascinated with folk music and learned to play guitar. He was the only member of The Monkees to learn about auditioning through the famous press ad looking for 4 zany guys for a Rock group for TV. As a member of the Monkees, the tall, thin Texan also wrote some of their material, and songs for others, including 'Different Drum' for the Stone Poney's, the breakthrough hit for Linda Ronstadt. Michael Nesmith was an only child and his parents separated when he was very young. With his father gone, Nesmith's mother worked as a secretary. Their fortunes changed when Mike's mom Bette invented typewriter correction fluid, later known commercially as 'Liquid Paper'. After the Monkees group and TV series ended, Nesmith had a few solo hits, and in 1977 he furthered his efforts in the form of music video by creating a TV chart show called 'Pop Clips'. In 1981, he became one of the creators of MTV and he won the very first Grammy Award in the category of video for 'Elephant Parts'. He founded Pacific Arts, a multi-media company specializing in commercial filmwork, music and video. In 1999, a jury awarded him over $46 million in a contract dispute with PBS. Michael Nesmith, who has been married three times, is a very talented, rich man who has been a singer, songwriter, actor, producer, novelist, businessman and philanthropist. He's worn many hats... but not the toque anymore.

♫ What 1968 song reached number 1 three months after this singer died?

♫ The brother of Actor Jon Voight (and Uncle of Angelina Jolie) wrote this million selling Top Ten single. What hit was it?

♫ When this hit was number one on the charts, this Soul singer lay wounded in a hospital as a result of injuries suffered while serving time in Vietnam. Who's the singer and what's the song?

♫ This British Actor gave us the surprise hit of the year with this unusual production which reached number two on the charts.

♫ He was the most popular instrumentalist of the 60's and the co-owner/founder of a successful record company. His biggest hit of all was his only vocal hit.

♫ She was the first singer signed to the Beatles' Apple label in 1968. She was discovered by supermodel Twiggy, who introduced her to Paul McCartney.

51

FIND OUT THAT…and MUCH MORE…INSIDE…1968!

1. **Hey Jude** by The Beatles was written by Paul McCartney for John Lennon's son Julian. This top hit of the entire year features Paul on lead vocals accompanied by John and George and a 40 piece orchestra. This was the Beatles first single on their own 'Apple' record label. **'Revolution'** was the 'B' side of this single. There were 3 versions of 'Revolution' recorded by the Beatles in 1968. The two others were a slower version and the psychedelic 'Revolution #9', both from the Beatles White album.

2. **Honey** was Bobby Goldsboro's biggest hit and it was written by Bobby Russell who also composed 'Little Green Apples', The Joker Went Wild' and 'The Light The Lights Went Out In Georgia' for his wife Vicki Lawrence.

3. **Mrs**. **Robinson** by Simon and Garfunkel was the Grammy Award winning Song of the Year from the movie 'The Graduate' starring Dustin Hoffman.

4. **(Sittin' On) The Dock Of The Bay** by Otis Redding was recorded just 3 days before he died when his private twin-engine plane crashed into the icy waters of Lake Monoma, near Madison , Wisconsin. It reached number one three months after his death.

5. **People Got to Be Free** by the Rascals was written by lead singer Felix Cavaliere as an expression of his feelings after the assassinations of Martin Luther King Jr. and Senator Bobby Kennedy in the spring of that year.

6. **Love Is Blue** by Paul Mauriat, a French conductor/arranger, was a number one hit for over a month, making it the second biggest instrumental hit of the 60's. The number one most popular instrumental was Theme From 'A Summer Place' by Percy Faith.

7. **This Guy's In Love with You** was the only vocal hit by Herb Alpert, the leader of The Tijuana Brass. This multi-week number one hit was composed by Burt Bacharach and Hal David.

8. **Tighten up** by Archie Bell and The Drells was a number one hit at the

time Archie was in a West German hospital recovering from being shot in the leg while serving in Vietnam.

9. **Young Girl** by Gary Puckett & the Union Gap was the biggest of their string of late 60's 'almost #1' hits.

10. **Love Child** by Diana Ross and The Supremes was a social comment hit co-written by Toronto's R. Dean Taylor, who later had hits of his own, including 'Indiana Wants Me'.

11. **Those Were the Days** was the first and biggest hit for Welsh singer Mary Hopkin. She was discovered by supermodel Twiggy, who introduced her to Paul McCartney who then signed her to the Beatles 'Apple' Record label.

12. **Born to Be Wild** was Steppenwolf's first and biggest hit. This Los Angeles based rock band featured Toronto's John Kay on lead vocals. This summer of '68 hit became a biker's anthem and was used in the film 'Easy Rider' starring Peter Fonda, Dennis Hopper and Jack Nicholson.

13. **Judy in Disguise (with glasses)** by John Fred and his Playboy band was inspired by The Beatles 'Lucy In The Sky With Diamonds'. John Fred Gourrier's father Fred played baseball with the Detroit Tigers.

14. **Hello I Love You (Won't You Tell Me Your Name**) by The Doors was one of Jim Morrison's least favorite songs, despite the fact that it reached number one in the summer of '68.

15. **A Beautiful Morning** was a happy-go-lucky goodtime hit by The Rascals. This single was their first hit without the 'Young' at the beginning of their name and was one of lead singer Felix Cavaliere's personal favorites.

16. **Harper Valley P.T.A.** by Jeannie C. Riley was a million selling Country crossover hit written by Tom T. Hall. The song was later made into a movie.

17. **Green Tambourine** was by The Lemon Pipers, another bubblegum group from Ohio. Ivan Browne was the lead singer on this simple, but popular number one hit in '68.

18. **Lady Madonna** by The Beatles was written solely by Paul McCartney, who also sang lead and played piano on this hit which featured backing vocals by John and George.

19. **Mony Mony** by Tommy James and The Shondells was their final hit produced by Bo Gentry and Ritchie Cordell. The song later became a number one hit for Billy Idol in 1987.

20. **Lady Willpower** was the third of four top ten hits in '68, the biggest year for Gary Puckett and The Union Gap.

21. **Grazing In The Grass** by Hugh Masekela was a number one instrumental hit by this South African born trumpeter/bandleader. A year later, a fast-paced vocal version was a top ten hit for The Friends Of Distinction. Masekela was married to Miriam Makeba from 1964 to 1966. She died in 2008.

22. **Cry Like A Baby** by the Memphis group The Box Tops featured the danelectric guitar, the sitar-sounding guitar that was also used on late 60's hits like 'Hooked On A Feeling' by B.J. Thomas and 'Games People Play' by Joe South.

23. **MacArthur Park** was a huge hit for actor-turned-singer Richard Harris. Songwriter Jim Webb talked him into recording the unique sounding song, despite Richard's doubts. A matter of fact, Richard Harris was so sure it wouldn't become a hit that he bet and lost his Silver Cloud Roll Royce to songwriter Jim Webb.

24. **Valley Of The Dolls** by Dionne Warwick was written by Burt Bacharach and Hal David and was the theme from the movie which starred Sharon Tate, who was murdered by the Manson family the following year in the summer of '69. Singer/actress Patty Duke also starred in the film.

25. **Magic Carpet Ride** was Steppenwolf's follow up to their 1968 anthem 'Born To Be Wild'. Both featured Toronto's John Kay on lead vocals.

26. **Jumpin' Jack Flash** by The Rolling Stones was their biggest hit of '68. The Rolling Stones have played this song during every tour since its release in '68.

27. **Classical Gas** was the only hit for Mason Williams, who at the time was an award-winning Head Writer for The Smothers Brothers Show, one of 1968's top rated TV shows.

28. **Little Green Apples** was a million selling hit by O. C. Smith written by Bobby Russell. Roger Miller made it a top ten hit on the Country charts that same year.

29. **For Once In My Life** by Stevie Wonder was yet another top ten hit for one of Motown's brightest stars. In the early 60's he also appeared on film performing in the movies 'Beach Party' and 'Muscle Beach Party' which starred Frankie Avalon and Annette Funiccllo.

30. **The Horse** was a top ten instrumental hit for Cliff Nobles and Co., a one hit wonder soul bandleader from Alabama.

31. **Fire** was the only hit for British theatrical rock singer Arthur Brown. He was billed as 'The Crazy World of Arthur Brown and made 'fire' a part of his wild and crazy act.

32. **The Good, The Bad and The Ugly** by Hugo Montenegro was the title track of the spaggetti western starring Clint Eastwood.

33. **Stoned Soul Picnic** was one of several 5th Dimension hits written by Laura Nyro. Others included 'Wedding Bell Blues', 'Sweet Blindness' and 'Save The Country'.

34. **Wichita Lineman** by Glen Campbell was one of many hits written by Jim Webb. This hit was top ten the same year his own TV variety show made it debut.

35. **Woman, Woman** was the first of a string of hits by Gary Puckett and The Union Gap, who dressed in civil war uniforms on stage, each bearing a different rank.

36. **Simon Says** by the 1910 Fruitgum Company was a million seller for this New Jersey based bubblegum group. The song was based on a popular children's game, similar to their top ten hit "1, 2, 3 Redlight".

36. **Valleri** was the Monkees' final top ten hit .This hastily-written Tommy Boyce and Bobby Hart song featured Davy Jones on lead vocals. Michael Nesmith despised the song. The group broke up shortly afterwards.

37. **Sunshine of Your Love** was one of only two top ten hits by the Super group known as Cream featuring Eric Clapton, Jack Bruce and Ginger Baker. After the short-lived Cream disbanded, Clapton and Baker formed Blind Faith along with Steve Winwood and Ric Grech.

38. **Midnight Confessions** was the biggest hit by The Grassroots, a goodtime group which featured Rob Grill on lead vocals.

39. **Abraham, Martin and John** was Dion's tribute to Abraham Lincoln, Martin Luther King Jr. and John F. and Bobby Kennedy. This was a complete change of direction from the former Belmonts' lead singer best known for hits like 'Runaround Sue' and 'The Wanderer' among others.

40. **Bend Me Shape Me** was a top 10 hit for The American Breed, an interracial rock group. Some members later joined Chaka Khan's group 'Rufus'.

41. **Yummy Yummy Yummy** was a bubblegum hit by The Ohio Express featuring the nasally-voiced lead singer Joey Levine. Levine later resurfaced as the lead singer of one hit wonder studio group Reunion on the 1974 hit Life Is a Rock (but the radio rolled me).

42. **La La Means I Love You** was a silky-smooth love ballad by Philadelphia's soul group The Delfonics. It reached top ten in the spring of '68.

43. **Angel of the Morning** was a Top ten hit by one hit wonder Merrilee

Rush which was written by Chip Taylor, the brother of actor Jon Voight and uncle of Angelina Jolie.

44. **Light My Fire** by Jose Feliciano was a completely different arrangement of the song which reached number one the previous summer for The Doors.

45. **I Wish It Would Rain** by The Temptations was popular in the same year group member David Ruffin, who sang lead on many of their hits, was replaced by Dennis Edwards.

46. **Love Is All Around** by The Troggs was the final top 10 hit in North America for this British rock group led by Reg Presley best known for the hit 'Wild Thing' from 1966.

47. **Hurdy Gurdy Man** by Donovan featured the unusual 'tambura' instrument, and although its widely believed that Jimmy Page played guitar, according to John Paul Jones who arranged and played bass on this hit, it was Alan Parker, not Jimmy Page playing electric guitar on Hurdy Gurdy Man.

48. **Hush** by Deep Purple was the first hit for this British hard rock band. 'Hush' was written by Joe South who wrote 'Down In The Boondocks' for Billy Joe Royal, 'Rose Garden' by Lynn Anderson' and 'Yo Yo for The Osmonds. He also won the song of the year Grammy Award in 1969 for 'Games People Play' which he wrote and recorded.

49. **Stormy** was the second of 4 top 20 hits for the Classics 4, a Jacksonville, Florida group which featured Dennis Yost on lead vocals.

50. **Girl Watcher** by The O'Kaysions was the only hit for this R & B sextet from North Carolina.

51. **1 2 3 Redlight** was a top ten hit by New Jersey bubblegum group 1910 Fruitgum Company. This hit was one of their 'kids games hits' which also included the popular 'Simon Says'.

52. **Dance To The Music** by Sly & The Family Stone was the first of a string of hits for this psychedelic San Francisco soul group led by former DJ Sylvester 'Sly Stone' Stewart.

53. **The Look of Love** by Sergio Mendes and Brazil '66 was written by Burt Bacharach and Hal David and featured in the film 'Casino Royale'. Many years later, Mike Myers heard this song on the radio and it inspired him to create the 'Austin Powers' character and movies.

54. **Just Dropped In (To See What Condition My Condition Was in)** was the psychedelic first hit by Kenny Rogers and The First Edition. The opening of the song featured the instruments played in reverse for a really far- out sound.

55. **Hold Me Tight** by Johnny Nash was one of the first reggae hits on the pop charts. He also sang the theme for the 'Hercules' cartoon TV series back then.

56. **Turn Around, Look At Me** was the first big hit by the Vogues with their softer, mellow sound similar to The Lettermen. This song was originally a minor hit in 1961 by a then-unknown Glen Campbell.

57. **You Keep Me Hangin' On** was a psychedelic rock remake of the Supremes number one hit from 2 years earlier. This New City Group included Tim Bogert, Carmine Appice and Mark Stein on lead vocals.

58. **Elenore** by The Turtles was written as a joke after their record company pressured the group into coming up with a hit that could be as successful as 'Happy Together' from the previous year. 'Elenore' is the only Top 40 hit which uses the word 'etcetera'.

59. **Slip Away** was the biggest 60's hit for Alabama singer Clarence Carter who was blind since the age of one.

60. **Cinnamon** was a Top Ten bubblegum hit by Derek, a singer/songwriter/producer who 5 years earlier had a hit with 'Mr. Bass Man' under the name Johnny Cymbal. Derek/Johnny Cymbal died of a heart attack at age 48 in 1993.

61. **The Mighty Quinn** by Manfred Mann, written by Bob Dylan was shown as 'Quinn the Eskimo' on some record releases.

62. **Baby Now That I've Found You** was the first hit by The Foundations, a British interracial group whose biggest hit was 'Build Me Up Buttercup'.

63. **Think** by Aretha Franklin was later performed by lady soul in the diner scene in the original Blues Brothers movie.

64. **The Unicorn** by The Canadian group The Irish Rovers was written by author/cartoonist/songwriter Shel Silverstein.

65. **White Room** by Cream was the second biggest of two 1968 hits they achieved with 'Sunshine Of Your Love' being the first. Their hits were produced by Felix Papalardi who was later a founding member of the group 'Mountain'.

66. **Ballad of Bonnie and Clyde** by Britain's Georgie Fame was inspired by the crime couple movie which starred Warren Beatty and Faye Dunaway.

67. **I've Gotta Get A Message To You** by The Bee Gees was a story song about a guy on death row. This was one of 15 top 10 hits achieved during the 60's and 70's.

68. **I Wonder What She's Doing Tonight** was the first and biggest hit for Tommy Boyce and Bobby Hart who were better known for writing some of the Monkees biggest hits including 'Last Train To Clarksville', 'Valleri' and 'The Monkees Theme'. In 1994, Tommy Boyce committed suicide by shooting himself in the head in his sitting room at his house.

69. **Over You** by Gary Puckett and The Union Gap was their only top ten hit of 5 songs which did not have 'Woman', 'Lady' or 'Girl' in the title. It still managed to sell over a million copies

70. **Cowboys to Girls** by The Intruders was written by Philadelphia's award-winning duo Kenny Gamble and Leon Huff.

71. **Time Has Come Today** was the only notable hit for The Chambers Brothers, a psychedelic soul group featuring 4 Mississippi-born brothers.

72. **Ain't Nothin' like the Real Thing** was one of three top 20 hits for Motown's Marvin Gaye with Tammi Terrell in 1968. She died of a brain hemorage in 1970 at the age of 24.

73. **(Sweet Sweet Baby) Since You've Been Gone** by Aretha Franklin, was one of 9 top 10 hits during 1967 - 1968, her most successful period of hits.

74. **Chewy Chewy** was one of 3 bubblegum hits from the Ohio Express in 1968. They all featured singer/songwriter Joey Levine on lead vocals.

75. **Both Sides Now** by Judy Collins was often referred to as 'Clouds'. This song was written by Canadian singer/songwriter Joni Mitchell.

76. **Do You Know The Way To San Jose** by Dionne Warwick was one of over a dozen hits for her written by Burt Bacharach and Hal David.

77. **The Fool on The Hill** by Sergio Mendez And Brazil '66 was written by John Lennon And Paul McCartney and featured on their 1967 album 'Magical Mystery Tour'. Herb Alpert's wife, Lani Hall was the lead singer of this group.

78. **Bottle of Wine** was a party hit by The Fireballs, the group that backed Jimmy Gilmer on the 1963 number one hit 'Sugar Shack'.

79. **My Special Angel** by The Vogues was originally a top ten hit 11 years earlier by Bobby Helms. This song demonstrated The Vogues' smooth harmony which became their new style after 'Five O'Clock World' in 1966.

80. **Piece of My Heart** by Big Brother and The Holding Company was the breakthrough hit for the legendary Janis Joplin, who died 2 years later of a drug overdose. This was a prime cut from the Cheap Thrills album which topped the album charts for 8 weeks in the fall of 1968.

81. **She's A Heartbreaker** by Gene Pitney was his final top 20 hit in North America, although he continued to have hits in Britain.

82. **Here Comes Da Judge** by Shorty Long was a Motown hit inspired by a gag line from 'Rowan & Martin's Laugh-In' TV Show. Alabama's Shorty Long drowned in Canada the following year in the summer of '69.

83. **Pictures of Matchstick Men** by The Status Quo was their only North American hit, even though they had no less than 20 hits in Britain.

84. **Nobody but Me** by the Human Beinz was a song written and originally recorded by the Isley Brothers, although it didn't become a hit for them. This one hit wonder rock band was from Youngstown, Ohio.

85. **I Love How You Love Me** was Bobby Vinton's final top 10 hit of the 60's. This song was a remake of the Paris Sisters hit from 1961.

86. **Reach Out Of the Darkness** was a groovy summer '68 hit by one hit wonder 'Friend and Lover' who were husband and wife team Cathy and James Post. Joe South produced this hit and Ray Stevens arranged the strings and played keyboards.

87. **Can't Take My Eyes Off You/Goin' Out Of My Head** by The Lettermen was a 'live' remake of two hits of the 60's by this L.A. based mellow harmonizing group.

88. **Indian Lake** was a top ten hit in the summer of '68 for the family act The Cowsills from Rhode Island. Lead singer Billy Cowsill died in 2006, just months after brother Barry died in late 2005.

89. **Different Drum** , written by Monkee Michael Nesmith was the first and last hit for the L.A.-based Folk-Rock Trio the Stone Poneys, but lead singer Linda Ronstadt went on to great fame as a soloist.

90. **Delilah** by Tom Jones was a great party song from this Welsh-born singer who hosted his own variety show from 1969 - '71.

91. **I Thank You** was a hit for the original Soul Men, Sam and Dave. Dave (Prater) was killed in a car accident in 1988.

92. **You're all I Need to get By** was the last of 5 top 20 hits by Marvin Gaye with Tammi Terrell. Aretha Franklin revived it three years later in 1971 and brought it into the top 20 again.

93. **Summertime Blues** by Blue Cheer was a hard rock remake of a song originally popular in the 50's by Eddie Cochran. The Who had a hit with it in 1970.

94. **Suzie Q** was the very first hit for the swamp rock group from California known as Creedence Clearwater Revival. This song was originally popular by Dale Hawkins in 1957.

95. **The House That Jack Built/I Say A Little Prayer** was a double-sided hit single for Lady Soul, Aretha Franklin. She revived 'I Say A Little Prayer' and made it a hit again a year after Dionne Warwick's version sold a million copies.

96. **Susan** was the final hit by The Buckinghams and their only hit that wasn't from 1967, a year they charted half a dozen hits.

97. **Words** by The Bee Gees was their first hit of 1968 after charting 5 hits in their debut year, 1967.

98. **I Love You** was by 'People', a one hit wonder 6 man band from San Jose, California. This ballad was one of the greatest psychedelic hits of the 60's.

99. **I Got The Feelin'** was a top ten hit on the pop charts and a number one hit on the R & B charts for James Brown, the Godfather of soul. The hardest working man in show business died suddenly on Christmas day 2006.

100. **On the Road Again** by Canned Heat was the first hit for this L.A-based blues/rock group. The unusual voice of Alan Wilson was featured on lead vocals. He died of a drug overdose two years later at the age of 27.

101. **In-A-Gadda-Da-Vida** by Iron Butterfly was a heavy metal anthem in 1968.The single version was just under 3 minutes while the most popular version ran over 17 minutes on the entire side of the album.

102. **Sky Pilot** by Eric Burdon and The Animals was their final top 20 hit in North America. Sky Pilot part two, on the 'B' side of the single prominently featured the sound of bagpipes, which was quite unusual for a rock song in the 60's.

103. **Master Jack** was a pop/folk hit for Four Jacks and A Jill, a one hit wonder act from South Africa.

104. **Love Makes A Woman** was a hit for Chicago soul singer/songwriter Barbara Acklin, who later co-wrote The Chi-Lites million seller 'Have You Seen Her'.

105. **Baby Come Back** by The Equals was led by singer/songwriter Eddy Grant who later had a big solo hit in the 80's with 'Electric Avenue'.

106. **Journey to the Centre Of Your Mind** was a psychedelic hit by The Amboy Dukes featuring Detroit rocker Ted Nugent on lead guitar.

107. **Tuesday Afternoon** by The Moody Blues was their first hit after the departure of Denny Laine and the arrival of Justin Hayward.

108. **Dream A Little Dream of Me** by Mama Cass Elliot with the Mamas and Papas was a remake of a 1931 number one hit for Wayne King. Mama Cass died in 1974.

109. **Shoot 'em Up Baby** by Montreal's Andy Kim was one of 5 notable solo hits he achieved from '68 to '69. Singer/songwriter Jeff Barry produced them all.

110. **Tip Toe Through The Tulips** was an oddball novelty hit by Tiny Tim which was originally popular in 1926 by Nick Lucas.

111. **Darlin** was a Beach Boys hit which featured Carl Wilson on lead vocals. Carl, who died of cancer in 1998, was also the lead singer on 'Good Vibrations' and 'God Only Knows'.

112. **Like to Get To Know You** by Spanky and Our Gang was the final top 20 hit for this harmonizing vocal group from Chicago featuring Elaine 'Spanky' McFarlane on lead vocals.

113. **Sweet Inspiration** was a hit for The Sweet Inspirations, an R & B quartet led by Cissy Houston, mother of Whitney. They were the backup singers on Elvis Presley's 'live' recording of "Suspicious Minds".

114. **Everything That Touches You** by The Association was the final top ten hit by this L.A. vocal group best known for hits like 'Cherish', 'Windy' and 'Never My Love'.

115. **Love Power** was a hit for the one hit wonder soul trio known as The Sandpebbles. This song was later redone by Luther Vandross.

116. **Don't Take It So Hard** by Paul Revere and The Raiders featured pony-tailed Mark Lindsay on lead vocals on all of their hits, which numbered almost a dozen.

117. **Wear Your Love like Heaven** was one of a string of late 60's hits for Scottish singer/poet Donovan Leitch. His daughter is actress Ione Skye and his actor son shares his name.

118. **Halfway To Paradise** by Bobby Vinton was written by Carole King and Gerry Goffin and was originally a hit for Tony Orlando in 1961.

119. **Alice Long (You're Still My Favorite Girlfriend)** was the second of two top 20 hits for singer/songwriters Tommy Boyce and Bobby Hart in 1968.

120. **See Saw** by lady soul, Aretha Franklin was one of 11 top 20 hits she achieved from 1967 - 1968 alone.

121. **A Man Without Love** was a middle-of-the-road hit for Madras, India born Engelbert Humperdinck, whose real name is Arnold George Dorsey.

122. **Promises, Promises** was another Dionne Warwick hit written by Burt Bacharach and Hal David. All of her 60's hits were recorded on the Scepter record label.

123. **Do It Again** by The Beach Boys was their return to the surf, sand and beach after a short-lived venture into a more progressive and experimental sound. This hit reached number one in the U.K., but failed to reach the top ten in North America.

124. **Suddenly You Love Me** by British vocal group the Tremeloes was their 4th and final top 40 hit in North America. This Italian-based song was reworked in English.

125. **Take Time To Know Her** was the final top 40 hit for Alabama's Percy Sledge, best known for his number one hit 'When A Man Loves A Woman' in 1966.

126. **Little Arrows** was a fun novelty hit by one hit wonder singer Leapy Lee. It was co-written by Albert Hammond, who not only later went on to have a top ten hit of his own with 'It Never Rains In Southern California', but co-wrote other hits which included 'The Air That I Breathe', 'Gimme Dat Ding' and 'When I Need You'..

127. **Soul Coaxing** was a big production instrumental hit by Raymond LeFevre, a conductor/pianist/flutist from Paris.

128. **Jennifer Juniper** was one of over half a dozen late 60's hits for Donovan on the Epic label produced by Mickie Most.

129. **Folsom Prison Blues** by Johnny Cash was actually recorded 'live' at this prison. The original studio version of this song was released by Cash in 1956.

130. **By the Time I Got to Phoenix** was another Glen Campbell hit written by Jim Webb which featured the name of a city in the title. The other two were 'Galveston' and 'Wichita'.

130. **Magic Bus** was a summer '68 hit for The Who. Their hits were written by guitarist Pete Townsend with Roger Daltry on lead vocals, accompanied by John Entwistle on guitar and the wild and legendary Keith Moon on drums.

131. **Mr**. **Businessman** was a serious social comment song by Ray Stevens, usually known for his funny novelty hits which included 'Ahab the Arab', 'Gitarzan' and 'The Streak'.

132. **She's A Rainbow** by The Rolling Stones was a prime cut from the album 'Their 'Satanic Majesties Request.' The LP stalled at number two because the Beatles held on to the number one spot for 8 consecutive weeks with 'Magical Mystery Tour'.

133. **Hey Western Union Man** by Jerry Butler was listed on some vinyl 45's as 'Send A Telegram', which was repeated prominently in the chorus..

134. **Down at Lulu's** was a bubblegum hit for the Ohio Express just after 'Yummy Yummy Yummy' and just before 'Chewy Chewy', all from 1968, their most successful year.

135. **How'd we Ever Get This Way** was the first of many hits for Andy Kim. The following year he wrote the multi-million selling 'Sugar Sugar' with songwriter/producer Jeff Barry for the Archies.

136. **Am I That Easy to Forget** was another easy going hit for Englebert Humperdick, who was managed by Gordon Mills - Tom Jones Manager.

137. **If You Can Want** was a moderate hit for Motown's Smokey Robinson and The Miracles. The multi-talented Robinson also produced and wrote the Temptations hits from 1964 - '66.

138. **Sweet Blindness** was a bouncy, bright-sounding 5th Dimension hit, which was one of 5 of their hits written by Laura Nyro.

139. **Shoo-Be-Do-Be-Do-Da-Day** by Stevie Wonder was a hit the same year he recorded a song as 'Eivets Rednow' - his name backwards.

140. **Red, Red Wine** by Neil Diamond didn't even reach the Top 40 but 20 years later UB40 revived this vintage song and brought it to number one..

141. **Son of Hickory Holler's Tramp** was a story song by O.C. Smith and was the first hit for this Louisiana-born singer who died in 2001.

142. **Soul Limbo** was a great instrumental hit by Booker T. and The MGs featuring Steve Cropper and Donald 'Duck' Dunn. 'MG' stood for 'Memphis Group'.

143. **I Put a Spell on You** was one of C.C.R.'s earliest hits. This song was originally recorded by Screamin' Jay Hawkins in 1956.

144. **With A Little Help from My Friends** was Joe Cocker's claim to fame. It was a reworking of The Beatles song. Jimmy Page was featured on guitar.

145. **Tell Mama** was a hit for L.A. based soul singer Etta James, who first recorded back in 1954. She was portrayed by Beyonce in the film 'Cadillac Records', the story of Chess Records.

146. **Dreams of An Everyday Housewife** was a hit for Glen Campbell, but was also a hit for Wayne Newton in 1968.

147.**Quick Joey Small** was by The Kasenetz-Katz Singing Orchestral Circus, a bubblegum music assemblage which included members from the Ohio Express, 1910 Fruitgum Company and the Music Explosion.

148. **The Eyes of a New York Woman** by B.J. (Billy Joe) Thomas was one of a dozen top 40 hits he achieved from the late 60's to early 70's.

149. **Stay in My Corner** by the Dells was a remake of their own hit from 1965. This one reached the top ten in the summer of '68.

150. **Shame, Shame** was a hit for the Magic Lanterns, a one hit wonder group from Lancashire, England who once had singer- songwriter Albert Hammond as a member.

151. **In the Midnight Hour** was a remake of the Wilson Pickett classic by former Ikettes members, the Mirettes.

152. **Jennifer Eccles** was the final Hollies hit featuring Graham Nash. After this hit, he left this popular British group to form 'Crosby, Stills and Nash'. Neil Young joined shortly afterwards.

153. **With Pen In Hand** was a heartfelt divorce song by Billy Vera written by Bobby Goldsboro. Billy Vera resurfaced two decades later with the number one hit 'At This Moment'.

154. **Help Yourself** was a sassy song from Tom Jones, who won the Best New Artist Grammy Award back in 1965.

155. **Sherry Don't Go** was a smooth, melodic hit by The Lettermen, a three man vocal from Los Angeles who formed in 1960 and had several middle-of-the-road hits during the decade.

156. **A Question of Temperature** by The Balloon Farm was a psychedelic hit featuring unusual sounds by a one hit wonder flower power quintet from New York.

157. **Bring A Little Lovin'** was the only other hit by the Spanish rock group Los Bravos, best known for their 1966 top 10 hit 'Black Is Black'.

158. **Black Day In July** was a social comment hit by Canadian singer/songwriter Gordon Lightfoot about the Detroit race riots during the summer of '67.

159. **Skip a Rope** by Henson Cargil was a country-crossover hit which topped the Country charts for 5 consecutive weeks in '68.

160. **Ride My See Saw** was a moderate hit for the Symphonic rock group the Moody Blues. It was from their 'Days of Future Past' album and was the follow up to their single 'Tuesday Afternoon'.

MORE HITS OF 1968

Street Fighting Man was a controversial hit by The Rolling Stones which was banned by many radio stations. Its lack of airplay resulted in missing the Top 40 on the charts.

My Name Is Jack was a catchy, but very oddball hit by Manfred Mann and was only a hit in Britain and Canada.

Baby Let's Wait was a serious hit by the Royal Guardsmen, the group primarily known for their 'Snoopy' novelty hits.

Call Me Lightning was a super-fast high energy hit by the legendary British group 'The Who'. They were inducted into the Rock And Roll Hall Of Fame in 1990.

Rainbow Ride was made popular by Andy Kim, whose real name is Andrew Joachim. This Montreal born and raised singer/songwriter had a string of bubblegum hits during the late 60's and early 70's. His voice was sped up on those recordings to make him sound even younger.

You've Had Better Times by Peter and Gordon was a hit only in Britain and Canada, the year after this popular British duo disbanded.

Cab Driver was an oddball hit in 1968 by The Mills Brothers, a popular act from another era.

Baby You Come Rollin' Cross My Mind was a mellow hit by one hit wonder act the Peppermint Trolley Company.

Sunday Sun was a goodtime, upbeat hit by singer/songwriter Neil Diamond which was more popular in Canada than it was in the U.S.

Loveitis was a hit by Toronto based blue-eyed soul group Mandala featuring George Oliver, Roy Kenner and Dominic Troiano.

Sunday Mornin' was the most progressive sounding hit for Spanky And Our Gang, usually known for their easy harmonizing vocal pop melodies.

Indian Reservation by British singer Don Fardon was the original version of the song Paul Revere and The Raiders revived and brought to number one in 1971.

Zabadak by British quintet Dave Dee, Dozy, Beaky, Mick and Tich was more popular in Britain and Canada than in the U.S. 'The Legend Of Xanadu' was another moderate British hit for this group in 1968. Dave Dee died of cancer in January of 2009 at age 67.

Competition Ain't Nothin' was the first hit for Little Carl Carlton who was 15 at the time he recorded this 1968 hit. He later had a big hit in 1974 with 'Everlasting Love'.

Lalena by Donovan was a lesser known follow up to 'Hurdy Gurdy Man'.

Unknown Soldier by The Doors featured a re-enactment of the event. Jim Morrison died mysteriously in Paris, France at age 27 in '71.

There Is was a great, upbeat hit for The Dells, an R & B vocal group that formed in the early 50's while in High School.

TOP 16 ALBUMS OF 1968

1. The Graduate - Soundtrack
2. Magical Mystery Tour - The Beatles
3. Cheap Thrills - Big Brother & The Holding Co.
4. Bookends - Simon & Garfunkel
5. Blooming Hits - Paul Mauriat
6. Waiting For The Sun - The Doors
7. Wheels Of Fire - Cream
8. Electric Ladyland - Jimi Hendrix
9. Witchita Lineman - Glen Campbell
10. Beat Of The Brass - Herb Alpert & The Tijuana Brass
11. Time Peace, The Rascals Greatest Hits - The Rascals
12. Their Satanic Majesties Request - The Rolling Stones
13. Greatest Hits - The Supremes
14. Lady Soul - Aretha Franklin
15. John Wesley Harding - Bob Dylan
16. Axis: Bold As Love - The Jimi Hendrix Experience

TOP 16 COUNTRY HITS OF 1968

1. Skip A Rope - Henson Cargill
2. Folsom Prison Blues - Johnny Cash
3. Mama Tried - Merle Haggard
4. For Loving You - Bill Anderson & Jan Howard
5. Stand By Your Man - Tammy Wynette
6. Honey - Bobby Goldsboro
7. Harper Valley P.T.A. - Jeannie C. Riley
8. D.I.V.O.R.C.E. - Tammy Wynette
9. A World Of Our Own - Sonny James
10. I Wanna Live - Glen Campbell
11. The Legend Of Bonnie & Clyde - Merle Haggard
12. Witchita Lineman - Glen Campbell
13. I Walk Alone - Marty Robbins
14. Sing Me Back Home - Merle Haggard
15. Then You Can Tell Me Goodbye - Eddy Arnold
16. Next In Line - Conway Twitty

TOP 16 ONE HIT WONDERS OF 1968

1. Paul Mauriat - Love Is Blue
2. Arthur Brown - Fire
3. Mason Williams - Classical Gas
4. The O'Kaysions - Girl Watcher
5. Merilee Rush - Angel Of The Morning
6. Friend And Lover - Reach Out Of The Darkness
7. Human Beinz - Nobody But Me
8. People - I Love You
9. Cliff Nobles & Co. - The Horse
10. Shorty Long - Here Come Da Judge
11. Leapy Lee - Little Arrows
12. Balloon Farm - A Question Of Temperature
13. Kasenetz Katz Singing Circus - Quick Joey Small
14. The Mirettes - In The Midnight Hour
15. Peppermint Trolley Co. - Baby You Come Rollin' 'Cross My Mind
16. The Magic Lanterns - Shame Shame

16 GREAT 'LOST' 45's FROM 1968

1. Do It Again - The Beach Boys
2. Summertime Blues - Blue Cheer
3. There Is - The Dells
4. Like To Get To Know You - Spanky & Our Gang
5. Master Jack - Four Jacks & A Jill
6. Soul Limbo - Booker T. & The MG's
7. Sweet Blindness - 5th Dimension
8. Hey Western Union Man - Jerry Butler
9. My Name Is Jack - Manfred Mann
10. You've Had Better Times - Peter & Gordon
11. A Question Of Temperature - Balloon Farm
12. Sunday Sun - Neil Diamond
13. Competition Ain't Nothin' - Little Carl Carlton
14. Sherry Don't Go - The Lettermen
15. Baby You Come Rollin' 'Cross My Mind - Peppermint Trolley Co.
16. Sunday Mornin' - Spanky & Our Gang

TOP 16 R & B/SOUL HITS OF 1968

1. Dock Of The Bay - Otis Redding
2. Tighten Up - Archie Bell & The Drells
3. Love Child - Diana Ross & The Supremes
4. Chain Of Fools - Aretha Franklin
5. For Once In My Life - Stevie Wonder
6. La La Means I Love You - The Delfonics
7. I Wish It Would Rain - The Temptations
8. Girl Watcher - The O'Kaysions
9. Dance To The Music - Sly & The Family Stone
10. Think - Aretha Franklin
11. Slip Away - Clarence Carter
12. Ain't Nothin' Like The Real Thing - Marvin G. & Tammi T.
13. Cowboys To Girls - The Intruders
14. Since You've Been Gone - Aretha Franklin
15. Here Come Da Judge - Shorty Long
16. I Got The Feelin' - James Brown

TOP 16 ROCK/HARD ROCK HITS OF 1968

1. Born To Be Wild - Steppenwolf
2. Jumpin' Jack Flash - The Rolling Stones
3. Sunshine Of Your Love - Cream
4. Magic Carpet Ride - Steppenwolf
5. Fire - Arthur Brown
6. Hush - Deep Purple
7. Hurdy Gurdy Man - Donovan
8. You Keep Me Hangin' On - Vanilla Fudge
9. White Room - Cream
10. Revolution - The Beatles
11. Piece Of My Heart - Big Brother & Holding Co.
12. Pictures Of Matchstick Men - Status Quo
13. In-A-Gadda-Da-Vida - Iron Butterfly
14. Summertime Blues - Blue Cheer
15. Journey To The Centre Of Your Mind - Amboy Dukes
16. Magic Bus - The Who

1. I Heard It Through The Grapevine - Marvin Gaye - 1969
2. I'm A Believer - Monkees - 1967
3. Theme From A Summer Place - Percy Faith - 1960
4. Pretty Woman - Roy Orbison - 1964
5. Are You Lonesome Tonight - Elvis Presley - 1960
6. Aquarius/Let The Sunshine In - 5th Dimension - 1969
7. It's Now Or Never - Elvis Presley - 1960
8. Happy Together - Turtles - 1967
9. I Got You Babe - Sonny & Cher - 1965
10. I Can't Stop Loving You - Ray Charles - 1962
11. Baby Love - Supremes - 1964
12. Good Vibrations - Beach Boys - 1966
13. Mrs. Robinson - Simon & Garfunkel - 1968
14. Tossin' & Turnin' - Bobby Lewis - 1961
15. Big Girls Don't Cry - Four Seasons - 1962
16. You've Lost That Loving Feeling - Righteous Bros. - 1965
17. The Letter - Box Tops - 1967
18. Dock Of The Bay - Otis Redding - 1968
19. Light My Fire - Doors - 1967
20. Suspicious Minds - Elvis Presley - 1969
21. The Twist - Chubby Checker - 1960
22. Runaway - Del Shannon - 1961
23. Cathy's Clown - Everly Bros. - 1960
24. Louie Louie - Kingsmen - 1963
25. Monday Monday - Mamas & Papas - 1966
26. Groovin' - Young Rascals - 1967
27. Crimson And Clover - Tommy James & Shondells - 1969
28. Stuck On You - Elvis Presley - 1960
29. Sherry - Four Seasons - 1962
30. I Get Around - Beach Boys - 1964
31. When A Man Loves A Woman - Percy Sledge - 1966
32. Honey - Bobby Goldsboro - 1968

33. The Lion Sleeps Tonight - Tokens - 1961
34. The Locomotion - Little Eva - 1962
35. Last Train To Clarksville - Monkees - 1966
36. People Got To Be Free - Rascals - 1968
37. Sugar Sugar - Archies - 1969
38. Sugar Shack - Jimmy Gilmer & Fireballs - 1963
39. Turn Turn Turn - Byrds - 1965
40. Unchained Melody - Righteous Brothers - 1965
41. Respect - Aretha Franklin - 1967
42. Proud Mary - C.C.R. - 1969
43. Georgia On My Mind - Ray Charles - 1962
44. Breaking Up Is Hard To Do - Neil Sedaka - 1962
45. Wipeout - Surfaris - 1963
46. I Can't Help Myself - Four Tops - 1965
47. El Paso - Marty Robbins - 1960
48. You Can't Hurry Love - Supremes - 1966
49. Windy - Association - 1967
50. My Girl - Temptations - 1965
51. Can't Help Falling In Love - Elvis Presley - 1962
52. Sounds Of Silence - Simon & Garfunkel - 1966
53. Daydream Believer - Monkees - 1967
54. Na Na Hey Hey Kiss Him Goodbye - Steam - 1969
55. Save The Last Dance For Me - Drifters - 1960
56. Big Bad John - Jimmy Dean - 1961
57. He's So Fine - Chiffons - 1963
58. Where Did Our Love Go - Supremes - 1964
59. This Guy's In Love With You - Herb Alpert - 1968
60. Stay - Maurice Williams & Zodiacs - 1960
61. California Girls - Beach Boys - 1965
62. Ode To Billie Joe - Bobbie Gentry - 1967
63. Everyday People - Sly & Family Stone - 1969
64. Will You Love Me Tomorrow - Shirelles - 1961
65. My Guy - Mary Wells - 1964
66. In The Year 2525 - Zager & Evans - 1969
67. Itsy Bitsy Teenie Weenie…Bikini - Brian Hyland - 1960
68. Hanky Panky - Tommy James & Shondells - 1966
69. Reach Out, I'll Be There - Four Tops - 1966
70. Hey Baby - Bruce Channel - 1962
71. These Boots Are Made For Walkin' - Nancy Sinatra - 1966
72. Dizzy - Tommy Roe - 1969
73. Blue Moon - Marcels - 1961
74. Rag Doll - Four Seasons - 1964
75. Stop In The Name Of Love - Supremes - 1965
76. Good Lovin' - Young Rascals - 1966
77. Mr. Tambourine Man - Byrds - 1965
78. Someday We'll Be Together - Supremes - 1969
79. I'm Sorry - Brenda Lee - 1960
80. Duke Of Earl - Gene Chandler - 1962

81. Summer In The City - Lovin' Spoonful - 1966
82. Somethin' Stupid - Nancy & Frank Sinatra - 1967
83. Take Good Care Of My Baby - Bobby Vee - 1961
84. It's My Party - Lesley Gore - 1963
85. Incense & Peppermints - Strawberry Alarm Clock - 1967
86. Love Child - Supremes - 1968
87. Pony Time - Chubby Checker - 1961
88. Walk Like A Man - Four Seasons - 1963
89. Help Me Rhonda - Beach Boys - 1965
90. Cherish - Association - 1966
91. Can't Take My Eyes Off You - Frankie Valli - 1967
92. Peppermint Twist - Joey Dee & The Starliters - 1962
93. Chapel Of Love - Dixie Cups - 1964
94. Leavin' On A Jet Plane - Peter, Paul & Mary - 1969
95. This Diamond Ring - Gary Lewis & The Playboys - 1965
96. Tighten Up - Archie Bell & The Drells - 1968
97. Good Luck Charm - Elvis Presley - 1962
98. Johnny Angel - Shelley Fabares - 1962
99. You Keep Me Hangin' On - Supremes - 1966
100. Wedding Bell Blues - 5th Dimension - 1969
101. Travelin' Man - Rick Nelson - 1961
102. Blue Velvet - Bobby Vinton - 1963
103. My Boyfriend's Back - Angels - 1963
104. Eve Of Destruction - Barry Mcguire - 1965
105. Kind Of A Drag - Buckinghams - 1967
106. Roses Are Red - Bobby Vinton - 1962
107. Surf City - Jan & Dean - 1963
108. Soul & Inspiration - Righteous Brothers - 1966
109. Sheila - Tommy Roe - 1962
110. Monster Mash - Bobby 'Boris' Pickett - 1962
111. Lightning Strikes - Lou Christie - 1966
112. Soldier Boy - Shirelles - 1962
113. Judy In Disguise - John Fred & His Playboy Band - 1968
114. There I've Said It Again - Bobby Vinton - 1964
115. Bad Moon Rising - C.C.R. - 1969
116. The Wanderer - Dion - 1962

♫ Mick Jagger was one of the several musical friends of the Beatles who played on this number one hit!

♫ This British classic hit was inspired by J.S. Bach's 'Sleeper's Awake', written in 1731!

♫ Otis Redding wrote two 1967 Million Selling hits for others in the year he would die in a plane crash!

♫ Screen legend Charlie Chaplin wrote this top ten hit for Petula Clark!

♫ A teenaged Steve Winwood sang lead on this top ten hit by the Spencer Davis Group!

♫ Neil Diamond wrote two 1967 major hits by The Monkees, including their most successful!

FIND OUT THAT...and MUCH MORE...INSIDE...1967!

1. **I'm A Believer /I'm Not Your Steppin' Stone** was a double-sided hit for The Monkees. 'I'm A Believer' written by Neil Diamond, became their biggest hit of all. The 'B' side 'I'm Not Your Steppin' Stone' was written by Boyce & Hart. Both songs featured Mickey Dolenz on lead vocals.

2. **The Letter** by The Box Tops featured 16 year old Alex Chilton on lead vocals. This was the first and biggest hit for this blue-eyed Memphis Soul group. Alex Chilton died Mar 17th 2010 at the age of 59.

3. **To Sir with Love** by Lulu was the title song of the film which starred Sidney Poitier and featured the singer of this multi-million seller. The 'B' side of this single was 'The Boat That I Row' written by Neil Diamond.

4. **Ode to Billie Joe** by Bobbie Gentry was one of the year's biggest hits. It was a story song about the mystery of Tallahatchie Bridge and later became a movie starring Robbie Benson. Bobbie Gentry was once married to Jim Stafford of 'Spiders & Snakes' fame.

5. **Happy Together** by The Turtles was the biggest hit for the goodtime 60's group led by 'Flo & Eddie', better known as Mark Volman & Howard Kaylan.

6. **Groovin'** was the second of three number one hits for this New York City group formed in 1964. Felix Cavaliere sang lead on this feel good hit from the summer of love. Group members Felix Cavaliere and Eddie Brigati were inspired to write this song after being away from their girlfriends all week, looking forward to Sundays when they could do some groovin'.

7. **All You Need Is Love** by The Beatles was recorded 'Live' worldwide via satellite. A gum-chewing John Lennon was featured on lead vocals with the Beatles musical friends which included Mick Jagger, Keith Richard, Donovan, Marianne Faithful and Keith Moon.

8. **Windy** by The Association was the 2nd and biggest of their two official number one hits. 'Cherish' from 1966 was their first number one hit.

9. **Light My Fire** was the first major hit by the legendary group the Doors, fronted by Jim Morrison. This Los Angeles-based rock group was formed in 1965 and continued until Morrison's death in 1971.

10. **Daydream Believer** was number one for the Monkees for a full month. This hit featured Davy Jones on lead vocals and was written by John Stewart, ex-member of The Kingston Trio and singer of the 70's hit 'Gold'.

11. **Hello Goodbye/I Am the Walrus** was a double-side hit single by The Beatles. The 'A' side was Paul's composition, Hello Goodbye, which featured him on piano and lead vocals. 'I Am The Walrus' was John's song as a composer and lead singer.

12. **Respect** was the signature hit for the lady dubbed 'Lady Soul', Aretha Franklin. This hit was written by Otis Redding and was number one the year he died.

13. **Kind Of A Drag** was the first and biggest of five 1967 hits for the Buckinghams, a Chicago-based brass rock band produced by James William Guercio, who later produced the hits of Chicago.

14. **Ruby Tuesday/Let's Spend the Night Together** was a great double-side hit single by The Rolling Stones. Mick Jagger was asked by Ed Sullivan to change 'Let's Spend the Night Together' to 'Let's Spend Some Time Together' before his performance on the show. Jagger decided to stick to the original.

15. **Somethin' Stupid** was a huge multi-week number one hit for father & daughter Frank and Nancy Sinatra. It was their only hit together.

16. **Incense and Peppermints** was a number one hit for the Strawberry Alarm Clock in the fall of 1967. Lead guitarist Ed King later joined Lynyrd Skynyrd.

17. **Penny Lane/Strawberry Fields Forever** was a doubled-sided hit single by The Beatles. 'Penny Lane' was written solely by Paul. He also sang lead and played piano on this number one hit. The 'B' side 'Strawberry Fields Forever' was John's song. He solely wrote it and sang lead on this far out psychedelic hit.

18. **Love Is Here & Now You're Gone** was a number one hit for The Supremes featuring spoken word by Diana Ross. Three years later she had a number one solo hit with spoken word, on 'Ain't No Mountain High Enough'.

19. **Can't Take My Eyes Off You** was the first solo hit for Frankie Valli who was still the lead singer of The Four Seasons when he recorded this top ten hit.

20. **The Happening** by The Supremes was the title song of the movie starring Anthony Quinn and Faye Dunaway. It was their only hit from 1964 to 1967 which was not written by Holland/Dozier/Holland.

21. **Snoopy vs. the Red Baron** was The Royal Guardsmen's first and biggest hit inspired by the Peanuts comic strip created by Charles Shultz. This was followed by 'The Return of the Red Baron' and 'Snoopy's Christmas'.

22. **Never My Love** was a beautiful love ballad by The Association written by Don and Dick Addrisi, also known as the Addrisi Brothers. They had a hit of their own in 1972 with 'We've Got To Get It on Again'.

23. **Soul Man** was the signature hit for Sam & Dave. This soul classic was co-written by Isaac Hayes and later made popular by The Blues Brothers in 1978.

24. **Dedicated to The One I Love** was the only Mamas & Papas hit which featured Michelle Phillips on lead vocals. This was a remake of The Shirelles hit from 1961.

25. **The Rain, The Park & Other Things** was the first hit for The Cowsills, the real life family act from Rhode Island which were the inspiration for the creation of the TV family act, The Partridge Family.

26. **Little Bit 'O Soul** was a major hit for The Music Explosion, a one hit wonder quintet from Ohio, produced by Jerry Kasenetz and Jeff Katz. Session player Kenny Laguna played on this and many other bubblegum hits including 'Simon Says', Yummy Yummy Yummy', '1,2,3 Redlight', 'Quick Joey Small' and several other late 60's hits.

27. **Georgy Girl** by The Seekers was the title song from the movie which starred Lynn Redgrave.

28. **I Heard It through the Grapevine** by Gladys Knight & The Pips was the original version of the song Marvin Gaye had a multi-week number one hit with a year later. Gladys Knight & The Pips version peaked at number two and was a completely different arrangement than the one presented by Marvin Gaye.

29. **Sweet Soul Music** was a million seller for Arthur Conley, a soul singer discovered by the writer of the song, Otis Redding . Sadly, it was also the year Otis died in a plane crash.

30. **A Little Bit Me, A Little Bit You** was the second major hit by The Monkees written by Neil Diamond and produced by Jeff Barry. This single had two different 'B' sides, 'The Girl I Knew Somewhere' and 'She Hangs Out' which was dropped a short time after its release.

31. **A Whiter Shade of Pale** by British group Procol Harum was based on the classical piece 'Sleeper's Awake' by J.S.Bach. The distinctive voice of Gary Brooker was featured on lead vocals.

32. **Come Back When You Grow Up** was the final top 10 hit for Fargo, North Dakota's Bobby Vee, whose real name was Robert Veline. Although some of his hits charted higher, this was his biggest selling single.

33. **Brown Eyed Girl** was Van Morrison's first solo hit after leaving the group 'Them'. The original title was proposed to be 'Brown Skinned Girl', but it was thought that it could cause negative reaction because of interracial content.

34. **I Was Made To Love Her** by 17 year old Stevie Wonder was number one on the R & B charts for four weeks. It was top ten on the pop charts.

35. **Reflections** was the first Supremes hit to show 'Diana Ross & The Supremes' as the name of the group on a 45 rpm single. This hit was a more progressive sounding Motown hit for the most popular girl group of the 60's.

36. **She'd Rather Be with Me** was The Turtles follow up to their number one hit 'Happy Together'. Both 1967 hits were written by Gary Bonner and Alan Gordon.

37. **Tell It Like It Is** was the first hit for legendary New Orleans singer, Aaron Neville.

38. **Pleasant Valley Sunday** by The Monkees was a social comment hit written by Carole King and Gerry Goffin. It was included of their number one album 'Pisces, Aquarius, Capricorn & Jones Ltd'.

39. **I Got Rhythm** by The Happenings was a remake of a song written in 1930 by George & Ira Gershwin for the show 'Girl Crazy'.

40. **Baby I Need Your Lovin'** was a 1967 Johnny Rivers remake of the Four Tops first hit from 1964.

41. **I Think We're Alone Now** was a big hit for Tommy James & The Shondells who recorded all their 60's hits on The Roulette label. In 1987, this song was remade by Tiffany and topped the charts. .

42. **This Is My Song** by Petula Clark was actually a song written by legendary film star Charlie Chaplin. They were neighbors at the time.

43. **I Say A Little Prayer** was a Burt Bacharach/Hal David composition popularized by Dionne Warwick. The following year, it made the top ten again by Aretha Franklin.

44. **There's a Kind Of Hush** was Herman's Hermits final top ten hit in North America. It was written by Geoff Stephens, who also composed 'Winchester Cathedral' for the New Vaudeville Band. The flip side of this single was 'No Milk Today', which was also a hit.

45. **I Second That Emotion** was another top ten hit for Motown's Smokey Robinson & The Miracles. William 'Smokey' Robinson wrote and produced most of their hits, as well as many hits for the Temptations up until 1966.

46. **Expressway to Your Heart** was a top ten hit for a blue-eyed soul group known as The Soul Survivors. This song was later remade by The Blues Brothers.

47. **San Francisco** by Scott McKenzie was an anthem song for the summer of love. This flower power favorite was written by John Phillips of The Mamas & Papas. Scott and John were once in the group The Journeyman together.

48. **How Can I Be Sure** was the third top ten hit in 1967 for The Young Rascals. Eddie Brigatti sang lead on this composition which he co-wrote with Felix Cavaliere.

49. **Release Me** was the signature hit for Engelbert Humperdinck. It was the first and biggest hit for the singer whose real name was Arnold George Dorsey.

50. **Baby I Love You** was one of five Top 10 hits Aretha Franklin achieved during her debut year of 1967.

51. **Good Thing** was a top ten hit for Paul Revere & The Raiders who were regulars on the music TV Shows 'Where The Action Is' and 'Happening '68'.

52. **Little Ol' Man** by Bill Cosby was a comical remake of Stevie Wonder's 'Uptight' which reached the top ten the previous year in 1966.

53. **Higher and Higher** was Jackie Wilson's best known hit of the 60's. In 1975, he collapsed on stage from a stroke and died nine years later in 1984.

54. **Somebody to Love** was the first of two 1967 top ten hits for Jefferson Airplane, a San Francisco group which featured Grace Slick upfront.

55. **Bernadette** was a top ten hit by The Four Tops who formed in 1953 and featured the same lead singer, Levi Stubbs on all their hits. Levi died in 2008.

56. **For What it's Worth** was an anti-war protest song by The Buffalo Springfield featuring Steve Stills on lead vocals and Neil Young on guitar.

57. **Words of Love** was the first Mamas & Papas hit to prominently display the vocal talents of Mama Cass Elliot. Although this was their 4th major hit released in their debut year of 1966, it peaked on the charts in early 1967.

58. **It Must Be Him** was a hit for Vicki Carr, a Texas born singer whose real name was Florencia Martinez Cardona. This song was the opposite of women's liberation.

59. **Your Precious Love** was one of Motown's greatest pairings with Marvin Gaye and Tammi Terrell, who died of a brain tumor in 1970 at age 24.

60. **Mercy, Mercy, Mercy** was The Buckinghams vocal remake of Cannonball Adderley's instrumental version from earlier that year.

61. **Up, Up & Away** flew the 5th Dimension into the top ten and songwriter Jim Webb's beautiful balloon song won him a Grammy Award for Song of The Year. This hit also won Record of The Year for 1967.

62. **Don't Sleep In The Subway** was the final top 10 hit in North America for British singer Petula Clark who achieved a long string of late 60's hits. She considered this song to be her personal favorite.

63. **Western Union** was the only top ten hit for a group from Dallas, Texas known as the Five Americans. Keyboardist John Durrill later wrote Cher's number one hit 'Dark Lady'. This hit was produced by Dale Hawkins, the singer/songwriter of the original 'Suzie Q' from 1957.

64. **Creeque Alley** by The Mamas & Papas was an autobiographical song about the group and their musical friends.

65. **Apples, Peaches, Pumpkin Pie** was the first and biggest hit for Jay & The Techniques, fronted by Jay Proctor. They recorded on the Smash label back then.

66. **Him or Me, What's It Gonna Be** was another hit by Paul Revere & The Raiders from the days they would average 3 hits a year from 1966 to 1969. Pony tailed lead singer Mark Lindsay would appear on the covers of the teen magazines on a regular basis.

67. **Come On Down To My Boat** was a summer delight by one hit wonder Every Mother's Son, a group from Greenwich Village led by two brothers.

68. **The Beat Goes On** by Sonny & Cher was a social comment and fashion scene statement hit for the times in '67. Sonny Bono wrote this and most of their hits during the 60's.

69. **To Love Somebody** by the Bee Gees was the second of four hits they charted in their debut year, 1967. They composed all of their own hits during the 60's.

70. **Don't You Care** was the third of five 1967 hits for The Buckinghams. This was their first hit on the Columbia Record Label.

71. **Standing In The Shadows Of Love** was one of many top ten hits for The Four Tops, a Motown group that were inducted into the Rock And Roll Hall of Fame in 1980.

72. **Then You Can Tell Me Goodbye** was a hit for The Casinos, a one hit wonder 9 man vocal group from Cincinnati which featured Gene Hughes on lead vocals.

73. **Carrie Anne** was a goodtime hit by The Hollies featuring both Graham Nash and Allan Clarke on lead vocals.

74. **Chain of Fools** by Aretha Franklin featured the bluesy guitar opening of Joe South on this 1967 million seller.

75. **Silence Is Golden** was a harmonizing hit by Britain's Tremeloes which was a remake of a lesser known recording by The Four Seasons.

76. **Gimme Some Lovin'** was the most successful hit for Britain's Spencer Davis Group featuring a then-17 year old Steve Winwood on lead vocals. The basic music of this top ten hit was written in 20 minutes.

77. **You Got What It Takes** was the final top ten hit in North America for The Dave Clark 5. It was an energetic reworking of the original version by Marv Johnson from 1960.The DC5 were finally inducted into the Rock And Roll Hall Of Fame in 2007, but sadly, lead singer Mike Smith died just a few weeks before the ceremony.

78. **Let's Live for Today** was the 2nd biggest hit for The Grassroots, a goodtime group formed in San Francisco featuring Rob Grill on lead vocals.

79. **Gimme Little Sign** was a catchy, top ten R & B hit for Brenton Wood, whose real name is Alfred Smith.

80. **98.6** by Keith featured The Tokens (The Lion Sleeps Tonight) on backup vocals. This Philadelphia-born singer's real name is James Keefer.

81. **I Can See For Miles** by The Who was the only official top ten hit in the U.S during the 60's for this legendary British rock band. They were inspired to write this song while on tour flying.

82. **A Natural Woman** by Aretha Franklin was written by Carole King and later included on her 'Tapestry' album.

83. **Please Love Me Forever** by Bobby Vinton was a remake of Cathy Jean & The Roommates hit from 1961.

84. **Sunday Will Never Be the Same** was the first and biggest hit for Spanky & Our Gang. This goodtime hit was written by Gene Pistilli and Tommy West, two thirds of The Buchanan Brothers of 'Medicine Man' fame..

85. **White Rabbit** by Jefferson Airplane was based on Lewis Carroll's Alice In Wonderland's pill scene. It was the second of two big 1967 hits for this San Francisco rock group.

86. **I Dig Rock & Roll Music** was a Peter, Paul & Mary hit that sounded more like The Mamas & Papas, who are mentioned in this song.

87. **Girl, You'll be A Woman Soon** by Neil Diamond was recorded on the Bang Record Label, and was produced by Jeff Barry and Ellie Greenwich.

88. **Sock It to Me Baby** by Mitch Ryder & The Detroit Wheels was very similar in sound to their previous hit 'Devil With A Blue Dress On/Good Golly Miss Molly'. They capitalized on the popular 'sock it to me' saying at the time.

89. **Tell It to the Rain** was one of the Four Seasons more progressive sounding 60's hits, - one of 12 during that incredible decade.

90.. **Spooky** was the first of four hits in the late 60's for the Classics 4, featuring Dennis Yost on lead vocals.

91. **Close Your Eyes** was the biggest 60's hit for the sweetheart duo known as Peaches and Herb. Peaches back then were Francine Baker and Herb was Herb Fame.

92. **59th Street Bridge Song (Feelin' Groovy)** was a hit written by Paul Simon, but made most popular by The California vocal group Harper's Bizarre. The lead singer was Ted Templeton who later went on to produce recordings by The Doobie Brothers and Van Halen.

93. **San Franciscan Nights** by Eric Burdon & the Animals was a psychedelic sound of the times in the summer of '67. It became their final top ten hit in the U.S.

94. **Mirage** by Tommy James & The Shondells was actually the music track of 'I Think We're Alone Now' backwards.

95. **Itchycoo Park** was a great psychedelic British hit by The Small Faces featuring Steve Marriot and Ronnie Lane.

96. **I Never Loved A Man (The Way I Love You)** was the very first hit for Lady Soul, Aretha Franklin.

97. **Boogaloo Down Broadway** was a top ten hit by one hit wonder soul singer, The Fantastic Johnny C. This singer from South Carolina was born Johnny Corley.

98. **A Girl like You** was The Young Rascals follow up to 'Groovin'. This one was top ten in the summer of love, 1967.

99. **The Tracks of My Tears** by Johnny Rivers was one of many remakes he had hits with in the 60's. This song was originally popular by Smokey Robinson & The Miracles.

100. **Cold Sweat** was one of many hits for James Brown who was also known as 'The Godfather of Soul' and 'The Hardest Working Man in Show Business'. He died on Christmas Day 2006

101. **You Better Sit Down Kids** was an unusual sing-speak song by Cher which was sung from a man's view to his kids about parents' separating.

102. **Lazy Day** was a fun, goodtime hit for Spanky & Our Gang, a Chicago folk-rock group which featured Elaine 'Spanky' McFarlane on lead vocals.

103. **We Ain't Got Nothin' Yet** was the only top 30 hit for a New York psychedelic rock quintet known as The Blues Magoos. It was a prime cut from their 'Psychedelic Lollipop' album.

104. **Hey Baby, They're Playing Our Song** was the 5th of 5 1967 hits by The Buckinghams, a pop brass group which featured Dennis Tufano on lead vocals.

105. **Summer Rain** was one of many 60's hits for Johnny Rivers, who discovered the 5th Dimension. They recorded on his own 'Soul City' record label beginning in 1967.

106. **Soul Finger** was a high-energy soul instrumental by The Barkays. They were Otis Redding's backup band, and most were killed in the same plane crash.

107. **Next Plane to London** was the only hit for The Rose Garden, a vocal group from West Virginia. The song begins with a boarding call P.A. announcement.

108. **Thank the Lord For the Nightime** was an upbeat, fun summer '67 hit by singer/songwriter Neil Diamond who worked in The Brill Building in the 60's.

109. **Keep the Ball Rollin'** by Jay & The Techniques was the second of two 1967 hits for this interracial R & B group from Allentown, Pennsylvania.

110. **On a Carousel** is a great harmony hit by The Hollies co-written by featured vocalist, Graham Nash.

111. **Go Where You Wanna Go** was the very first hit for the 5th Dimension and was written by John Phillips of The Mamas & Papas.

112. **Ding Dong the Witch Is Dead** was a novelty bubblegum hit by The Fifth Estate. The song was originally used in the 1939 film 'The Wizard of Oz'.

113. **Friday on My Mind** was the most notable hit for The Easybeats who formed in Australia, then moved to England in 1966. This rock group featured George Young, - brother of AC/DC's Angus and Malcolm.

114. **Skinny Legs and All** by Joe Tex was a humorous soul hit recorded 'live' at a nightclub.

115. **I'm A Man** was the second major hit for The Spencer Davis group featuring a teenaged Steve Winwood on lead vocals. The group Chicago had a hit with it in the early 70's.

116. **Everlasting Love** by one hit wonder Robert Knight was the original version of a song that's been a hit for others including Carl Carlton in 1974.

117. **New York Mining Disaster 1941** was the very first hit for Barry, Robin and Maurice Gibb - The Bee Gees. The title of this song is never mentioned in the song, however the 'Have You Seen My Wife Mr. Jones' is the most memorable line.

118. **Stagger Lee** by Wilson Pickett was a fast-paced remake of the Lloyd Price hit from 1959. This hit was also known as 'Stag-O-Lee.' The 'B' side of this single was the popular soulful love ballad 'I'm In Love'.

119. **Society's Child** was perhaps the most talked about hit of the year. This social comment song about an unaccepted interracial teen romance was written by Janis Ian when she was only 14 years old. She was 16 when it became a hit. Record Arranger Artie Butler used the same keyboard ending on this hit as he did on the end of 'Indian Reservation' by The Raiders.

120. **People Are Strange** was the Doors follow up to their first and biggest hit 'Light My Fire' from that same year, 1967.

121. **Massachusetts** was two of four 1967 Bee Gees hits which had American States in the title. The other was New York Mining Disaster 1941. The Bee Gees were inspired to write this song after they heard the flower power hit 'San Francisco' by Scott McKenzie.

122. **Monterey** by Eric Burdon & The Animals was a song about their experiences playing at this three day festival from earlier that year. Many of the music artists who played at this pre-Woodstock music celebration were mentioned in this song.

123. **Music to Watch Girls By** was a popular instrumental by The Bob Crewe Generation which began as a Diet Pepsi TV commercial. Bob Crewe produced and co-wrote most of the hits of The Four Seasons.

124. **Do It Again a Little Bit Slower** was the most famous hit for Jon and Robin. It was produced by Dale Hawkins, who did the original Suzie Q in the late 50's. He also produced the group the Five Americans in 1967. Both of these acts recorded for the Abnak record label.

125. **Here Comes My Baby** was a goodtime hit by Britain's Tremeloes written by Cat Stevens. In North America, it was their first of four late 60's hits.

126. **I've Been Lonely Too Long** was the first of five hits the Young Rascals charted in 1967 alone. Felix Cavaliere sang lead on most of their hits, including this one.

127. **Get On Up** was an R & B dance hit by The Esquires, a soul quintet from Milwaukee.

128. **Memphis Soul Stew** was a top ten hit for King Curtis, a popular R & B session player on many hits from that period. He was stabbed to death in New York City in 1971.

129. **When I Was Young** by Eric Burden and The Animals was a nostalgic look back at growing up. It was the first of three 1967 hits for them. Most of their hits in North America were released on the MGM record label.

130. **Jimmy Mack** was one of six top ten hits for Motown girl group Martha & The Vandellas.

131. **Funky Broadway** was the 'wicked' Wilson Pickett's final hit to reach the top ten.

132. **Yellow Balloon** by The Yellow Balloon was a goodtime, harmonizing hit by a group formed by Don Grady, who was still actively playing the role of Robbie Douglas on 'My Three Sons' when this was a hit.

133. **I Wanna Testify** was a great soul hit by The Parliaments, led by George Clinton, later of Funkedelic fame.

134. **My Mammy** by The Happenings was a remake of Al Jolson's theme song, written in 1920. Most of the late 60's hits of the Happenings were produced by the similar-sounding group, The Tokens.

135. **In And Out Of Love** was the fourth top ten hit of 1967 for Diana Ross & The Supremes.

136. **Kentucky Woman** by Neil Diamond was his final release on the 'Bang' record label. His next notable hit didn't arrive until 1969 with 'Brother Love's Traveling Salvation Show' on the 'UNI' label. 'Kentucky Woman' was revived by hard rock band Deep Purple the following year.

137. **Let It All Hang Out** by The Hombres was one of the year's strangest hits. Random thoughts/words were chosen for this offbeat one hit wonder group.

138. **Gentle on My Mind** was Glen Campbell's breakthrough hit, written by John Hartford. Back in the mid-60's, Glen played on some of the Beach Boys hits and was one of the members of 'the Wrecking Crew', a group of session musicians who played on hundreds of big hits of the 60's.

139. **Heroes & Villains** was a very creative, intricate and ambitious recording by The Beach Boys. This Van Dyke Parks production was their follow up to Good Vibrations.

140. **The Last Waltz** was the third of four hits for Engelbert Humperdinck during his debut year on the charts, 1967.

141. **I Had Too Much To Dream Last Night** was one of only two hits achieved by The Electric Prunes, a Seattle psychedelic rock quintet. Their other hit was 'Get Me To The World On Time'.

142. **I've Passed This Way Before** was Jimmy Ruffin's follow up to his biggest hit 'What Becomes of the Broken Hearted'. Jimmy's brother was David Ruffin of The Temptations.

143. **Foxey Lady** by the legendary progressive guitarist Jimi Hendrix failed to reach the top 40, but this recording went on to become a rock classic. Hendrix died in 1970 at age 27 from a drug overdose. The 'B' side of this single was 'Hey Joe', which was a huge hit in Britain.

144. **So You Want To Be a Rock & Roll Star** was one of The Byrds more progressive hits. David Crosby left shortly afterwards to form Crosby, Still and Nash, and later Young.

145. **Hello Hello** was a 1930's sounding hit by Sopwith Camel, a one hit wonder band from San Francisco. They recorded on the Kama Sutra record label, the home for the Lovin' Spoonful's hits of the 60's.

146. **Beautiful People** was the only hit for Kenny O'Dell, however under his real name, Kenny Gist, he wrote 'Behind Closed Doors' for Charlie Rich.

147. **I Was Kaiser Bill's Batman** was an oddball British instrumental hit by one hit wonder Whistling Jack Smith, a.k.a. Billy Moeller from Liverpool.

148. **Sit Down I Think I Love You** was the only hit for the American band known as The Mojo Men. Steve Stills wrote this hit which was popular at the time he sang lead on 'For what its Worth' by The Buffalo Springfield.

149. **It's Wonderful** was a very abstract, psychedelic hit by The Young Rascals, complete with crazy sound effects. Members Felix Cavaliere and Eddie Brigatti wrote most of their hits together.

150. **Honey Chile** was a hit for Martha & The Vandellas, the second most popular female Motown group next to the Supremes.

151. **Purple Haze** was the very first hit for the Jimi Hendrix Experience. It included that well known line '…'scuse me while I kiss the sky'.

152. Niki Hoeky by P.J. Proby was written by the Vegas brothers of 'Redbone' fame. Proby, whose real name was James Marcus Smith was born in Houston, Texas, but settled in Los Angeles.

153. **If You're Thinkin' What I'm Thinkin'** was a minor hit written by Boyce & Hart for teen idols Dino, Desi & Billy. Dino was Dean Martin's son and Desi was the son of Desi Arnez and Lucille Ball. Billy Hinsche later went on to perform on the road with the Beach Boys.

154. **Jackson** by Nancy Sinatra and Lee Hazelwood was one of their most popular hits together. The country version was a hit for Johnny Cash and his wife June Carter.

155. **Dandelion/We Love You** was one of The Rolling Stones most progressive recordings of the late 60's. 'Dandelion' was the 'A' side of the single backed with 'We Love You' which featured backing vocals by John Lennon and Paul McCartney.

156. **Stand By Me** was the only hit for Spyder Turner, who impersonates various soul singers as they would perform this classic hit originally popular by Ben E. King.

157. **Pretty Ballerina** was The Left Banke's classically-inspired follow up to 'Walk Away Renee'. Keyboardist Mike Brown later joined The Stories of 'Brother Louie' fame.

158. **Happy** was a hit for The Sunshine Company, a Southern California pop quintet who charted two hits in 1967. 'Back on My Feet Again' was the other.

159. **Happy Jack** was the Who's first top 30 hit in the U.S. At The end of the song, guitarist Pete Townsend can be heard yelling 'I Saw Ya' to drummer Keith Moon.

160. **There Is a Mountain** was an abstract hit by flower power singer/poet Donovan Leitch from Glasgow, Scotland.

MORE 1967 HITS!

Even The Bad Times Are Good was The Tremeloes' follow up to 'Silence Is Golden' and was before their third hit of the year.

She Is Still A Mystery was the final top 30 hit for The New York City goodtime group, The Lovin' Spoonful, headed by lead singer/songwriter John Sebastian.

Alfie was another Burt Bacharach/Hal David composition which Dionne Warwick had success with. However, it was Cher's version that was used in the film, (which starred Michael Caine), but Warwick's version charted higher.

Deadend Street was a Kinks hit in the UK and Canada, but not in the U.S. All of their 60's hits were produced by Shel Talmy.

Mercy, Mercy, Mercy was the original instrumental hit version by Saxman Cannonball Adderly who died of a stroke in 1975. The Buckinghams had a vocal hit with this song in the summer of '67.

Bowling Green was a smooth and melodic hit by The Everly Brothers which was more popular in Canada than in the U.S.

With This Ring by The Platters was one of the surprise hits of the year, since they hadn't charted anything in 7 years. This became the final hit for this very popular vocal group from the 50's.

You Got to Me by Neil Diamond was recorded in the same session as 'Cherry, Cherry', and both were produced by Jeff Barry & Ellie Greenwich, who also did the backup vocals and handclapping on each session.

There Goes My Everything was Engelbert Humperdick's follow up to his biggest hit 'Release Me'. His Manager, Gordon Mills named him after the German opera composer.

Sunday for Tea was Peter & Gordon's final top 40 hit in North America. Peter Asher went on to produce the hits of James Taylor and Linda Ronstadt.

I Take It Back was the third and final pop hit for Sandy Posey, the singer who was best known for the 1966 hits 'Born A Woman' and 'Single Girl'.

Gettin' Together was one of five 1967 hits from Tommy James & The Shondells, a pop/rock group from Dayton, Ohio.

Six O'Clock was a lesser known hit by The Lovin' Spoonful who charted 10 hits in the short span of 1966 to 1967.

Holiday was another Bee Gees hit from their first year on the charts, 1967. The Gibb Brothers were born in England, but moved to Australia in 1958.

Two In The Afternoon by Dino, Desi & Billy was written by Bonner/ Gordon who wrote 'Happy Together' & 'She'd Rather Be With Me' for The Turtles and 'Celebrate' for 3 Dog Night.

The Other Man's Grass Is Always Greener was one of many notable hits for Petula Clark who also starred in the films 'Finian's Rainbow' and 'Goodbye Mr. Chips'.

Where Will the Words Come From by Gary Lewis & The Playboys was on the charts when Gary was drafted into the U.S. Army. They performed this song on The Ed Sullivan Show just before departing.

Go Go Round by Gordon Lightfoot was a song inspired by a go-go dancer he knew from downtown Toronto.

Travelin' Man was a moderate Motown hit for the singer born blind as Steveland Morris, better known as Stevie Wonder.

I Had a Dream was Paul Revere & the Raiders final top 20 hit with Terry Melcher, (Doris Day's son) as the Producer.

I've Got To Have A Reason was a hit on the tail end of the career of Rock And Roll Hall Of Fame group The Dave Clark Five featuring keyboardist Mike Smith on lead vocals.

All I Need was a Temptations hit co-written by R. Dean Taylor of 'Indiana Wants Me' fame.

Knight in Rusty Armor by Peter & Gordon was their follow up to 'Lady Godiva' making it another historic reference hit.

At The Zoo by Simon & Garfunkel was the 'B' side to the original version of 'The 59th Street Bridge Song' written by Paul Simon, but made famous by Harper's Bizarre.

Pay You Back With Interest was a moderately successful hit for The Hollies and their last on the Capitol record label before moving to Epic records.

Let's Fall in Love was the first hit for the soul sweetheart couple Peaches and Herb. This song was originally popular in 1934 by Eddie Duchin.

TOP 16 ALBUMS OF 1967

1. Sgt. Pepper's Lonely Heart's Club Band - The Beatles
2. More of The Monkees - The Monkees
3. Diana Ross & The Supremes Greatest Hits - The Supremes
4. Pisces, Aquarius, Capricorn & Jones - The Monkees
5. Ode To Billie Joe - Bobbie Gentry
6. The Doors - The Doors
7. Revenge - Bill Cosby
8. Headquarters - The Monkees
9. Sounds Like - Herb Alpert & The Tijuana Brass
10. Surrealistic Pillow - Jefferson Airplane
11. Strange Days - The Doors
12. I Never Loved A Man - Aretha Franklin
13. S.R.O. - Herb Alpert & The Tijuana Brass
14. Aretha Arrives - Aretha Franklin
15. Born Free - Roger Williams
16. The Temptations Greatest Hits - The Temptations

TOP 16 COUNTRY HITS OF 1967

1. There Goes My Everything - Jack Greene
2. It's The Little Things - Sonny James
3. All The Time - Jack Greene
4. Where Does The Goodtimes Go - Buck Owens
5. I'll Never Find Another You - Sonny James
6. Sam's Place - Buck Owens
7. I Don't Wanna Play House - Tammy Wynette
8. Walk Through The World With Me - George Jones
9. You Mean The World To Me - David Houston
10. My Elusive Dreams - David Houston
11. It's Such A Pretty World Today - Jack Greene
12. Need You - Buck Owens
13. Lonely Again - Sonny James
14. The Fugitive - Merle Haggard
15. Don't Come Home A-Drinkin' - Loretta Lynn
16. I Won't Come In While He's There - George Jones

TOP 16 ONE HIT WONDERS OF 1967

1. Scott McKenzie - San Francisco
2. Music Explosion - Little Bit O' Soul
3. Every Mother's Son - Come On Down To My Boat
4. Blues Magoos - We Ain't Got Nothin' Yet
5. The Casinos - Then You Can Tell Me Goodbye
6. Robert Knight - Everlasting Love
7. Fantastic Johnny C - Boogaloo Down Broadway
8. Rose Garden - Next Plane To London
9. Hombres - Let It All Hang Out
10. Spyder Turner - Stand By Me
11. Yellow Balloon - Yellow Balloon
12. Mojo Men - Sit Down I Think I Love You
13. Sopwith Camel - Hello Hello
14. Whistling Jack Smith - I Was Kaiser Bill's Batman
15. The Forum - The River Is Wide
16. Bob Crewe Generation - Music To Watch Girls By

16 GREAT LOST 45'S FROM 1967

1. Sunshine Girl - The Parade
2. I Wanna Testify - The Parliaments
3. California Nights - Lesley Gore
4. Pretty Ballerina - Left Banke
5. Heroes & Villains - Beach Boys
6. I've Passed This Way Before - Jimmy Ruffin
7. Where Will The Words Come From - Gary Lewis & The Playboys
8. Epistle To Dippy - Donovan
9. The River Is Wide - The Forum
10. Happy - The Sunshine Company
11. Yellow Balloon - Yellow Balloon
12. Bowling Green - Everly Brothers
13. Niki Hoeky - P.J.Proby
14. If You're Thinkin' What I'm Thinkin' - Dino, Desi & Billy
15. Lightning's Girl - Nancy Sinatra
16. Beautiful People - Kenny O'Dell

TOP 16 R & B/ SOUL HITS OF 1967

1. Respect - Aretha Franklin
2. Soul Man - Sam & Dave
3. I Never Loved A Man - Aretha Franklin
4. Tell It Like It Is - Aaron Neville
5. I Heard It Through The Grapevine - Gladys Knight & The Pips
6. I Was Made To Love Her - Stevie Wonder
7. Cold Sweat - James Brown
8. Are You Lonely For Me - Freddie Scott
9. Love Is Here & Now You're Gone - The Supremes
10. Baby I Love You - Aretha Franklin
11. Make Me Yours - Bettye Swann
12. Higher And Higher - Jackie Wilson
13. Jimmy Mack - Martha & The Vandellas
14. Funky Broadway - Wilson Pickett
15. Sweet Soul Music - Arthur Conley
16. Reflections - Diana Ross & The Supremes

TOP 16 ROCK/HARD ROCK HITS OF 1967

1. Light My Fire - The Doors
2. Hello Goodbye/I Am The Walrus - The Beatles
3. Ruby Tuesday/Let's Spend The Night - Rolling Stones
4. Somebody To Love - Jefferson Airplane
5. I Can See For Miles - The Who
6. White Rabbit - Jefferson Airplane
7. San Franciscan Nights - Eric Burdon & The Animals
8. Foxey Lady - Jimi Hendrix
9. Friday On My Mind - Easybeats
10. Itchycoo Park - Small Faces
11. Purple Haze - Jimi Hendrix
12. Monterey - Eric Burdon & The Animals
13. Break On Through - The Doors
14. When I Was Young -Eric Burdon & The Animals
15. People Are Strange - The Doors
16. Dandelion/We Love You - Rolling Stones

(* indicates number one only in Britain)

1. I Want To Hold Your Hand - Beatles - 1964
2. Hey Jude - Beatles - 1968
3. A Whiter Shade Of Pale - Procol Harum - 1967
4. House Of The Rising Sun - Animals - 1964
5. Hello Goodbye - Beatles - 1967
6. Satisfaction - Rolling Stones - 1965
7. Yesterday - Beatles - 1965
8. Telstar - Tornadoes - 1962
9. She Loves You - Beatles - 1964
10. Green Green Grass Of Home - Tom Jones - 1966
11. Glad All Over * - Dave Clark Five - 1964
12. Can't Buy Me Love - Beatles - 1964
13. Honky Tonk Women - Rolling Stones - 1969
14. Summer Holiday * - Cliff Richard - 1963
15. Help - Beatles - 1964
16. To Sir With Love - Lulu - 1967
17. All You Need Is Love - Beatles - 1967
18. I Remember You * - Frank Ifield - 1962
19. Those Were The Days * - Mary Hopkin - 1968
20. Puppet On A String * - Sandie Shaw - 1967
21. Downtown - Petula Clark - 1965
22. From Me To You * - Beatles - 1964
23. Do Wah Diddy Diddy - Manfred Mann - 1964
24. Ruby Tuesday - Rolling Stones - 1967
25. Love Me Do - Beatles - 1964
26. Where Do You Go To My Lovely * - Peter Sarstedt - 1969
27. A World Without Love - Peter & Gordon - 1964
28. Ballad Of John & Yoko * - Beatles - 1969
29. The Young Ones * - Cliff Richard - 1962
30. Game Of Love - Wayne Fontana & Mindbenders - 1965
31. Paint It Black - Rolling Stones - 1966

32. I Like It * - Gerry & The Pacemakers - 1963
33. Get Back - Beatles - 1969
34. Wild Thing - Troggs - 1966
35. Something In The Air * - Thunderclap Newman - 1969
36. A Hard Day's Night - Beatles - 1964
37. Needles And Pins * - Searchers - 1964
38. Lily The Pink * - Scaffold - 1968
39. My Love - Petula Clark - 1966
40. Over And Over - Dave Clark Five - 1965
41. Ticket To Ride - Beatles - 1965
42. Winchester Cathedral - New Vaudeville Band - 1966
43. Pretty Flamingo * - Manfred Mann - 1966
44. Sunshine Superman - Donovan - 1966
45. You're My World * - Cilla Black - 1964
46. I'm Henry The 8th - Herman's Hermits - 1965
47. How Do You Do It * - Gerry & The Pacemakers - 1963
48. Baby Come Back * - Equals - 1968
49. Sweets For My Sweets * - Searchers - 1963
50. Have I The Right * - Honeycombs - 1964
51. Come Together - Beatles - 1969
52. Baby Now That I've Found You * - Foundations - 1967
53. My Old Man's A Dustman * - Lonnie Donegan - 1960
54. Paperback Writer - Beatles - 1966
55. Release Me * - Engelbert Humperdinck - 1967
56. She's Not There * - Zombies - 1964
57. Don't Throw Your Love Away * - Searchers - 1964
58. Twist And Shout - Beatles - 1964
59. It's Not Unusual * - Tom Jones - 1965
60. I Feel Fine - Beatles - 1964
61. A Groovy Kind Of Love * - Mindbenders - 1966
62. Mellow Yellow - Donovan - 1966
63. Eight Days A Week - Beatles - 1965
64. Massachusetts * - Bee Gees - 1967
65. Walkin' Back To Happiness * - Helen Shapiro - 1961
66. Mrs. Brown You've Got A Lovely Daughter - Herman's Hermits - 1965
67. Ob-La-Di-Ob-La-Da * - Marmalade - 1969
68. Penny Lane - Beatles - 1967
69.With A Girl Like You * - Troggs - 1966
70.Get Off Of My Cloud - Rolling Stones - 1965
71. Sunny Afternoon * - Kinks - 1966
72. Long Live Love * - Sandie Shaw - 1965
73. We Can Work It Out - Beatles - 1966
74. Yeh Yeh * - Georgie Fame - 1965
75. Georgy Girl - Seekers - 1967
76. Macarthur Park - Richard Harris - 1968
77. You Were On My Mind * - Crispian St. Peters - 1966
78. I've Gotta Get A Message To You * - Bee Gees - 1968
79. Do You Want To Know A Secret - Beatles - 1964

80. Congratulations * - Cliff Richard - 1968
81. I'm Telling You Now - Freddie & The Dreamers - 1965
82. Apache * - Shadows - 1960
83. Yellow Submarine - Beatles - 1966
84. Can't You Hear My Heartbeat - Herman's Hermits - 1965
85. Anyone Who Had A Heart * - Cilla Black - 1964
86. 19th Nervous Breakdown - Rolling Stones - 1966
87. The Last Waltz * - Engelbert Humperdinck - 1967
88. Do You Love Me * - Brian Poole & The Tremeloes - 1963
89. Fire * - Arthur Brown - 1968
90. I'm Alive * - Hollies - 1965
91. Please Don't Tease * - Cliff Richard - 1960
92. Please Please Me - Beatles - 1964
93. Tears * - Ken Dodd - 1965
94. Build Me Up Buttercup - Foundations - 1969
95. Tie Me Kangeroo Down, Sport - Rolf Harris - 1963
96. Nowhere Man - Beatles - 1966
97. You Don't Know * - Helen Shapiro - 1961
98. Love Potion Number 9 - Searchers - 1965
99. Because - Dave Clark Five - 1964
100.Confessin' * - Frank Ifield - 1963
101.Jumpin' Jack Flash - Rolling Stones - 1968
102.Something - Beatles - 1969
103.All Or Nothing * - Small Faces - 1966
104.Diamonds * - Jet Harris & Tony Meehan - 1963
105.Dance On * - Shadows - 1963
106.Somebody Help Me * - Spencer Davis Group - 1966
107.Everlasting Love * - Love Affair - 1968
108.The Carnival Is Over * - Seekers - 1965
109.Wonderful Land * - Shadows - 1962
110.Johnny Remember Me * - John Leyton - 1961
111.Cinderella Rockefella * - Esther & Abi Ofarim - 1968
112.Tower Of Strength * - Frankie Vaughan - 1961
113.There's A Kind Of Hush - Herman's Hermits - 1967
114.Lady Madonna - Beatles - 1968
115.You Don't Have To Say You Love Me - Dusty Springfield - 1966
116.The Pied Piper - Crispian St. Peters - 1966

♫ Paul McCartney made a cameo appearance on this million seller by Donovan!

♫ Paul Simon co-wrote this hit by the only American act managed by Brian Epstein!

♫ The lead singer of this group died mysteriously in 1966... the same year as his only top 10 hit!

♫ This number one hit sat on a shelf for 3 years before it reached number one!

♫ Denny Doherty wrote the lyrics of this Mamas & Papas hit about his affair with Michelle Philips!

♫ The lead singer on this Beach Boys hit was not a member of the group!

FIND OUT THAT...and MUCH MORE...INSIDE...1966!

1. **We Can Work It Out/Day Tripper** was a double-sided hit single by The Beatles.
' We Can Work It Out' was written solely by Paul, who also sang lead on this number one hit.
'Day Tripper' was written solely by John Lennon and featured John and Paul sharing lead vocals.

2. **Cherish** by the Association was the first number one hit for this six man band from Los Angeles. 'Cherish' was written by group member Terry Kirkman.

3. **Monday Monday** was the only official number one hit by The Mamas & Papas, who charted six top ten hits from 1966 to 1967.

4. **Good Vibrations** was a true masterpiece by The Beach Boys. It was the most expensive single produced up to 1966 and was recorded in several studios at the persistence of perfectionist Brian Wilson. Carl Wilson sang lead on this number one hit, and Mike Love played the unusual instrument known as the theremin.

5. **The Sounds of Silence** was Simon and Garfunkel's very first hit and was written by Paul Simon a few months after the shocking 1963 assassination of John F. Kennedy. In early 1966 this hit reached number one where it remained for several weeks.

6. **When a Man Loves a Woman** was the first and biggest hit for Percy Sledge, a soul singer from Alabama. Although Percy Sledge apparently wrote this classic, he gave the songwriting credits to Calvin Lewis and Andrew Wright, two of the musicians on this recording.

7. **You Can't Hurry Love** was a number one hit for The Supremes, the most successful girl group in pop music history. Phil Collins later remade this song and brought it back for an encore at number one.

8. **Summer in the City** was the Lovin' Spoonful's only official number one hit. This summer sizzler was co-written by John Sebastian's brother Mark and featured different sounds of the city including car horns and a very prominent jackhammer.

9. **Winchester Cathedral** by The New Vaudeville Band was written and produced by Geoff Stephens, who also sung this hit through a megaphone to give it that old Rudy Vallee effect.

10. **(You're My) Soul And Inspiration** was the Righteous Brothers first major hit after parting ways with their producer Phil Spector. This number one hit was written by the songwriting team of Barry Mann and Cynthia Weil.

11. **Reach Out I'll Be There** was the second and only other official Number one hit for the Four Tops. 'I Can't Help Myself' was their first and Levi Stubbs sang lead on all of their 20 top 40 hits.

12. **Wild Thing** by The Troggs was a number one hit written by Chip Taylor, the brother of actor Jon Voight. Reg Presley was the front man for this British rock group popular during the late 60's.

13. **You Keep Me Hangin' On** was one of 12 official number one hits achieved by The Supremes from 1964 - 1969. The hard rock group Vanilla Fudge revived this song their way two years later in 1968 and brought it into the top ten again.

14. **My Love** by Petula Clark was the first of five top 20 hits from 1966 for this popular British singer.

15. **Sunshine Superman** by Scottish singer/songwriter Donovan featured Jimmy Page of the Yardbirds and Led Zeppelin fame on guitar. This hit reached number one for Donovan Leitch in the late summer of 1966.

16. **Last Train to Clarksville** was the first hit by the Monkees and was number one on the charts when their TV Show debuted in September of 1966. This hit was written by Tommy Boyce & Bobby Hart and featured Mickey Dolenz on lead vocals.

17. **96 Tears** by ? & The Mysterians was a number one hit for this garage band from Saginaw, Michigan, which featured Rudy Martinez on lead vocals. The song was originally named '69 Tears' but the band's record label made them remove it out of fear that it would cause controversy because of the '69' sexual position.

18. **These Boots Are Made For Walkin'** by Nancy Sinatra was written and produced by Lee Hazelwood, who would later record some duet hits with the daughter of 'ol blue eyes'. This original version of 'Boots' reached number one and sold millions.

104

19. **Paint It Black** by The Rolling Stones featured Brian Jones on the sitar opening of this number one hit. This hit was later used in the War in Vietnam movie 'Full Metal Jacket' closing credits and the opening of the TV Series 'Tour of Duty'.

20. **Paperback Writer/Rain** was a double-sided hit single by The Beatles. 'Paperback Writer' was written solely by Paul McCartney, who also sang lead on this 'A' side hit. The 'B' side, 'Rain' was written solely by John Lennon, who sang lead on this progressive recording which used some abstract techniques.

21. **Lightning Strikes** was the biggest hit for the falsetto-voiced Lou Christie, whose real name is Lugee Sacco.

22. **Strangers In The Night** became Frank Sinatra's signature hit in the 60's, especially for his 'doo be doo be doo ending'. This hit was co-written by Bert Kaempfert which won the Record of the Year Grammy Award in 1966.

23. **Good Lovin'** was the first of three official number one hits for the blue-eyed soul group The Young Rascals. It was a remake of a lesser known version by The Olympics.

24. **Hanky Panky** by Tommy James & The Shondells was actually recorded three years before it became a number one hit. It was written by Jeff Barry & Ellie Greenwich who originally recorded the song as 'The Raindrops' as a 'B' side.

25. **Ballad Of The Green Berets** by Staff Sgt. Barry Sadler was a real life Green Beret who was later shot in the head in 1988. He died in 1989.

26. **Poor Side Of Town** was the first official number one hit for Johnny Rivers and the first original composition for the singer whose real name is Johnny Ramistella. He had almost ten 60's hits prior to this one.

27. **Mellow Yellow** was a million seller by Donovan which featured Paul McCartney supplying the whispering vocals.

28. **Sunny** was the biggest hit for Bobby Hebb, an R & B singer who was born in Nashville and played The Grand Ol' Opry at age 12. He wrote 'Sunny' in 1963 after being devastated by the knifing death of his brother Harold the day after the assassination of JFK.

29. **Lil Red Riding Hood** by Texas group Sam The Sham & The Pharoahs, was a million seller based on the children's story. Domingo Samudio was lead singer Sam.

30. **19th Nervous Breakdown** was a Rolling Stones hit written while they were on tour in the U.S. This was one of 3 songs they performed on the Ed Sullivan Show that year.

31. **Nowhere Man** by The Beatles was written solely by John Lennon, who also sang lead on this major hit which was popular the year the Fab 4 went on tour for the last time.

32. **California Dreamin'** was the very first hit for The Mamas and Papas. This John Phillips composition featured Denny Doherty on lead vocals.

33. **Daydream** was one of six notable hits by The Lovin' Spoonful in their most successful year on the pop charts.

34. **A Groovy Kind Of Love** by The Mindbenders was co-written by a then-teenaged Carole Bayer Sager, who years later would marry Burt Bacharach.

35. **Barbara Ann** by The Beach Boys featured Dean Torrence of Jan & Dean fame on lead vocals. He just happened to take a break while recording down the hall and dropped in on his Beach Boy buddies who were recording at the time. This was a remake of The Regents hit from 1961.

36. **Yellow Submarine/Eleanor Rigby** was a double-sided hit single by The Beatles. 'Yellow Submarine' was written by both Lennon & McCartney and featured Ringo Starr on lead vocals accompanied by the other Beatles and many others in attendance in the recording studio. 'Eleanor Rigby' was composed by both Lennon and McCartney featuring Paul on lead vocals. This was the first Beatles hit to feature strings, complete with 4 violins, 2 violas and 2 cellos.

37. **Red Rubber Ball** was the first and biggest hit for The Cyrkle, the only American group managed by Brian Epstein. The song was co-written by Paul Simon.

38. **Did You Ever Have To Make Up Your Mind** was a decision song in a banner year for The Lovin' Spoonful in which they charted six successful hits. John Sebastian wrote the lyrics of this song in the backseat of a cab on the way to a recording session.

39. **Green, Green Grass of Home** by Tom Jones was a song about a man in prison dreaming of being back home. This song was originally a hit for Porter Wagoner in 1964. Tom Jones' version was number one for almost 2 months in the U.K.

40. **Rainy Day Women # 12 & 35** was a top ten hit by Bob Dylan which never mentions the title anywhere in the song. This unusual hit featured a brass band, Bob Dylan's varied harmonica playing and the line 'everybody must get stoned'.

41. **See You In September** was the first of a string of hits for The Happenings. This summer of '66 hit was originally made popular by The Tempos in 1961.

42. **Five O'Clock World** was the second hit for The Vogues. It was later used for the opening theme on the Drew Carey Show.

43. **Secret Agent Man** was another Johnny Rivers hit recorded 'live' at The Whiskey A-Go-Go. This was the theme for the TV series which starred Patrick McGoohan.

44. **Uptight (Everything's Alright)** was a goodtime Motown hit for Stevie Wonder when he was only 15 years old.

45. **Sloop John B** by The Beach Boys was a folk song that originated from the West Indies in 1927. Brian Wilson and Mike Love shared lead vocals on this single from the 'Pet Sounds' album.

46. **I Am a Rock** was a hit for Simon & Garfunkel in their debut year, when they charted more hits than any other year afterwards.

47. **Bus Stop** was the Hollies first North American top ten hit. Allan Clarke sang lead on this hit written by Graham Gouldman of The Mindbenders and 10 C.C. fame. The Hollies were inducted into the Rock and Roll Hall of Fame in March 2010.

48. **Devil with A Blue Dress/Good Golly Miss Molly** by Mitch Ryder & The Detroit Wheels was a medley of two songs for one fast moving top ten hit. The group was produced and named by Bob Crewe, the man responsible for much of the Four Seasons' success.

49. **Kicks** by Paul Revere & The Raiders was an anti-drug message song written by Barry Mann and Cynthia Weil.

50. **Time Won't Let Me** was the first and biggest hit for The Outsiders. Lead singer Sonny Geraci later resurfaced as the lead singer of Climax, known for their hit 'Precious and Few'.

51. **She's Just My Style** by Gary Lewis & The Playboys featured Leon Russell on keyboards on this top ten recording. This was the personal favorite of Gary Lewis, who was going after the Beach Boys sound on this recording.

52. **Over And Over** was the only official number one hit for The Dave Clark Five in the U.S. The upbeat hit by one of Britain's best was a remake of the Bobby Day hit from 1958.

53. **The Pied Piper** was a substantial hit for British singer/songwriter Crispian St. Peters, whose real name is Peter Smith. The song, complete with a prominent flute, was inspired by the legend of the Pied Piper of Hamelin.

54. **Listen People** by Herman's Hermits was a top ten hit from the movie 'When The Boys Meet The Girls' with Connie Francis, Peter Noone, Louis Armstrong and Liberace.

55. **They're Coming To Take Me Away** by Napoleon the 14th was a million selling novelty hit. The 'B' side was the same song backwards. Napoleon the 14th was actually Jerry Samuels, who wrote Sammy Davis Jr's 1963 hit 'The Shelter of Your Arms'.

56. **Flowers on The Wall** by The Statler Brothers was the most successful hit on the pop charts for this Country music act from Virginia. This recording was later used in the film 'Pulp Fiction'.

57. **Walk Away Renee** by The Left Banke was a classically-inspired song co-written by a then 16 year old keyboardist Michael Brown about his infatuation with Renee, the girlfriend of one of the members of the group.

58. **You Don't Have To Say You Love Me** was a reworking of an Italian song by British singer Dusty Springfield, whose real name was Mary O'Brien.

59. **Black Is Black** was a hit for Los Bravos, the first rock group from Spain to have a top ten hit. Many thought it was Gene Pitney who was the singer of this hit because the voice was very similar.

60. **No Matter What Shape (Your Stomach's In)** was a top ten instrumental hit which was a popular Alka-Selzer TV commercial in 1966. It was a hit for the T-Bones, who later resurfaced as the group 'Hamilton, Joe Frank & Reynolds, best known for their hit 'Don't Pull Your Love'.

61. **Ain't Too Proud To Beg** by The Temptations was their first hit written and produced by Norman Whitfield. Motown boss Berry Gordy wanted to give Whitfield a chance after Smokey Robinson's production of 'Get Ready' did not live up to expectations. David Ruffin sang lead on this Motown classic.

62. **Sweet Pea** was a popular summer of '66 hit for Tommy Roe, a bubblegum music singer from Atlanta, Georgia who had six top ten hits during this decade.

63. **That's Life** was the 4th of 4 hits for Frank Sinatra in his comeback year of 1966.

64. **Psychotic Reaction** was a top ten psychedelic hit by The Count Five, a one hit wonder group from San Jose, California.

66. **Land Of 1000 Dances** by Wilson Pickett was a remake of the 1963 song by Chris Kenner. This hit became the 'wicked' Wilson Pickett's biggest hit of all. He died in 2006.

67. **Sugar Town** was a top ten hit for Nancy Sinatra who was married to actor/singer Tommy Sands from 1960 to 1965. The 'B' side of this 45 single was 'Summer Wine', a duet with Lee Hazelwood, the writer/producer of Nancy's hits.

68. **Elusive Butterfly** was the only hit for folk/pop singer/songwriter Bob Lind, who many believed would be the next Bob Dylan. Bob Lind later became successful as a regular contributing writer for the Weekly World News publication and book author .

69. **Cherry, Cherry** was one of Neil Diamond's early hits from his debut year in the top 40. Songwriters Jeff Barry & Ellie Greenwich also supplied the backup singing and handclapping on this classic hit.

70. **I Saw Her Again** by The Mamas & Papas was co-written by group member Denny Doherty about his affair with 'Mama' Michelle Phillips, wife of John Phillips.

71. **Homeward Bound** by Simon and Garfunkel was the second of five consecutive hits in their debut year on the charts.

72. **My World Is Empty Without You** was the first of four major Supremes hits in 1966 alone.

73. **Dandy** by Herman's Hermits was written by Ray Davies of The Kinks.

74. **I'm Your Puppet** was the biggest hit for cousins James & Bobby Purify. The following year they revived 'Shake A Tail Feather', making it one of the best R & B party hits of the year.

75. **Lady Godiva** was Peter & Gordon's top ten hit about the legendary 'bare all' horse rider.

76. **As Tears go By** was a Rolling Stones' ballad that was also a hit for Mick Jagger's then-girlfriend Marianne Faithful.

77. **What Becomes of The Broken Hearted** was the biggest hit for Motown's Jimmy Ruffin. He is the brother of the late David Ruffin, former lead singer of The Temptations.

78. **Wouldn't It Be Nice/God Only Knows** was a double-sided hit single by The Beach Boys from their most critically-acclaimed album, 'Pet Sounds'. It was Carl Wilson who sang lead on 'God Only Knows'.

79. **Along Comes Mary** was the very first hit for the Association and was controversial because of the reference 'Mary' possibly being connected with 'Mary juana'. Their style changed to a softer, mellower sound after this hit.

80. **Crying Time** by Ray Charles was a pop hit that also charted on the Country charts in 1966. The song was written by Don Gibson, best known for his hit 'Oh Lonesome Me'.

81. **Hungry** was one of five hits in 1966 charted by Paul Revere & The Raiders, featuring Mark Lindsay on lead vocals.

82. **Cool Jerk** was the only hit for Detroit R & B trio, The Capitols. The lead singer Sam George was murdered in 1982.

83. **Mother's Little Helper/Lady Jane** was a double-sided hit single by The Rolling Stones. Mick Jagger was only 23 when he sang the opening line 'what a drag it is getting old' on 'Mother's Little Helper'. The 'B' side 'Lady Jane' featured Brian Jones on the unusual instrument, the dulcimer.

84. **I'm so Lonesome I Could Cry** was the first of a long string of hits for B. J. Thomas. This song was written by Country music legend Hank Williams.

85. **I Fought The Law** was a top ten hit for the Bobby Fuller Four the same year Bobby Fuller died under mysterious circumstances. He was found dead in his car apparently of asphyxiation, but there are some who believe he was murdered.

86. **Working in a Coal Mine** was a hit written by Allen Toussaint for Lee Dorsey, a prize fighting boxer -turned-singer. Devo revived the song in 1981 for the movie 'Heavy Metal'. Lee Dorsey died in 1986.

87. **Stop Stop Stop** by The Hollies was their follow up to 'Bus Stop' and it also reached the top ten in '66. Group members were inspired to write the song after watching a belly dancer in a club in New York City.

88. **Working My Way Back To You** was a Four Seasons hit written by Sandy Linzer and Denny Randell, who also wrote their hits 'Let's Hang On' and 'Opus 17'.

89. **Green Grass** by Gary Lewis & The Playboys featured session player Leon Russell on keyboards, especially prominent on the song's opening. This hit was written by the British songwriting team of Roger Cook and Roger Greenaway.

90. **If I Were a Carpenter** was Bobby Darin's final top ten hit. When he recorded this Tim Hardin composition, he was still married to Sandra Dee. Bobby Darin died in 1973 at age 37.

91. **Barefootin'** was a hit for one hit wonder Saxman/vocalist/bandleader Robert Parker from Louisiana. It later became a popular tune for a TV commercial for a floor cleaning product.

92. **Born Free** by pianist Roger Williams was the Academy Award winning Best Song from the movie of the same name.

93. **It's a Man's, Man's, Man's World** by James Brown was a thought-provoking top 10 hit from The Godfather Of Soul.

94. **Message to Michael** was another Burt Bacharach/Hal David composition made popular by Dionne Warwick, a cousin of Whitney Houston.

95. **Little Girl** was a top ten hit for The Syndicate Of Sound, a one hit wonder garage band from San Jose, California.

96. **A Must to Avoid** was one of six 1966 hits by Herman's Hermits. This song was written by Graham Gouldman of Mindbenders/10 C.C. fame who also wrote 'Bus Stop' for the Hollies' and 'Heart Full Of Soul' for The Yardbirds.

97. **Don't Mess with Bill** by The Marvelettes was the only top 10 late 60's hit for this Motown girl group. Their biggest hit 'Please Mr. Postman' reached number one in 1961.

98. **Oh How Happy** was a soul hit by one hit wonder Detroit act the Shades Of Blue. They were discovered by Edwin Starr, who wrote this top ten hit under his real name, Charles Hatcher.

99. **Beauty Is Only Skin Deep** is a Temptations hit about inner beauty delivered by Motown's most successful male group. David Ruffin sang lead on this top ten hit.

100. **Mustang Sally** by Wilson Pickett became more popular years after it was a 1966 hit, when it didn't even peak in the top 20. It became a staple R & B hit, covered by many acts through the years.

101. **Bang Bang** was Cher's first solo hit, while continueing a successful career as half of the top husband and wife duo of the 60's. She was married to Sonny Bono from 1963 to 1974.

102. **Fever** by The McCoys was a rock reworking of the Peggy Lee hit of the 50's. Lead singer Rick Zehringer was just a teenager when he had all his hits with the McCoys. He later changed his name to 'Derringer' and had solo hits and a 70's hit with 'Rock 'N Roll Hootchie Koo'.

103. **You Didn't Have To Be So Nice** was one of six 1966 hits by The Lovin' Spoonful led by singer/songwriter John Sebastian. They recorded their hits on the eye-catching Kama Sutra record label.

104. **But Its Alright** by J. J. Jackson was the only notable hit for this soul singer from Brooklyn, New York.

105. **Summertime** by R & B singer Billy Stewart was a George Gershwin song from Porgy and Bess three decades earlier. Sadly, the very talented Billy Stewart died in a car accident in 1970.

106. **It's My Life** by The Animals featured Eric Burden on lead vocals. Keyboardist Alan Price had just left the group and Bass player Chas Chandler discovered Jimi Hendrix and became a member of the Experience.

107. **Solitary Man** was Neil Diamond's first hit. His first seven hits were all recorded on the 'Bang' record label. His follow up, 'Cherry Cherry' was recorded in the same session.

108. **Get Ready** by The Temptations was written and produced by Smokey Robinson. This Motown favorite featured Eddie Kendricks on lead vocals. Surprisingly, this classic never reached the top ten. Four years later, Rare Earth brought it into the top five.

109. **Ebb Tide** was the final Righteous Brothers hit produced by Phil Spector. Ebb Tide was a major hit back in 1953 by Frank Chacksfield.

110. **Born A Woman** was the first of two social comment hits for Sandy Posey in 1966. The other one was 'Single Girl'.

111. **The Men In My Little Girl's Life** was a surprise hit by TV Talk Show host Mike Douglas. This top ten hit was half narration and half singing as he looked back on his girl growing up.

112. **See See Rider** by Eric Burden and The Animals was actually a song that dates back to 1925 as 'See See Rider Blues'.

113. **Double Shot (Of My Baby's Love)** was a party hit for a one hit wonder 8 man band from Greenwood, South Carolina known as The Swingin' Medallions. The song was considered too suggestive by many at the time because of the lyrics 'She loved me so long and she loved me so hard'.

114. **Sunny Afternoon** by The Kinks was a lazy, summer '66 hit which featured the nasally voice of singer/songwriter Ray Davies.

115. **Sweet Talkin' Guy** was the third and final major hit for The Chiffons, a black female group that scored with early 60's hits like 'He's So Fine' and 'One Fine Day'.

116. **The Cheater** by Bob Kuban & the 'In' Men featured Walter Scott on lead vocals. In 1983, he disappeared and was found murdered, shot in the back. His ex wife and her husband, were charged with the 1983 murder three years later.

117. **The Sun Ain't Gonna Shine Anymore** by the Walker Brothers was written by Bob Crewe and Bob Gaudio who were responsible for the hits of The Four Seasons. The Walker Brothers were an unrelated duo from Los Angeles that were most popular in Britain, where they charted almost a dozen hits.

118. **Leaning On A Lampost** was a top ten hit by Herman's Hermits which was originally popular by George Formby many years earlier.

119. **A Well Respected Man** was a hit by The Kinks about the average working man's 9 to 5 routine. Ray Davies was lead singer on all of the hits for this British group and brother Dave Davies was a guitarist.

120. **Hold On I'm Comin'** is a classic from the original Soul Men, Sam & Dave. This hit was co-written by The 'Shaft' man, Isaac Hayes. He died in 2008.

121. **Where Were You When I Needed You** was the first hit by The Grassroots, although it was singer/songwriters Steve Barri and P.F.Sloan who created the group after this recording. The actual group didn't exist until their next hit 'Let's Live For Today' in 1967.

122. **Dirty Water** by the Los Angeles- based punk rock band the Standells featured former Mouseketeer Dick Dodd on lead vocals and drums. The opening talk/sing was made up on the spot at the time of recording.

123. **The Joker Went Wild** was a Brian Hyland hit written by Bobby Russell of 'Honey' and 'Little Green Apples' fame. Leon Russell arranged and played keyboards on this top 20 hit from the summer of '66.

124. **Call Me** was the first of many hand clapping sound-a-like hits for Chris Montez, who first hit the charts in 1962 with 'Let's Dance'.

125. **Woman** by Peter & Gordon was written by Paul McCartney under the name Bernard Webb to see if it could become a hit without his successful name. Years later John Lennon would write his own song titled 'Woman' which also became a top ten hit.

126. **England Swings** by Roger Miller took us on a trip to where we'd see Westminster Abbey, the Tower Of Big Ben and many other noteworthy sights of England. This was Roger Miller's final top ten hit on the pop charts.

127. **Shapes of Things** was a progressive hit by the British group the Yardbirds featuring Jimmy Page on guitar. Eric Clapton and Jeff Beck were also members of this group at various times.

128. **A Place in the Sun** was a social comment hit by Stevie Wonder when he was only 16 years old. This was one of three top ten hits he achieved in 1966 alone.

129. **I've Got You under My Skin** by The Four Seasons was a remake of a Cole Porter song made famous by Frank Sinatra. It was a great production, complete with a false ending.

130. **Single Girl** was one of two equally popular 1966 'woman's view' hits by Sandy Posey written by Martha Sharp.

131. **Turn Down Day** was The Cyrkle's follow up to 'Red Rubber Ball'. John Lennon chose the name of the group with its unusual spelling. The Cyrkle, managed by Brian Epstein, opened for the Beatles at their final concert in 1966 at Candlestick Park.

132. **Somewhere My Love** by The Ray Coniff Singers was also known as 'Lara's Theme' from the film Dr. Zhivago.

133. **Knock on Wood** became a soul classic for Eddie Floyd, who was replaced by Wilson Picket in the original 'Falcons' vocal group. This number one R & B hit was written by Eddie Floyd and Steve Cropper.

134. **It Was a Very Good Year** was a very good comeback hit for 'ol blue eyes', who hadn't had a top ten hit since 1958 until the release of this song in 1966.

135. **What Now My Love** by Herb Alpert & The Tijuana Brass was one of seven instrumental hits they charted in 1966 alone. This was the title track of their number one album. Sonny & Cher charted a vocal version of this song that same year.

136. **Coming on Strong** was one of the final notable hits by Brenda Lee, Little Miss Dynamite. Golden Earring referred to this song in their 1974 hit 'Radar Love' with the line 'Brenda Lee is coming on strong'.

137. **Opus 17 (Don't You Worry 'Bout Me)** was a Four Seasons hit which did not mention the title anywhere in the lyrics of the song.

138. **Respectable** was an Isley Brothers composition popularized by Cleveland, Ohio rock group The Outsiders, featuring Sonny Geraci on lead vocals.

139. **Blowin' In The Wind** by Stevie Wonder was a remake of the Bob Dylan protest song which was also previously a hit for Peter, Paul & Mary.

140. **Mama** by B.J. Thomas was a tribute song to mothers everywhere in his first year on the charts.

141. **Batman Theme** was a hit by The Marketts in the year the TV series with Adam West and Burt Ward made its debut. Neal Hefti's less popular hit version was the one used as the theme on the original TV Show.

142. **Don't Bring Me Down** by The Animals was written by the husband and wife songwriting team of Carole King and Gerry Goffin. The hit features the unusual fuzz guitar played by Hilton Valentine, bass guitar played by Chas Chandler and the pulsating organ by Dave Rowberry.

143. **Tijuana Taxi** was a hit for the most successful instrumental act of the 60's, Herb Alpert & the Tijuana Brass. In 1966, Herb Alpert & the Tijuana Brass had 3 number one albums.

144. **I'm Ready For Love** by Martha & The Vandellas was originally offered to The Supremes, but they turned it down because it sounded too similar to 'You Can't Hurry Love'. This Motown hit was written and produced by Holland/Dozier/Holland.

145. **A Sign Of The Times** was one of many late 60's hits for Petula Clark, who was born in Epsom, England in 1932. She was on the radio singing 'live' when she was only 9 years old.

146. **I Know I'm Losing You** was a Temptations hit featuring David Ruffin on lead vocals. The song later became a top ten hit for Rare Earth in 1970.

147. **Hooray For Hazel** was Tommy Roe's follow up to his million selling top ten hit 'Sweet Pea'.

148. **Have You Seen Your Mother Baby** was the fifth of five top ten hits by The Rolling Stones in 1966.

149. **Lies** was the only hit for this New Jersey band, The Knickerbockers, whose sound resembled the early Beatles. Buddy Randall was the lead singer.

150. **634-5789** by Wilson Pickett was coincidentally the same phone number as 'Beechwood 4 - 5789 by The Marvelettes in their 1962 hit. It's believed that it was a safe number to use since it wasn't a problem the first time around.

151. **It's Good News Week** was a hit for one hit wonder British band, Hedgehopper's Anonymous, the brainchild of Producer/writer/singer Jonathan King.

152. **Nashville Cats** was a salute to Nashville's musicians from the Lovin' Spoonful featuring John Sebastian front and centre. This was the last of six consecutive 1966 hits by the Lovin' Spoonful.

153. **Over, Under, Sideways, Down** by The Yardbirds featured Jeff Beck on lead guitar. The lead singer/harmonica player was Keith Relf who was electrocuted to death on stage in 1976.

154. **I Love Onions** was a novelty hit by Susan Christie complete with a kazoo and Elmer Fudd's voice at the end.

155. **Love Is Like an Itching In My Heart** was a hit for the Supremes, who were originally known as The Primettes. They followed this top ten hit with four consecutive number one singles.

156. **Walkin' My Cat Named Dog** was an oddball folk/pop song by Norman Tanega, a one hit wonder singer/songwriter/guitarist from California.

157. **One Has My Name** was the only hit for Barry Young, a singer many believed was Dean Martin because of the uncanny resemblance in his voice.

158. **Just Like Me** by Paul Revere & The Raiders featured Mark Lindsay on lead vocals. He also co-wrote most of their hits.

159. **Mr. Dieingly Sad** was the second of 2 1966 soft rock hits for the New Jersey vocal group, The Critters.

160. **Rain on The Roof** was a very laid back folksy song by The Lovin' Spoonful, led by John Sebastian. This was one of six 1966 hits for this folk rock band.

More Hits of 1966

Talk Talk by the Music Machine was a fast and progressive hit for this Los Angeles based rock quintet, led by Sean Bonniwell.

How Sweet It is (To Be Loved By You) by Jr. Walker & the All-Stars was a great remake of Marvin Gaye's 1964 hit with a 'live party' feel to it and lots of good sax.

Say I Am (What I Am) was Tommy James & The Shondells lesser known follow up to their first big hit 'Hanky Panky'.

Sweet Dreams was the only notable hit for falsetto- voiced Tommy McClain. His great version of this Don Gibson-penned hit was originally a hit for Patsy Cline in 1963, two months after she was killed in a plane crash.

Going to a Go-Go was a popular Motown hit by The Miracles featuring Smokey Robinson. Go-Go nightclubs with Go-Go dancers were 'in' at the time this hit was popular in '66.

Phoenix Love Theme by The Brass Ring was an instrumental hit from the movie 'Flight of The Phoenix' starring James Stewart.

Yesterday Man was a major hit in the U.K for singer/songwriter Chris Andrews from Essex, England.

With a Girl like You by The Troggs was their follow up to their biggest hit 'Wild Thing', also in 1966.

Michelle by David & Jonathan was a cover of the Beatles song which the Fab 4 never released as a single. Britain's David & Jonathan were actually songwriters Roger Cook and Roger Greenaway, known for composing many hits including 'You've Got Your Troubles' and 'My Baby Loves Lovin' to name just a couple.

You Make Me Feel So Good was a moderate hit for the Indiana based rock group, The McCoys featuring Rick Zehringer (Derringer) on lead vocals.

Billy & Sue was a sad story song by B.J. Thomas in his debut year.

Lovedrops was a Canadian hit for singer/songwriter Barry Allen from British Columbia.

River Deep, Mountain High was only a minor success for Ike and Tina Turner. Producer Phil Spector was so disappointed by the results, that he retired and went into seclusion.

Pretty Flamingo was a hit for South African born Manfred Mann, leader and keyboardist of this popular British band. Paul Jones was the lead singer on this summer 1966 hit.

Girl In Love by The Outsiders was a love ballad about a girl on her wedding night. It was one of three notable hits they achieved in their only year on the pop charts.

Cloudy Summer Afternoon was a goodtime hit by Barry McGuire, the singer of 'Eve of Destruction' the year before. Barry was a former member of The New Christy Minstrels and lead singer on their big hit 'Green Green'.

The More I See You by Chris Montez was a remake of a song originally a hit in 1945 by Dick Haymes.

Lovin' Sound was a Canadian hit for folk duo Ian and Sylvia. Ian Tyson wrote 'Four Strong Winds' and Sylvia Fricker (later Tyson) wrote the top ten hit 'You Were On My Mind' for We Five.

Love Is a Hurtin' Thing was the first hit by smooth soul singer Lou Rawls, who was also Garfield The Cat's singing voice on the TV Specials. This song reached number one on the R & B chart.

Jenny Take a Ride by Mitch Ryder & the Detroit Wheels was a medley of Little Richard's Jenny Jenny and Chuck Willis 'C. C. Rider'.

East West by Herman's Hermits was one of three of their hits written by Mindbenders member Graham Gouldman. The other two were 'A Must to Avoid' and 'No Milk Today'.

My Heart's Symphony by Gary Lewis & The Playboys was one of six top 20 hits in '66 for one of Jerry's real kids.

Ashes to Ashes was a moderate hit for The Mindbenders, the group that performed in the prom scene in the film 'To Sir with Love' starring Sidney Poitier and singer Lulu.

Just Like a Woman by Bob Dylan was on the charts at the time of his near-fatal motorcycle accident in 1966.

Happy Summer Days was a lesser known hit for Ronnie Dove, who despite his popularity, never managed to make the top ten.

Popsicle was a fun song about one of the most popular summer foods for kids of all ages. This was Jan & Dean's final top 30 hit. This record debuted on the charts about two months after Jan was critically injured in an auto accident.

Girl on A Swing by Gerry & The Pacemakers was their final top 40 hit in North America.

(Clear The Track) Here Comes Shack by Douglas Rankin & the Secrets was a big hit in Canada about one of the Toronto Maple Leafs' most popular players, Eddie Shack. The song was written by Hockey commentator Brian McFarlane.

Juanita Banana was a one hit wonder novelty hit by The Peels. The melody of this song was adapted from 'Caro Nome' from Verdi's opera 'Ringoletto'.

Wade in The Water was an instrumental hit by The Ramsey Lewis Trio. The other two members who made up this jazz trio were Eldee Young and Isaac Holt, later known as 'Young-Holt Unlimited' of 'Soulful Strut' fame.

This Door Swings Both Ways was a summer of 1966 hit by Herman's Hermits, whose name was derived from 'Sherman' on TV's Bullwinkle Show.

It's Too Late was an up tempo hit by Bobby Goldsboro, who toured with Roy Orbison from 1962 to '64 before launching his own successful solo career.

Zorba the Greek by Herb Alpert & The Tijuana Brass was the title tune from the movie which starred Anthony Quinn.

Get Away was a British hit for Georgie Fame & The Blue Flames. Georgie Fame's real name is Clive Powell.

Trains & Boats & Planes by Dionne Warwick was another Burt Bacharach/Hal David composition. It was also a hit for Billy J. Kramer the previous year.

Dedicated Follower of Fashion was one of four 1966 hits by The Kinks, a group which formed in London, England in 1963. Their string of hits began in 1964.

118

Go Away Little Girl by The Happenings was a remake of the number one Steve Lawrence hit written by Carole King and Gerry Goffin. Five years later, Donny Osmond brought it to the number one chart position.

The Work Song by Herb Alpert & The Tijuana Brass was one of a dozen instrumentals they charted from 1962 - 1968.

(I Washed My Hands In) Muddy Water was the last of a string of hits recorded 'live' at The Whiskey -A-Go-Go for Johnny Rivers.

Younger Girl by The Critters was a song written by The Lovin' Spoonful's John Sebastian. Their version was never released as a single.

Flamingo by Herb Alpert & the Tijuana Brass was a remake of a hit originally popular by Duke Ellington back in 1941.

Mr. Spaceman was a fun, lighthearted look at extraterrestrial life by The Byrds. Longtime member Gene Clark had just left the band.

A Hazy Shade of Winter was another notable hit by Simon and Garfunkel in their first unstoppable year. This successful duo split in 1971 after over a dozen hits from 1966 on.

I Love You Drops by Vic Dana was written by Bill Anderson who charted this song on the Country charts.

Eight Miles High was a hit by The Byrds which many believed was drug related, but apparently it was just about the band's plane trip and touring England in 1965.

Brainwashed was a Canadian hit by David Clayton-Thomas three years before he fronted Blood, Sweat & Tears on all their hits.

Rhapsody in the Rain by Lou Christie was banned on some radio stations due to some suggestive lyrics around the backseat of a car and the rhythm of the windshield wipers in a rainstorm.

Jug Band Music was a hit for The Lovin' Spoonful in Canada. This catchy tune failed to make any notable impact on the charts in the U.S.

The Little Girl I Once Knew was a Beach Boys single which was not included on any of their albums at the time. It was innovative, but not well-received by radio and record sales. 'Barbara Ann' quickly followed the release of this Beach Boys single.

Changes by Crispian St. Peters, written by folk singer/songwriter Phil Ochs, followed 'The Pied Piper'. The use of Crispian St. Peters' overdubbed voice was very effective on this 1966 hit.

TOP 16 ALBUMS OF 1966

1. The Monkees - The Monkees
2. What Now My Love - Herb Alpert & The Tijuana Brass
3. Revolver - The Beatles
4. Rubber Soul - The Beatles
5. Going Places - Herb Alpert & The Tijuana Brass
6. Yesterday & Today - The Beatles
7. Supremes A Go-Go - The Supremes
8. Ballad Of The Green Berets - Sgt. Barry Sadler
9. Strangers In The Night - Frank Sinatra
10. Doctor Zhivago - Soundtrack
11. If You Can Believe Your Eyes & Ears - Mamas & Papas
12. Big Hits (High Tide & Green Grass) - The Rolling Stones
13. Color Me Barbra - Barbra Streisand
14. Aftermath - The Rolling Stones
15. The Mamas & Papas - Mamas & Papas
16. Lou Rawls 'Live'! - Lou Rawls

TOP 16 COUNTRY HITS OF 1966

1. Almost Persuaded - David Houston
2. Waitin' In Your Welfare Line - Buck Owens
3. Giddyup Go - Red Sovine
4. I Want To Go With Him - Eddy Arnold
5. Think Of Me - Buck Owens
6. Distant Drums - Jim Reeves
7. Open Up Your Heart - Buck Owens
8. Somebody Like Me - Eddy Arnold
9. Take Good Care Of Her - Sonny James
10. Blue Side Of Lonesome - Jim Reeves
11. I Get The Fever - Bill Anderson
12. There Goes My Everything - Jack Greene
13. Flowers On The Wall - Statler Brothers
14. England Swings - Roger Miller
15. I Love You Drops - Bill Anderson
16. Husbands & Wives - Roger Miller

TOP 16 ONE HIT WONDERS OF 1966

1. New Vaudeville Band - Winchester Cathedral
2. Bob Lind - Elusive Butterfly
3. Count Five -Psychotic Reaction
4. Napoleon X1V - They're Coming To Take Me Away
5. T -Bones - No Matter What Shape Your Stomach's In
6. Robert Parker - Barefootin'
7. The Capitols - Cool Jerk
8. Syndicate Of Sound - Little Girl
9. Shades Of Blue - Oh How Happy
10. Tommy McClain - Sweet Dreams
11. Knickerbockers - Lies
12. Music Machine - Talk Talk
13. Swinging Medallions - Double Shot (Of My Baby's Love)
14. Bob Kuban & The In Men - The Cheater
15. J.J. Jackson - But Its Alright
16. Hedgehopper's Anonymous - It's Good News Week

16 GREAT 'LOST 45's' FROM 1966

1. The Joker Went Wild - Brian Hyland
2. Talk Talk - Music Machine
3. Lies - Knickerbockers
4. Mr. Dieingly Sad - The Critters
5. Changes - Crispian St. Peters
6. How Sweet It Is - Jr. Walker & The All-Stars
7. It's Too Late - Bobby Goldsboro
8. Respectable - The Outsiders
9. Yesterday Man - Chris Andrews
10. Holy Cow - Lee Dorsey
11. Get Away - Georgie Fame
12. Cloudy Summer Afternoon - Barry McGuire
13. You Make Me Feel So Good - McCoys
14. This Door Swings Both Ways - Herman's Hermits
15. Ashes To Ashes - The Mindbenders
16. Jug Band Music - Lovin' Spoonful

TOP 16 R & B/ SOUL HITS OF 1966

1. Ain't Too Proud To Beg - The Temptations
2. 634 - 5789 - Wilson Pickett
3. Uptight (Everything's Alright) - Stevie Wonder
4. When A Man Loves A Woman - Percy Sledge
5. Reach Out, I'll Be There - Four Tops
6. You Keep Me Hangin' On - The Supremes
7. Land Of 1000 Dances - Wilson Pickett
8. You Can't Hurry Love - The Supremes
9. It's A Man's, Man's, Man's World - James Brown
10. Get Ready - The Temptations
11. Hold On, I'm Comin' - Sam & Dave
12. Knock On Wood - Eddie Floyd
13. Baby Scratch My Back - Slim Harpo
14. Love Is A Hurtin' Thing - Lou Rawls
15. What Becomes Of The Broken Hearted - Jimmy Ruffin
16. Mustang Sally - Wilson Pickett

1. Paint It Black - The Rolling Stones
2. 96 Tears - ? & the Mysterians
3. Wild Thing - The Troggs
4. Psychotic Reaction - Count Five
5. My Generation -The Who
6. 19th Nervous Breakdown - The Rolling Stones
7. Talk Talk - Music Machine
8. Devil With A Blue Dress/Good Golly - Mitch Ryder & Detroit Wheels
9. Shapes Of Things - The Yardbirds
10. Little Girl - Syndicate Of Sound
11. Don't Bring Me Down - The Animals
12. Dirty Water - The Standells
13. Mother's Little Helper - The Rolling Stones
14. Over, Under, Sideways, Down - The Yardbirds
15. Have You Seen Your Mother - The Rolling Stones
16. 7 And 7 Is - Love

1. Born To Be Wild - Steppenwolf - 1968
2. These Eyes - Guess Who - 1969
3. Spinning Wheel - Blood, Sweat & Tears - 1969
4. No Time - Guess Who - 1969
5. You've Made Me So Very Happy - Blood, Sweat & Tears - 1969
6. Laughing - Guess Who - 1969
7. Baby I Love You - Andy Kim - 1969
8. Which Way You Going Billy? - Poppy Family - 1969
9. Magic Carpet Ride - Steppenwolf - 1968
10. Bo Diddley - Ronnie Hawkins - 1963
11. Fortune Teller - Bobby Curtola - 1962
12. Clap Your Hands - Beau Marks - 1960
13. When I Die - Motherlode - 1969
14. The Weight - The Band - 1969
15. One Tin Soldier - Original Caste - 1969
16. Shakin' All Over - Chad Allen & The Expressions - 1965
17. And When I Die - Blood, Sweat & Tears - 1969
18. Undun - Guess Who - 1969
19. Charlena - Richie Knight & The Midnights - 1963
20. Gaslight - Ugly Ducklings - 1967
21. 3 Rows Over - Bobby Curtola - 1963
22. We'll Sing In The Sunshine - Gale Garnett - 1964
23. Ringo - Lorne Greene - 1964
24. Four Strong Winds - Ian & Sylvia - 1963
25. So Good Together - Andy Kim - 1969
26. What In The World's…Over - Jack Scott - 1960
27. The Unicorn - Irish Rovers - 1968
28. Black Day In July - Gordon Lightfoot - 1968
29. Any Other Way - Jackie Shane - 1963
30. Rock Me - Steppenwolf - 1969
31. Unless You Care - Terry Black - 1964
32. How'd We Ever Get This Way - Andy Kim - 1968

33. Lovin' Sound - Ian & Sylvia - 1967
34. Big Town Boy - Shirley Matthews - 1964
35. Opportunity - Mandala - 1967
36. Cornflakes & Ice Cream - Lords Of London - 1967
37. If I Call You By Some Name - Paupers - 1967
38. Canada - Young Canada Singers - 1967
39. Indian Giver - Bobby Curtola - 1963
40. Go Go Round - Gordon Lightfoot - 1967
41. Loveitis - Mandala - 1968
42. Here Comes Shack - Douglas Rankine & The Secrets - 1966
43. Burning Bridges - Jack Scott - 1960
44. Lovedrops - Barry Allen - 1966
45. The French Song - Lucille Ball - 1964
46. Hello Young Lovers - Paul Anka - 1960
47. Looking At A Baby - Collectors - 1967
48. Hitch Hiker - Bobby Curtola - 1961
49. Half Past Midnight - Staccatos - 1967
50. Shoot 'Em Up Baby - Andy Kim - 1968
51. Goodnight My Love - Paul Anka - 1969
52. Brainwashed - David Clayton-Thomas - 1966
53. Alladin - Bobby Curtola - 1962
54. Tears Of Misery - Pat Hervey - 1963
55. Rainbow Ride - Andy Kim - 1968
56. Jolie Jacqueline - Lucille Starr - 1964
57. A Steel Guitar & A Glass Of Wine - Paul Anka - 1962
58. Cool Water - Jack Scott - 1960
59. Love Me Warm & Tender - Paul Anka - 1962
60. Only 16 - Terry Black - 1965
61. Twilight Woman - 49th Parallel - 1969
62. Home From The Forest - Ronnie Hawkins - 1967
63. Mr. Heartache - Pat Hervey - 1962
64. Spin Spin - Gordon Lightfoot - 1966
65. Keep On Running - Grant Smith & The Power - 1967
66. Give Me Time - Last Words - 1967
67. I Would Be The One - Kensington Market - 1968
68. It Was I - Big Town Boys - 1965
69. You Really Got A Hold On Me - Little Caesar & The Consuls - 1965
70. Boom Boom - David Clayton-Thomas - 1964
71. Bluebirds Over The Mountain - Ronnie Hawkins - 1965
72. Nothin' - Ugly Ducklings - 1966
73. Got To Get You Into My Life - Stitch In Tyme - 1967
74. Eso Beso - Paul Anka - 1962
75. Off To Dublin/Merry Ploughboy Abbet Tavern Singers - 1966
76. Walk That Walk - David Clayton-Thomas - 1965
77. Fannie Mae - Robbie Lane - 1964
78. My Girl Sloopy - Little Caesar & The Consuls - 1965
79. Does Your Mama Know... Me - Bobby Taylor & The Vancouvers - 1968
80. Terry - Leigh Bell & The Chimes - 1960

81. I Symbolize You - Last Words - 1966
82. Don't You Sweetheart Me - Bobby Curtola - 1961
83. If (I Found A New Girl) - Little Caesar & The Consuls - 1963
84. My Hometown - Paul Anka - 1960
85. Stood Up - Larry Lee - 1963
86. My Kinda Guy - Willows - 1966
87. Me And You - Regents - 1965
88. Dance On Little Girl - Paul Anka - 1961
89. Rainbow - Terry Black - 1966
90. Baby Ruth - Butterfingers - 1965
91. Hands Of The Clock - Life - 1969
92. The Way I Feel - Gordon Lightfoot - 1967
93. Better Watch Out - Mckenna-Mendelson Mainline - 1969
94. Poor Little Fool - Terry Black - 1965
95. Somebody Help Me - British Modbeats - 1967
96. And She's Mine - Guess Who - 1966
97. Just Like Tom Thumbs Blues - Gordon Lightfoot - 1965
98. If You Don't Want My Love - Jack London & The Sparrows - 1965
99. Ship Of Dreams - Quiet Jungle - 1967
100.Simple Deed - Paupers - 1967
101.I'm A Loner - Jaybees - 1966
102.Like A Dribblin' Fram - Race Marbles - 1966
103.The Cruel War - Sugar & Spice - 1969
104.Little Liar - Terry Black - 1965
105.Tonight My Love Tonight - Paul Anka - 1961
106.Bitter Green - Gordon Lightfoot - 1968
107.Makin' Love - Bobby Curtola - 1965
108.Give And Take - Mandala - 1967
109.I'm Losing Tonight - Passing Fancy - 1967
110.Johnny Take Your Time - Bobby Curtola - 1962
111.Walkin' In Bonnie's Footsteps Pat Hervey - 1964
112.Walk On By - Bobby Kris & The Imperials - 1966
113.The Stones That I Throw - Levon & The Hawks - 1965
114.I'm Movin' On - Matt Lucas - 1963
115.Private Property - Shirley Matthews - 1964
116.Little Reuben - Al Gardner – 1961

60's!... 1965 HITS INSIDE! FIND OUT...

♫ The words from this number one hit came from the bible!

♫ 3 of The Beatles contributed to this hit by a one hit wonder group managed by Brian Epstein!

♫ Legendary guitarist Jimmy Page played on this first hit by Tom Jones!

♫ This was the only Beach Boys hit which featured Al Jardine on lead vocals and it reached number one!

♫ This top ten hit for Peter & Gordon was written by Del Shannon!

♫ This was the biggest solo hit for the former lead singer of The Dovells!

FIND OUT THAT...and MUCH MORE...INSIDE...1965!

I WANT TO HOLD YOUR HAND
(Lennon–McCartney)

Capitol
5112
(45-X44711)

Duchess
Music Corp.
BMI–2:24

THE BEATLES

HONEY COME BACK
(Jimmy Webb)

STEREO

Capitol
2718

GLEN CAMPBELL

Arranged & Conducted
by Al De Lory

Produced by
AL
DE LORY

ATLANTIC

45-2478

TIGHTEN UP – PART II

ARCHIE BELL & THE DRELLS

LONDON

DR. 33923

L. 9726

GO NOW
(Banks; Bennett)
THE MOODY BLUES

45 RPM

ATCO
RECORDS

ATCO
6639X

Side 1
(BMI) 3:04
Pub. Cotrerole

I STARTED A JOKE
(From Atco LP 33-253)
(Barry, Robin & Maurice Gibb)
THE BEE GEES

MANUFACTURED IN CANADA BY QUALITY RECORDS LIMITED

LAURIE
LAURIE RECORDS INC. NEW YORK

Record No.
LR 3308
Elmwin Mus.
Inc., BMI

Time: 2:12

54KM 6320

ARE YOU A BOY OR
ARE YOU A GIRL
(D. Morris–R. Morris)
THE BARBARIANS
"PROD. BY DOUG MORRIS"
RECORDED AT ALLEGRO
SOUND STUDIOS"

M·G·M

3

K13721

WHEN I WAS YOUNG

EPIC

45 RPM

5-10345
ZSP 137733
3:15

A Mickie Most
Production

HURDY GURDY MAN
(D. Leitch)
DONOVAN
Produced by Mickie Most

"EPIC", "CBS", MARCAS REG. T.M. PRINTED IN CAN. A PRODUCT OF CBS

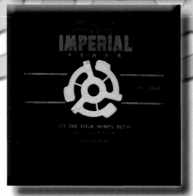

1. **Yesterday** by The Beatles was the most recorded Beatles song of all time by other artists. Paul McCartney wrote this with the working title 'Scrambled Eggs'. Paul was the only Beatle present on this recording. The 'B' side was 'Act Naturally' featuring Ringo on lead vocals.

2. **Satisfaction** was the biggest hit of all for The Rolling Stones. While on tour in a hotel room, Keith Richards came up with the guitar riff while in bed trying to sleep and got up to record it on a tape machine so he wouldn't forget it. Mick Jagger was 22 when he sang what became a Rock music anthem.

3. **I Got You Babe** was the first and biggest hit for Sonny and Cher. Sonny Bono wrote this and other major hits for this popular 60's duo.

4. **Turn Turn Turn** was a number one hit by The Byrds with lyrics adapted by Pete Seeger from the Bible's book of Ecclesiastes. This hit has the oldest lyrics of any pop hit in the history of music.

5. **Help** by the Beatles was the title song from their second movie. Although Lennon/McCartney appear as the writers of this song, it was composed solely by John Lennon, who also sings lead.

6. **Mrs**. **Brown you've Got A Lovely Daughter** by Herman's Hermits was their biggest hit of all, selling over 2 million copies and outselling all other singles that year.

7. **You've lost That Loving Feeling** by The Righteous Brothers was the most played song of the 20th century according to the Broadcast Music Inc (BMI). The most successful hit by the Righteous brothers was written by Barry Mann, Cynthia Weil and Producer Phil Spector.

8. **Downtown** became Petula Clark's signature hit. It was the first of many of her 60's hits written by Tony Hatch.

9. **Unchained Melody** by The Righteous Brothers was produced by Phil Spector and featured Bobby Hatfield on lead vocals. This song was previously a hit for Al Hibbler and Les Baxter. It was revived in 1990 when it was featured in the movie 'Ghost'.

10. **I Can't Help Myself** was the first and biggest number one hit for the Four Tops. Lead singer Levi Stubbs, died at the age of 72 after a lengthy illness on October 17th 2008.

11. **Help Me Rhonda** was a number one hit by The Beach Boys featuring Al Jardine on lead vocals. This hit was featured on their 'Summer Days and Summer Nights' album.

12. **Stop In The Name Of Love** was the fourth of five consecutive number one hits for The Supremes from 1964 - '65.

13. **This Diamond Ring** was the first and biggest hit for Gary Lewis & The Playboys, who were discovered while performing at Disneyland. This hit was co-written by Al Kooper, a session musician who played on dozens of hits and later formed Blood, Sweat & Tears.

14. **Eight Days a Week** by The Beatles was the first of five number 1 hits of 1965 - from the LP Beatles V1.

15. **Get Off Of My Cloud** was The Rolling Stones follow up to Satisfaction. It also reached number one.

16. **My Girl** was the first number one hit for the legendary Motown group The Temptations. It was written and produced by the Miracle man, Smokey Robinson.

17. **I Hear a Symphony** was another super hit by The Supremes featuring Diana Ross on lead vocals. They were inducted into the Rock And Roll Hall Of Fame in 1988.

18. **Mr. Tambourine Man** was the Byrds' first hit and this Bob Dylan composition went all the way to the top of the charts. The only member of the Byrds to play on this hit was Roger McGuinn, who played the 12 string Rickenbacker guitar. All other instruments were played by session players.

19. **Eve of Destruction** was a social comment hit by Barry McGuire, a former member of The New Christy Minstrels and lead singer on their biggest hit 'Green Green'. The Turtles were originally offered this song by writer P.F.Sloan, but they turned it down, instead recording 'Let Me Be', written by P.F.Sloan and Steve Barri.

20. **Hang On Sloopy** by The McCoys featured a teenaged Rick Zehringer (later Derringer) on lead vocals. It was a remake of 'My Girl Sloopy' by The Vibrations from 1964.

21. **Game of Love** was a number one hit in 1965 for the British group Wayne Fontana & The Mindbenders. Wayne Fontana left the same year and The Mindbenders continued until they evolved into Hotlegs, then 10 C.C.

22. **Ticket to Ride** by The Beatles featured John Lennon singing lead on this number one hit from their second movie, 'Help'.

23. **California Girls** was a summer '65 hit by The Beach Boys featuring Mike Love on lead vocals. This was the first Beach Boys hit to feature new member Bruce Johnston, who took Brian Wilson's place on the road. Studio musicians featured on this recording include Hal Blaine on drums and Leon Russell on piano.

24. **Like a Rolling Stone** is considered to be Bob Dylan's best ever recording. In 2004, Rolling Stone Magazine declared it 'The Greatest Song of All Time'. This cut from the album 'Highway 61 Revisited' produced by Tom Wilson, featured Mike Bloomfield on guitar and Al Kooper on organ. At 6 minutes in length, it was the longest hit up to 1965 to reach the top ten.

25. **I'm Telling You Now** was the first and biggest hit for Freddie (Garity) & The Dreamers. It reached number one in March of '65.

26. **I'm Henry The 8th** by Herman's Hermits was a big hit for Herman's Hermits in 1965.The song was written in 1911 and popularized in England by Harry Champion.

27. **Wooly Bully** was the first of two million selling singles for Sam the Sham & the Pharoahs. The other was 'Lil Red Riding Hood' in the summer of '66. Sam's real name was Domingo Samudio.

28. **Back In My Arms Again** by The Supremes was the last of 5 Supremes hits in a row to go to number one. Lead singer Diana Ross mentions 'Mary and Flo' in the song, referring to Supremes' members Mary Wilson and Florence Ballard.

29. **You Were on My Mind** was the California group We Five's only hit. It was written by Canadian folk singer Sylvia Fricker before she married Ian Tyson, recording together as Ian & Sylvia.

30. **Crying In The Chapel** by Elvis Presley became a hit 5 years after it was featured as an album cut. Sonny Til & the Orioles recorded the original version in the 50's.

31. **1 2 3** was the biggest solo hit for Len Barry, the former lead singer of The Dovells, best known for their hits 'Bristol Stomp' and 'You Can't Sit Down'. The group The Tymes sang backup on this top five hit.

32. **A Lover's Concerto** by The Toys was credited to Sandy Linzer and Denny Randell based on a piece of classical music by J.S Bach.

33. **Can't You Hear My Heartbeat** by Herman's Hermits was the first of six top 10 hits of 1965, two of which reached number one. Peter 'Herman' Noone sang lead on all of their hits. According to Peter Noone, this song was Herman's Hermits tribute to Buddy Holly.

34. **I Got You (I Feel Good)** was the signature hit for James Brown, the Godfather of Soul.

35. **The Birds and The Bees** was the only hit for Jewel Akens, a singer from Houston, Texas. His parents named him Jewel because they wanted a girl.

36. **Save Your Heart for Me** by Gary Lewis & The Playboys was a summertime classic produced by Snuff Garrett. The son of comedian Jerry Lewis had his name changed when he was two years old from Cary Levitch to Gary Lewis.

37. **Treat Her Right** almost reached number one for Roy Head, a one hit wonder singer/guitarist from Texas.

38. **Let's Hang On** was one of 15 Top 10 hits for the Four Seasons which featured Frankie Valli on all but one major hit, - December 63 (Oh What A Night) which highlighted drummer Gerri Polci upfront on lead vocals.

39. **Love Potion Number 9** was a top ten hit by The Searchers written by Jerry Leiber and Mike Stoller. The Searchers version was more popular than the original by the Clovers from 1959, which failed to reach the top ten.

40. **I Know a Place** was Petula Clark's follow up to her first major hit 'Downtown'. This hit was written and produced by Tony Hatch who was responsible for most of Petula Clark's early hits.

41. **You're The One** was the first hit by The Vogues from Turtle Creek, Pennsylvania. The song was co-written by Petula Clark and was originally featured on her 'I Know a Place' album.

42. **What's New Pussycat** by Tom Jones was the title song of the movie which starred Peter Sellers and Woody Allen. The song was written by Burt Bacharach and Hal David.

43. **King of The Road** was Roger Miller's signature hit, having spent 5 weeks at number one on the Country Chart, top ten on the pop chart and also winning a Grammy Award in the year he won several.

44. **The Name Game** was a fun audience participation novelty hit by Bronx-born singer/songwriter Shirley Ellis.

45. **Shotgun** was the first notable hit for Motown Sax man Jr. Walker with his group The All-Stars. He died in 1995.

46. **Rescue Me** was the only top ten hit for St. Louis singer Fontella Bass. This hit was produced by Maurice White who later led Earth, Wind and Fire to great success.

47. **Cara Mia** demonstrated the powerful vocal range of Jay Black of Jay and the Americans on this 1965 top ten hit which was originally popular in 1954 by David Whitfield.

48. **Keep on Dancing** by The Gentrys featured wrestling's 'Mouth of The South' Jimmy Hart. This was their only top 30 hit.

49. **I'll Never Find Another You** by The Seekers was the first North American hit for this folk-rock Australian quartet.

50. **Count Me In** by Gary Lewis & The Playboys was their follow up to the number one hit 'This Diamond Ring'. This song was written by Glen Hardin, who wrote two other singles for Gary Lewis. All of their pre-1967 hits were arranged by Leon Russell. According to Gary Lewis, this was the most important record to him, because this second hit proved that he wasn't a One Hit Wonder.

51. **Catch Us If You Can** was a fun song by The Dave Clark Five featured in their film 'Having A Wild Weekend'.

52. **Wonderful World** by Herman's Hermits was a very fast-paced remake of the Sam Cooke classic from 1960.

53. **It's The Same Old Song** was the second top 10 hit for the Four Tops following 'I Can't Help Myself'. Most of their hits were written by the Motown songwriting team of Holland/Dozier/Holland.

54. **Everybody Loves A Clown** by Gary Lewis And The Playboys was their 4th top 5 hit in 1965. It was co-written by Leon Russell who also played keyboards on this and several other Gary Lewis hits in '65 and '66, even though he was never a member of the group.

55. **The 'In' Crowd** was one of only two hits for Dobie Gray. His next hit came 8 years later with 'Drift Away'.

56. **Ferry Cross the Mersey** was a movie hit by Gerry & The Pacemakers, who also starred in the film. This British group was also from Liverpool and managed by Brian Epstein.

57. **What the World Needs Now** was Jackie DeShannon's first top ten hit and was written by Burt Bacharach and Hal David.

58. **Yes, I'm Ready** was the only top ten hit for Barbara Mason, a singer/songwriter from Philadelphia.

59. **You've Got Your Troubles** was the biggest hit in North America by British group The Fortunes. Many compared them to Britain's answer to the Four Seasons because of their great harmonizing. This hit was written by Roger Cook and Roger Greenaway who composed dozens of top 40 hits for British music acts during the 60's and 70's.

60. **A Taste of Honey** was The Grammy Award Winning Record of The Year for Herb Alpert and The Tijuana Brass, the top selling instrumental group of the 60's.

61. **How Sweet It Is (To Be Loved By You)** by Marvin Gaye was the original version of a song that was later a hit for Jr. Walker & The All-Stars the following year and James Taylor in the mid-70's.

62. **For Your Love** was one of two 1965 Yardbirds' hits written by Graham Gouldman of Mindbenders/10CC fame. The other was 'Heart Full Of Soul'. Jimmy Page, Jeff Beck and Eric Clapton were all members of The Yardbirds at various times.

63. **Silhouettes** by Herman's Hermits was a much faster-paced version of the song The Rays made famous in 1957. Jimmy Page, who was a session guitarist at the time, played on this top ten hit.

64. **Baby Don't Go** was Sonny & Cher's successful follow up one month after their first hit 'I Got You Babe'. Sonny Bono wrote this and most of their big hits.

65. **All Day And All Of The Night** was the second North American hit for Britain's Kinks led by Ray Davies. This hit was similar in sound to the hit it immediately followed, 'You Really Got Me'.

66. **Tell Her No** by The Zombies featured Colin Blunstone on lead vocals and songwriter Rod Argent on keyboards.

67. **Hold Me, Thrill Me, Kiss Me** was an emotional soulful song by Cincinnati born Mel Carter. It was his only top ten hit, although he continued afterwards with a career in acting.

68. **Do You Believe In Magic** was the first of many late 60's hits for The Lovin' Spoonful featuring John Sebastian on lead vocals.

69. **In the Midnight Hour** became a signature hit for the 'Wicked' Wilson

Pickett. This soul classic was co-written by Steve Cropper who also played guitar on this and dozens of other hits of the 60's on the Atlantic and Stax record label.

70. **Hold What You've Got** was the first hit for Texas-born soul singer Joe Tex. It was an advice song about not taking the person you're with for granted, because there's always someone else who will appreciate them.

71. **Down in The Boondocks** was the biggest hit for Billy Joe Royal. It was written by Joe South, who also wrote his hits 'I Knew You When' and 'Yo-Yo' also recorded by The Osmonds.

72. **Seventh Son** by Johnny Rivers was a cover of a Willie Dixon song and was recorded 'live' at The Whiskey a Go-Go.

73. **Make the World Go Away** was the biggest hit on the pop charts for legendary Country singer Eddy Arnold who died in 2008 at the age of 89. He died two months after Sally, his wife of 65 years.

74. **I Like It Like That** by The Dave Clark Five was a remake of the Chris Kenner song from 1961. Dave Clark Five's version was faster and typical of their signature beat.

75. **Tired Of Waiting For You** was the third consecutive top ten hit for The Kinks featuring Ray Davies on lead vocals.

76. **Goldfinger** by Shirley Bassey was one of the most memorable themes from a James Bond film. This song was written by John Barry who scored over 10 James Bond movies and the music for Midnight Cowboy and Born Free.

77. **The Jerk** was a song by Los Angeles R & B group The Larks about a popular dance of the day. It became their only notable hit.

78. **It's Not Unusual** was the first hit in North American for Tom Jones. Jimmy Page, who was a session musician back then, played guitar on this light-hearted hit.

79. **It Ain't Me Babe** was the very first notable hit for the Turtles. It was written by the legendary Bob Dylan.

80. **Positively 4th Street** was a social comment hit which reached the top ten for Bob Dylan, whose real name is Robert Zimmerman.

81. **Don't Let Me Be Misunderstood** was a top ten hit for British band The Animals, who were inducted into the Rock And Roll Hall Of Fame in 1994.

82. **Hush, Hush Sweet Charlotte** by Patti Page was the title song from the film which starred Bette Davis and Olivia DeHavilland. Patti Page is best

known for all her hits in the 50's including 'Tennessee Waltz' and 'Doggie in The Window'.

83. **Papa's Got A Brand New Bag** was one of two big hits for James Brown in 1965. The other was 'I Got You (I Feel Good).

84. **Just A Little Bit Better** by Herman's Hermits was the last of six top ten hits they achieved in 1965 alone.

85. **You Turn Me On** was a fun, upbeat hit top ten hit for Ian Whitcomb, a British born singer, songwriter and author.

86. **Heart Full of Soul** by The Yardbirds was written by Graham Gouldman of Mindbenders/10C.C. fame. Jeff Beck's guitar work was highlighted on this top ten hit.

87. **I Can Never Go Home Anymore** was a song by The Shangrilas that really tugged at the heart strings. This was the final hit for this girl group which consisted of two sets of sisters.

88. **Go Now** was the first hit for Britain's Moody Blues. Denny Laine, who joined Paul McCartney's Wings in 1971 was the lead singer on this top ten hit.

89. **Cast Your Fate To The Wind** by Sounds Orchestral was an instrumental written by Vince Guaraldi, who also composed The Peanuts theme.

90. **I'll Be Doggone** was a number one hit on the R & B charts for Marvin Gaye, who was a member of The Moonglows before going solo.

91. **I Go to Pieces** was a Peter and Gordon hit written by Del Shannon, best known for his hit 'Runaway'.

92. **Nowhere To Run** by Martha & The Vandellas was another great Motown hit written and produced by Holland/Dozier/Holland. This recording has been featured in several movies and TV Shows through the years.

93. **Do the Freddie** was the signature hit for British Band Freddie & The Dreamers and it also became a popular dance. It's interesting to note that all five of their hits charted in the same year, 1965.

94. **Engine, Engine #9** was one of three top ten hits Roger Miller achieved in 1965, the same year he won 6 Grammy Awards.

95. **The Last Time** by The Rolling Stones was their first hit to reach number one in the U.K. written by Mick Jagger and Keith Richards. Phil Spector assisted on this session which was their hit just before 'Satisfaction'.

96. **Laugh Laugh** by San Francisco group Beau Brummels was produced by Sly (of Family) Stone three years before he had his first hit.

97. **The Jolly Green Giant** was inspired by the popular TV commercial from then. The Kingsmen, who were best known for the party anthem 'Louie, Louie' had a top ten hit with this silly song.

98. **The Boy from New York City** was a goodtime hit by one hit wonder The Ad Libs, a quintet from Newark, New Jersey. Several years later, The Manhatten Transfer made it their biggest hit.

99. **Sunshine, Lollipops And Rainbows** was a Lesley Gore hit written by a then-unknown Marvin Hamlisch. It was featured in the film 'Ski Party' which starred Dwayne Hickman and Frankie Avalon with appearances by James Brown, The Hondells and Lesley Gore singing this hit.

100. **Shake** was Sam Cooke's final hit. It was Top 10 a month after he was shot and killed by a motel owner under mysterious circumstances.

101. **Baby I'm Yours** was a beautiful soulful ballad by Barbara Lewis written by a then-unknown Van McCoy, who a decade later would have a number one hit with 'The Hustle'.

102. **We Gotta Get Out Of This Place** by The Animals, featuring Eric Burdon, was a social comment hit popular during the Vietnam War. It was written by the Brill Building songwriting team Barry Mann and Cynthia Weil.

103. **Little Things** by Bobby Goldsboro was a hit during his up tempo era in the mid 60's.

104. **Just Once In My Life** was one of four 1965 hits for The Righteous Brothers. This song was written by Carole King, Gerry Goffin and Phil Spector.

105. **You Baby** by The Turtles was an upbeat, goodtime hit written by P.F. Sloan and Steve Barri and was completely different in style to the other hit they wrote that year, - 'Eve Of Destruction' for Barry McGuire.

106. **She's About A Mover** was the first and biggest hit for Tex Mex group Sir Douglas Quintet, led by Doug Sahm.

107. **A World of Our Own** was a hit for Australian pop-rock quartet The Seekers who charted 3 top 20 hits in North America.

108. **Here Comes the Night** was the follow up to 'Gloria' by Them. Both were written by and featured Van Morrison on lead vocals before he sought a very successful solo career.

109. **You Got To Hide Your Love Away** was a Lennon/McCartney composition by the British folk group Silkie. Three of the four members of the Beatles participated in recording this song because Brian Epstein managed this group of University students.

110. **Some Enchanted Evening** by Jay & The Americans was a remake of a song used in the 1949 film 'South Pacific'. This song was a perfect match for the powerful voice of lead singer Jay Black.

111. **Don't Just Stand There** was a top ten hit for Patty Duke when The Patty Duke Show was popular. This hit sounded quite similar to Lesley Gore's 'You Don't Own Me' from two years earlier.

112. **Everyone's Gone to The Moon** was the only North American hit for Jonathan King, a British music mogul who wrote and produced hits for others.

113. **Spanish Eyes** was Al Martino's biggest hit of the 60's. In the 70's he played singer Johnny Fontaine in The Godfather. Al Martino died on OCt 13th 2009 at the age of 82.

114. **Shakin' All Over** by Chad Allen & The Expressions was a remake of a song by British act Johnny Kidd. Chad Allen & The Expressions evolved into Canadian Supergroup 'The Guess Who'.

115. **Take Me Back** was the final top 30 hit for Brooklyn, New York's Little Anthony & The Imperials, who were inducted into The Rock And Roll Hall Of Fame in April of 2009 by Smokey Robinson.

116. **Voodoo Woman** was one of many hits for Bobby Goldsboro during the 60's. He had his own syndicated TV show from 1972 to '75.

117. **Baby the Rain Must Fall** was the title song from the movie which starred Steve McQueen and Lee Remick. This was a hit for Glenn Yarborough, a former singer with the folk trio The Limeliters.

118. **Ain't That Peculiar** reached number one on the R & B charts for Marvin Gaye. He was fatally shot by his father on April 1 1984, one day before his 45th birthday.

119. **Yeh Yeh** was a hit for Georgie Fame, a British jazz/pop singer whose real name is Clive Powell.

120. **Houston** was one of five hits Dean Martin charted in 1965, the year his TV Show debuted. It ran until 1974.

121. **Tijuana Taxi** was one of many 60's instrumental hits for Herb Alpert & The Tijuana Brass. Los Angeles born Herb Alpert played trumpet since the age of 8.

140

122. **Heart of Stone** was a soulful, dramatic ballad by The Rolling Stones, who took their name from a Muddy Waters song.

123. **I Want Candy** by The Strangeloves was an example of a song that used the Bo Diddley beat. The writers/producers of this song also composed the number one hit 'My Boyfriend's Back' from 1963.

124. **One Kiss for Old Times Sake** was the highest charting hit for Ronnie Dove, a singer from Herndon, Virginia. This hit was arranged by Ray Stevens.

125. **Action** by Freddie Cannon was his final top 20 hit. This energetic, goodtime hit was from the TV Show 'Where The Action Is'. It was a rock 'n roll variety show hosted by Dick Clark and featuring Paul Revere, Mark Lindsay, Linda Scott and Steve Alaimo as regulars.

126. **Liar Liar** was a hit for one hit wonder group, the Castaways. The song was inspired by the nursery rhyme 'Liar Liar, pants on fire…'. They were a teen quintet from Minnesota.

127. **(Remember Me) I'm The One Who Loves You** was one of several pop hits by Dean Martin during this time period. His 60's hits were all on the Reprise record label, founded by fellow Rat Pack member Frank Sinatra.

128. **Too Many Rivers** was one of 12 top ten hits in the 60's for Brenda Lee, who was nicknamed 'Little Miss Dynamite' because of her small stature and big voice.

129. **Mohair Sam** was a hit for Charlie Rich in his pre-Silver Fox days when he was still rockin'. This great feel good hit was written by Dallas Frazier who also wrote 'Alley Oop', 'Elvira' and other notable hits.

130. **My Generation** was a teenage anthem by The Who featuring a stuttering Roger Daltry on lead vocals.

131. **Ooh Baby Baby** by The Miracles was a Smokey Robinson song which was later a hit for Linda Ronstadt.

132. **Catch the Wind** by Donovan was his first hit and popular when he was just 19 years old.

133. **Just A Little** was one of two 1965 hits charted by The Beau Brummels. This band from San Francisco failed to chart any hits outside of '65.

134. **Nothing but Heartaches** was The Supremes' only hit from 1965 to 1967 which did not reach the top 10.

135. **Gloria** by the British group Them featured Van Morrison on lead vocals. He also wrote this classic rock song two years before his solo career began. The Shadows of Knight had a hit with this song the following year in 1966.

136. **A Walk in The Black Forest** was a popular instrumental hit by jazz pianist Horst Jankowski from Berlin, Germany.

137. **I Can't Explain** by The Who, was the first hit in North America for this British Rock 'N Roll Hall Of Fame Quartet.

138. **Don't Think Twice** was an offbeat, fun version of this Bob Dylan composition performed by The Four Seasons in disguise as 'The Wonder Who'.

139. **Concrete and Clay** was a catchy hit with great hooks by British pop sextet Unit Four Plus Two. An American single version was released by Eddie Rambeau.

140. **Not The Lovin' Kind** was a hit for Dino, Desi & Billy of which two were sons of celebrities Dean Martin and Desi Arnez. Dean Martin's son Dino was killed piloting a jet that crashed in 1987. He was only 35 years old when he died.

141. **The Door Is Still Open To My Heart** was one of several mid 60's hits for Dean Martin, whose real name is Dino Crocetti.

142. **I'm Yours** was an Elvis Presley ballad that he actually recorded four years earlier in 1961.

143. **Bring It on Home to Me** was a hit for The Animals in 1965. It was a remake of Sam Cooke's classic from 1962. Eddie Floyd also had a hit with this song before the decade ended.

144. **Make It Easy On Yourself** was the first hit by unrelated act, The Walker Brothers, a trio from Los Angeles who were very popular in the U.K. This song was written by Burt Bacharach and Hal David and was originally a hit for Jerry Butler in 1962.

145. **True Love Ways** by Peter and Gordon was a remake of a Buddy Holly non- charted hit he co-wrote with Norman Petty.

146. **I'll Be There** was a ballad from Gerry & the Pacemakers written by Bobby Darin, who originally recorded it with little success.

147. **Under Your Spell Again** was one of four hits Johnny Rivers charted in 1965. This song was written by Country singer/songwriter Buck Owens.

148. **I'm A Fool** was the first hit for Dino, Desi and Billy, who appeared

142

on the covers of 'Hit Parader', '16 Magazine' and 'Tiger Beat' back then. This hit was produced by Lee Hazelwood, who also produced the hits for another celebrity offspring, - Nancy Sinatra.

149. **Are You a Boy Or Are You a Girl** was a hit for The Barbarians, a 60's punk garage band from Cape Cod, Massachusetts which featured 'Moulty', a one-armed drummer.

150. **Say Something Funny** was a hit for actress Patty Duke, who won an Oscar for The Miracle Worker three years earlier.

151. **New York's A Lonely Town** was a hit for The Tradewinds, who were the New York pop singing duo Peter Anders and Vinnie Poncia.

152. **I Will** by Dean Martin was the last of 5 charted hits from '65. Dean died Christmas day 1995.

153. **Puppet on a String** was a ballad from Elvis Presley from his movie 'Girl Happy' starring Shelley Fabares.

154. **Here It Comes Again** was The Fortunes follow up to 'You've Got Your Troubles' also from 1965.

155. **May The Bird Of Paradise Fly Up Your Nose** was a humorous Country hit for Little Jimmy Dickens, a 4 foot 11 inch tall Country Hall Of Famer.

156. **Lemon Tree** was a more up tempo hit version by Trini Lopez, of a song Peter, Paul and Mary had a hit with three years earlier.

157. **Its Alright** was a powerful song by British singer/songwriter/producer/actor Adam Faith, who later managed the career of Leo Sayer.

158. **I'm A Man** by The Yardbirds was a very progressive recording for its time. The group eventually evolved into Led Zeppelin. The song was written and originally recorded in 1955 by Ellas McDaniel, who is better known as Bo Diddley.

159. **Let Me Be** was the Turtles follow up to their first hit 'It Ain't Me Babe'

160. **Marie** was a hit for The Bachelors, a trio from Dublin, Ireland. This was a remake of the song Tommy Dorsey brought to number one in 1937.

MORE HITS FROM 1965

You Were Made for Me was the final North American hit for Freddie & The Dreamers, a British band from Manchester. Lead singer Freddie Garrity wore glasses similar to the style of Buddy Holly.

143

Hang on Sloopy by The Ramsey Lewis Trio was a very successful instrumental version of a song the McCoys had a number one hit with in the same year.

Roses Are Red My Love was a recording by the 'You Know Who' Group, a one hit wonder American group that tried to sound British.

Twine Time was mostly an instrumental by Alvin Cash, a one hit wonder soul man from St. Louis.

I Found a Girl was one of the final hits for Jan and Dean, a popular surf rock duo during the early 60's. Jan Berry died in 2004 from complications from his serious car crash in 1966.

Sunday and Me by Jay & The Americans was Neil Diamond's first major hit as a songwriter. His string of hits began the following year in 1966.

Laugh at Me was a moderate solo hit for Sonny Bono while Sonny & Cher's hit 'I Got You Babe' was number one on the charts.

Red Roses for a Blue Lady was a hit by Buffalo, New York's Vic Dana. This tune was also an instrumental hit by Bert Kaempfert in 1965.

Operator was a hit for Brenda Holloway, a California Motown singer/ songwriter who co-wrote and recorded 'You've Made Me So Very Happy' which Blood, Sweat & Tears had a major hit with in 1969. Smokey Robinson wrote 'Operator'.

It's Gonna Be Alright was a fast-paced goodtime hit by Gerry & the Pacemakers which was featured in their film 'Ferry Cross The Mersey'.

For Lovin' Me by folk trio Peter, Paul & Mary was written by Canadian folk/ singer songwriter Gordon Lightfoot.

(Such An) Easy Question by Elvis Presley was from his film 'Tickle Me', where he played the part of a guy working at an all-girl dude ranch.

Second Hand Rose by Barbara Streisand was originally a song from 1922 for Fanny Brice, subject of 'Funny Girl'.

A Little Bit of Heaven was a hit for Virginian-born singer Ronnie Dove. This hit was arranged by funnyman Ray Stevens.

TOP ALBUMS OF 1965

1. Mary Poppins - Original Cast
2. Help - Beatles
3. Beatles '65 - Beatles
4. Whipped Cream & Other Delights - Herb Alpert & The Tijuana Brass
5. Beatles V1 - Beatles
6. Out Of Our Heads - Rolling Stones
7. Goldfinger - Shirley Bassey
8. The Sound Of Music - Soundtrack
9. Roustabout - Elvis Presley
10. Herman's Hermits On Tour - Herman's Hermits
11. Summer Days & Summer Nights - Beach Boys
12. Highway 61 Revisited - Bob Dylan
13. Look At Us - Sonny & Cher
14. You've Lost That Loving Feeling - Righteous Brothers
15. 12 X 5 - Rolling Stones
16. Where Did Our Love Go - Supremes

1. Before You Go - Buck Owens
2. King Of The Road - Roger Miller
3. I've Got A Tiger By The Tail - Buck Owens
4. You're The Only World I Know - Sonny James
5. Make The World Go Away - Eddy Arnold
6. Behind The Tear - Sonny James
7. Is It Really Over - Jim Reeves
8. This Is It - Jim Reeves
9. Hello Vietnam - Johnny Wright
10. May The Bird Of Paradise - Little Jimmy Dickens
11. Girl On The Billboard - Del Reeves
12. What's He Doing In My World - Eddy Arnold
13. The First Thing Ev'ry Morning - Jimmy Dean
14. Yes, Mr. Peters - Roy Drusky & Priscilla Mitchell
15. Ribbon Of Darkness - Marty Robbins
16. Buckaroo - Buck Owens

TOP 16 ONE HIT WONDERS OF 1965

1. Roy Head - Treat Her Right
2. We Five - You Were On My Mind
3. Jewel Akens - The Birds & The Bees
4. The Ad Libs - The Boy From New York City
5. Silkie - You've Got To Hide Your Love Away
6. The Larks - The Jerk
7. Barbara Mason - Yes I'm Ready
8. The Castaways - Liar, Liar
9. Ian Whitcomb - You Turn Me On
10. The Strangeloves - I Want Candy
11. Alvin Cash - Twine Time
12. Unit Four Plus Two - Concrete & Clay
13. Barbarians - Are You A Boy Or Are You A Girl?
14. Sounds Orchestral - Cast Your Fate To The Wind
15. The Tradewinds - New York's A Lonely Town
16. The 'You Know Who' Group - Roses Are Red My Love

1. Sunday & Me - Jay & The Americans
2. Puppet On A String - Elvis Presley
3. Here Comes The Night - Them
4. Voodoo Woman - Bobby Goldsboro
5. Take Me Back - Little Anthony & The Imperials
6. I'm A Man - Yardbirds
7. Marie - The Bachelors
8. I Found A Girl - Jan & Dean
9. Action - Freddy Cannon
10. Laurie (Strange Things Happen) - Dickey Lee
11. Here It Comes Again - Fortunes
12. Mohair Sam - Charlie Rich
13. Houston - Dean Martin
14. I'll Be There - Gerry & The Pacemakers
15. One Kiss For Old Time's Sake - Ronnie Dove
16. Laugh At Me - Sonny

TOP 16 R & B/SOUL HITS OF 1965

1. I Can't Help Myself - Four Tops
2. Papa's Got A Brand New Bag - James Brown
3. I Got You (I Feel Good) - James Brown
4. Rescue Me - Fontella Bass
5. Stop In The Name Of Love - Supremes
6. My Girl - Temptations
7. I Hear A Symphony - Supremes
8. I Want To (Do Everything For You) - Joe Tex
9. Ain't That Peculiar - Marvin Gaye
10. We're Gonna Make It - Little Milton
11. In The Midnight Hour - Wilson Pickett
12. Shotgun - Jr. Walker & The All Stars
13. Back In My Arms Again - Supremes
14. It's The Same Old Song - Four Tops
15. How Sweet It Is - Marvin Gaye
16. Hold What You've Got - Joe Tex

TOP 16 ROCK HITS OF 1965

1. Satisfaction - Rolling Stones
2. Get Off Of My Cloud - Rolling Stones
3. Help - Beatles
4. Hang On Sloopy - McCoys
5. For Your Love - Yardbirds
6. Tell Her No - Zombies
7. Catch Us If You Can - Dave Clark Five
8. All Day & All Of The Night - Kinks
9. Heart Full Of Soul - Yardbirds
10. I Like It Like That - Dave Clark Five
11. The Last Time - Rolling Stones
12. Don't Let Me Be Misunderstood - Animals
13. My Generation - Who
14. We Gotta Get Outa This Place - Animals
15. She's About A Mover - Sir Douglas Quintet
16. Gloria - Them

TOP 16 HITS OF THE 60's

1. Hey Jude - The Beatles
2. Theme From A Summer Place - Percy Faith
3. I Heard It Through…Grapevine - Marvin Gaye
4. I Want To Hold Your Hand - The Beatles
5. I'm A Believer - The Monkees
6. Aquarius/Let The Sunshine In - The 5th Dimension
7. Tossin' And Turnin' - Bobby Lewis
8. Are You Lonesome Tonight - Elvis Presley
9. Yesterday - The Beatles
10. Satisfaction - The Rolling Stones
11. I Can't Stop Loving You - Ray Charles
12. Sugar Shack - Jimmy Gilmer & Fireballs
13. Oh Pretty Woman - Roy Orbison
14. It's Now Or Never - Elvis Presley
15. The Twist - Chubby Checker
16. Big Girls Don't Cry - The Four Seasons

Top 16 Music Artists Of The 60's

1. The Beatles
2. Elvis Presley
3. The Supremes
4. The Rolling Stones
5. The Beach Boys
6. The Four Seasons
7. Brenda Lee
8. Stevie Wonder
9. Ricky Nelson
10. Connie Francis
11. The Everly Brothers
12. Aretha Franklin
13. Neil Diamond
14. Ray Charles
15. Marvin Gaye
16. C.C.R.

Top 16 One Hit Wonders Of The 60's

1. Zager And Evans - In The Year 2525
2. New Vaudeville Band - Winchester Cathedral

3. Steam - Na Na Hey Hey …Goodbye
4. Kyu Sakamoto - Sukiyaki
5. Bruce Channel - Hey Baby
6. Tornadoes - Telstar
7. Paul Mauriat - Love Is Blue
8. J. Frank Wilson - Last Kiss
9. Arthur Brown - Fire
10. Ernie K. Doe - Mother-In-Law
11. Scott Mackenzie - San Francisco
12. Music Explosion - Little Bit O' Soul
13. Jewel Aikens - The Birds And The Bees
14. Mark Dinning - Teen Angel
15. Roy Head -Treat Her Right
16. Mercy - Love Can Make You Happy

Top 16 Motown Hits Of The 60's

1. I Heard It Through…Grapevine - Marvin Gaye
2. Baby Love - The Supremes
3. My Girl - The Temptations
4. I Can't Help Myself - The Four Tops
5. Someday We'll Be Together - The Supremes
6. You Can't Hurry Love - The Supremes
7. Reach Out I'll Be There - The Four Tops
8. My Guy - Mary Wells
9. Love Child - The Supremes
10. Fingertips Part 2 - Stevie Wonder
11. Stop In The Name Of Love - The Supremes
12. Do You Love Me - The Contours
13. Shop Around - The Miracles
14. I Can't Get Next To You - The Temptations
15. Come See About Me - The Supremes
16. I Was Made To Love Her - Stevie Wonder

Top 16 Soul/R & B Hits Of The 60's

(Excluding Motown)

1. Respect - Aretha Franklin
2. Dock Of The Bay - Otis Redding
3. I Got You (I Feel Good) - James Brown
4. Soul Man - Sam & Dave
5. When A Man Loves A Woman - Percy Sledge
6. Land Of 1000 Dances - Wilson Pickett
7. Chain Of Fools - Aretha Franklin
8. Everyday People - Sly & The Family Stone
9. Tighten Up - Archie Bell & The Drells
10. In The Midnight Hour - Wilson Pickett
11. Sweet Soul Music - Arthur Conley
12. La La Means I Love You - The Delfonics
13. Higher And Higher - Jackie Wilson
14. Mustang Sally - Wilson Pickett
15. Stand By Me - Ben E. King
16. It's Your Thing - The Isley Brothers

Top 16 Country Hits Of The 60's

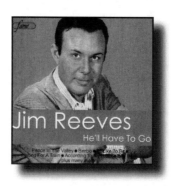

1. He'll Have To Go - Jim Reeves
2. Walk On By - Leroy Van Dyke
3. Wolverton Mountain - Claude King
4. Daddy Sang Bass - Johnny Cash & June Carter
5. Skip A Rope - Henson Cargil
6. Almost Persuaded - David Houston
7. King Of The Road - Roger Miller
8. Once A Day - Connie Smith
9. There Goes My Everything - Jack Greene
10. A Boy Named Sue - Johnny Cash
11. Don't Let Me Cross Over - Carl Butler
12. Ring Of Fire - Johnny Cash
13. Please Help Me I'm Falling - Hank Locklin
14. Folsom Prison Blues - Johnny Cash
15. El Paso - Marty Robbins
16. My Heart Skips A Beat - Buck Owens

Top 16 Male Artists Of The 60's

1. Elvis Presley
2. Stevie Wonder
3. Ricky Nelson
4. Neil Diamond
5. Marvin Gaye
6. Ray Charles
7. Roy Orbison
8. Chubby Checker
9. Neil Sedaka
10. James Brown
11. Gene Pitney
12. Fats Domino
13. Bobby Vinton
14. Bobby Vee
15. Dion
16. Paul Anka

Top 16 Female Artists Of The 60's

1. Brenda Lee
2. Connie Francis
3. Aretha Franklin
4. Lesley Gore
5. Dionne Warwick
6. Petula Clark
7. Dusty Springfield
8. Jackie Deshannon
9. Patsy Cline
10. Mary Wells
11. Cher
12. Lulu
13. Dee Dee Sharp
14. Betty Everett
15. Nancy Sinatra
16. Barbara Lewis

Top 16 Duos Of The 60's

1. Simon And Garfunkel
2. The Everly Brothers
3. The Righteous Brothers
4. Sonny And Cher

5. Jan And Dean
6. Peter And Gordon
7. Sam And Dave
8. Paul And Paula
9. Chad And Jeremy
10. Marvin Gaye & Tammi Terrell
11. Tommy Boyce & Bobby Hart
12. Nino Tempo & April Stevens
13. James & Bobby Purify
14. Dale And Grace
15. The Poppy Family
16. Mel And Tim

Top 16 Novelty Hits Of The 60's

1. Winchester Cathedral - New Vaudeville Band
2. Alley Oop - Hollywood Argyles
3. Snoopy Vs. The Red Baron - Royal Guardsmen
4. Gitarzan - Ray Stevens
5. Surfin' Bird - Trashmen
6. They're Coming To Take Me Away Napoleon X1v
7. Ahab The Arab - Ray Stevens
8. Ringo - Lorne Greene
9. Hello Muddah Hello Faddah - Allan Sherman
10. Tie Me Kangeroo Down Sport - Rolf Harris
11. These Boots Are Made For Walkin' - Nancy Sinatra
12. Lil Red Riding Hood - Sam The Sham & Pharoahs
13. Harry The Hairy Ape - Ray Stevens
14. Does Your Chewing Gum Lose - Lonnie Donegan
15. Mr. Custer - Larry Verne
16. The Name Game - Shirley Ellis

Top 16 Bubblegum Hits Of The 60's

1. Sugar Sugar - The Archies
2. Dizzy - Tommy Roe
3. Hanky Panky - Tommy James & Shondells
4. Green Tambourine - Lemon Pipers
5. Simon Says - 1910 Fruitgum Co.
6. Yummy Yummy Yummy - Ohio Express
7. Little Woman - Bobby Sherman
8. 1 2 3 Redlight - 1910 Fruitgum Co.
9. Cinamon - Derek
10. Chewy Chewy - Ohio Express
11. Tracy - The Cuff Links
12. Sweet Pea - Tommy Roe
13. Gimme Gimme Good Lovin' - Crazy Elephant
14. Baby I Love You - Andy Kim
15. Jam Up & Jelly Tight - Tommy Roe
16. So Good Together - Andy Kim

Top 16 Girl Groups Of The 60's

1. The Supremes
2. The Shirelles
3. Martha & The Vandellas
4. The Crystals
5. The Chiffons
6. The Marvelettes
7. The Ronettes

8. The Shangrilas
9. The Angels
10. The Cookies
11. The Dixie Cups
12. The Paris Sisters
13. The Chordettes
14. The Murmaids
15. The Caravelles
16. The Jelly Beans

Top 16 Folk Hits Of The 60's

1. Blowin' In The Wind - Peter, Paul & Mary
2. Like A Rolling Stone - Bob Dylan
3. Puff The Magic Dragon - Peter, Paul & Mary
4. Walk Right In - The Rooftop Singers
5. The Sounds Of Silence - Simon & Garfunkel
6. Michael (Row The Boat Ashore) - The Highwaymen
7. Elusive Butterfly - Bob Lind
8. Greenfields - Brothers Four
9. Leavin' On A Jet Plane - Peter, Paul & Mary
10. Don't Let The Rain Come Down- Serendipity Singers
11. Greenback Dollar - The Kingston Trio
12. If I Had A Hammer - Peter, Paul & Mary
13. Green Green - New Christy Minstrels
14. Lemon Tree - Trini Lopez
15. Baby The Rain Must Fall - Glenn Yarborough
16. Washington Square - Village Stompers

Top 16 Beach And Surf Hits Of The 60's

1. Surfin' U.S.A. - The Beach Boys
2. Surf City - Jan & Dean
3. California Girls - The Beach Boys
4. Itsy Bitsy Teenie Weenie…Bikini - Brian Hyland
5. Wipeout - The Surfaris
6. Surfer Girl - The Beach Boys
7. Surfin' Safari - The Beach Boys
8. California Sun - The Rivieras
9. Perfidia - The Ventures
10. Ride The Wild Surf - Jan & Dean
11. Under The Boardwalk - The Drifters
12. Surfin' Bird - The Trashmen
13. Pipeline - The Chantays
14. Honolulu Lulu - Jan & Dean
15. Catch A Wave - The Beach Boys
16. Surfer Joe - The Surfaris

Top 16 Psychedelic Hits Of The 60's

1. Crimson And Clover - Tommy James & Shondells
2. Light My Fire - The Doors

3. Incense And Peppermints - Strawberry Alarm Clock
4. Born To Be Wild - Steppenwolf
5. Fire - Arthur Brown
6. Paint It Black - The Rolling Stones
7. Hurdy Gurdy Man - Donovan
8. Sunshine Of Your Love - Cream
9. Hush - Deep Purple
10. You Keep Me Hangin' On - Vanilla Fudge
11. Time Has Come Today - Chambers Brothers
12. Magic Carpet Ride - Steppenwolf
13. Somebody To Love - Jefferson Airplane
14. Pictures Of Matchstick Men - Status Quo
15. San Fransican Nights - Eric Burdon & The Animals
16. Itchycoo Park - Small Faces

Top 16 Instrumental Hits Of The 60's

1. Theme From A Summer Place - Percy Faith
2. Love Is Blue - Paul Mauriat
3. Wonderland By Night - Bert Kaempfert
4. Telstar - The Tornadoes
5. Stranger On The Shore - Mr. Acker Bilk
6. Walk Don't Run - The Ventures
7. Last Date - Floyd Cramer
8. Calcutta - Lawrence Welk
9. Wipeout - The Surfaris
10. The Stripper - David Rose
11. Green Onions - Booker T. & The Mg's
12. Grazing In The Grass - Hugh Masekela
13. Classical Gas - Mason Williams
14. Theme From Romeo & Juliet - Henry Mancini
15. Exodus - Ferrante & Teicher
16. The Horse - Cliff Nobles & Co.

♫ Accidental guitar feedback became legendary on this Beatles number one hit!

♫ This major hit featured a then-unknown Rod Stewart on harmonica!

♫ Paul McCartney wrote 3 of this British duos' hits in 1964!

♫ Glen Campbell played guitar on this Beach Boys hit from 1964!

♫ Chuck Berry changed the lyrics and title of his own hit 'School Days' from 1957 and had a top ten hit in 1964!

♫ This hit became a tragic reality for the singer two years later!

FIND OUT THAT...and MUCH MORE...INSIDE...1964!

1. **I Want To Hold Your Hand/I Saw Her Standing There** was one of several double-sided hit singles by The Beatles. 'I Want to Hold Your Hand' was the ultimate Beatlemania song from the year the Fab Four dominated the North American music scene. John Lennon and Paul McCartney wrote and shared lead vocals on this multi-week number one hit. The 'B' side, 'I Saw Her Standing There' was Paul's song and he was featured on lead vocals. Paul performed it on the Grammy Awards in February 2009.

2. **Can't Buy Me Love** by The Beatles featured Paul McCartney on lead vocals and was one of the tracks from the soundtrack of their first film, 'A Hard Day's Night'. This hit was the fastest selling Beatles single ever.

3. **Oh Pretty Woman** was Roy Orbison's biggest hit of all time and one that continues to appeal to large numbers to this day. He wrote this song with songwriter Bill Dees one afternoon while his wife Claudette, the pretty woman went shopping. It was completed by the time she had returned home.

4. **Baby Love** by the Supremes was a 4 week number one hit for the most successful girl group of all time. Holland/Dozier/Holland wrote and produced this and most of their major hits.

5. **House of The Rising Sun** by The Animals was originally a traditional folk song dating back many decades before this British rock group resurrected it. This multi million seller featured the powerful, soulful voice of Eric Burden and the haunting organ of Alan Price, who received songwriting credits for this number one hit.

6. **Chapel of Love** by The Dixie Cups was originally intended for The Ronettes, but songwriter/producers Jeff Barry and wife Ellie Greenwich decided to record it with this girl group from New Orleans. Phil Spector was co-writer and Leiber & Stoller were co-producers of this instant hit.

7. **I Feel Fine** by The Beatles was written by John Lennon, who is also credited for the opening guitar lick with the first feedback ever recorded on a major hit. John and Paul shared lead vocals. The 'B' side, 'She's A Woman' was written by Paul, who sings lead and plays piano.

8. **There, I've Said It Again** was a multi-week number one hit for balladeer Bobby Vinton just before The Beatles arrived in North America and changed the music scene. It was the Beatles' first number one North American hit 'I Want to Hold Your Hand' that replaced this Bobby Vinton hit in the number one position.

9. **She Loves You** by The Beatles replaced 'I Want To Hold Your Hand' as the number one hit in North America. John and Paul wrote this song together while touring in England the year before.

10. **A Hard Day's Night** was the title song from The Beatles first movie. John Lennon wrote and also sang lead on this number one hit.

11. **I Get Around/Don't Worry Baby** was a double-sided hit single by The Beach Boys. Brian Wilson and Mike Love wrote and shared lead vocals on 'I Get Around'. 'Don't Worry Baby' was written by Brian Wilson and radio DJ Roger Christian, who also co-wrote 'Little Deuce Coupe', 'Shut Down' and many hits for Jan and Dean.

12. **My Guy** was a number one hit by Motown's first female artist, Mary Wells. This classic Motown hit was written and produced by Smokey Robinson while he was having hits with his group The Miracles.

13. **Rag Doll** was The Four Season's 4th number one hit and one of many written by Bob Crewe and group member Bob Gaudio, who was also the group's keyboardist/singer.

14. **Where Did Our Love Go** was the first number one hit for the Supremes, a group formerly known as The Primettes. Diana Ross, Mary Wilson and Florence Ballard had a long string of hits together into the late 60's.

15. **Do Wah Diddy Diddy** by Manfred Mann was a number one hit written by Jeff Barry and Ellie Greenwich. John Paul Jones sang lead on this hit which was originally recorded by The Exciters, but failed to make any impact until British group Manfred Mann recorded it.

16. **Come See about Me** was The Supremes third consecutive number one hit in their debut year on the charts.

17. **Everybody Loves Somebody** was Dean Martin's signature hit. Although the song was written in 1949, and recorded by several artists through the years, it was never a hit until Dean Martin recorded it and brought it to number one in 1964.The following year it became the theme for 'The Dean Martin Show'.

164

18. **Hello Dolly** by Louis Armstrong was the surprise hit of the year, especially since a 63 year old Jazz great knocked the Beatles out of the number one position. The song that became Armstrong's biggest hit of his illustrious career was from the Broadway musical that opened earlier that year starring Carol Channing.

19. **Love Me Do//P.S.I Love You** was a doubled-sided hit single by The Beatles. 'Love Me Do' was actually recorded in 1962, making it their first hit. Original drummer Pete Best played drums on the version released in North America, while his replacement, Ringo Starr played drums on the British released version of the song. 'P. S I love You' was written by Paul with John and Paul sharing lead vocals. Ringo played maracas and Andy White played drums on this Beatles hit recorded in 1962.

20. **A World Without Love** by Peter & Gordon was written by Paul McCartney and became the biggest hit for this British duo. Peter Asher's sister, Jane was dating Paul at the time.

21. **Mr. Lonely** became Bobby Vinton's fourth number one single, and second for 1964, the year of Beatlemania. This self-penned hit is Bobby Vinton's personal favorite. The 'Polish Prince' went on to have over a dozen more top ten hits.

22. **Leader of The Pack** by The Shangrilas actually featured a real motorcycle in the studio for an authentic motor sound. This was one of three official number one hits in 1964 written by Jeff Barry and Ellie Greenwich with 'Do Wah Diddy Diddy' and 'Chapel of Love' being the other two.

23. **Twist And Shout** by The Beatles was a remake of The Isley Brothers hit from 1962. John sang lead on this dance party favorite.

24. **Ringo** by Lorne Greene was a number one hit by this TV star who played Ben Cartwright, the head of the Ponderosa on Bonanza every week on prime time TV. Like Paul Anka, Lorne Greene was also born in the Capitol of Canada, Ottawa, Ontario.

25. **Dancing in the Street** by Martha & The Vandellas was a goodtime, fun Motown favorite co-written by label mate Marvin Gaye. Rolling Stone Magazine named it song number 40 on the 500 Greatest Songs Of All Time.

26. **Last Kiss** by J. Frank Wilson was a song written by Wayne Cochran inspired by a real life tragedy that took place on a highway near his home in Georgia where two teens were killed and others seriously injured. It became J. Frank Wilson's only hit.

27. **Bread And Butter** was a fun song by The Newbeats, a trio featuring the falsetto-voiced Larry Henley on lead. He later became known as co-writer of the song 'Wind beneath My Wings' made famous by Bette Midler.

28. **Memphis** was the first hit for Johnny Rivers. It was a remake of Chuck Berry's classic and Johnny recorded it 'live' at The Whiskey a Go-Go in Los Angeles.

29. **My Boy Lollipop** by Millie Small from Jamaica featured a then-unknown Rod Stewart playing harmonica.

30. **She's Not There** was the first hit for the British group The Zombies featuring Colin Blunstone on lead vocals and Rod Argent on keyboards. Argent later had a hit of his own in 1972 with 'Hold Your Head Up'.

31. **Do You Want to Know a Secret** by The Beatles was written by John Lennon and sung by George Harrison. This single was backed with 'Thank You Girl' and both were featured on the 'Please Please Me' album.

32. **You Don't Own Me** by Lesley Gore was ahead of its time lyrically in regards to the woman's liberation movement a decade later. Although she had hits after this song, this was Lesley's last official top ten hit.

33. **Suspicion** was Terry Stafford's only top ten hit. This Oklahoma born and raised singer had a voice that sounded like Elvis Presley, who originally recorded this song two years earlier. It was the 'B' side of Elvis Presley's single 'Kiss Me Quick'.

34. **Please Please Me/From Me To You** was a double-sided hit single by The Beatles recorded on a two track tape machine two years earlier in 1962. 'Please Please Me' was written by John and featured John and Paul sharing lead vocals. 'From Me to You' was written by John and Paul, who shared lead vocals on this song.

35. **Little Old Lady from Pasadena** by Jan and Dean was inspired by a line a local used car salesmen would use. They would say that the previous owner was a little old lady from Pasadena who only drove it to church on Sundays.

36. **Come A Little Bit Closer** was a Jay & The Americans hit co-written by Tommy Boyce and Bobby Hart who would begin writing many of the hits for the Monkees two years later in 1966.

37. **Dawn (Go Away)** by The Four Seasons didn't reach number one because The Beatles 'I Want to Hold Your Hand' and 'She Loves You' had a firm grip for several weeks at the top spot on the charts. 'Dawn' was written by Bob Gaudio and Sandy Linzer and produced by Bob Crewe.

38. **Under the Boardwalk** by The Drifters featured group member Johnny Moore on lead vocals and was the group's final top ten hit.

166

39. **Because** by The Dave Clark Five was one of the few ballads from this British group known for its fast-paced tempo.

40. **Popsicles and Icicles** was a top five hit for the Los Angeles trio of girls known as The Murmaids. Their one and only hit was written by David Gates who resurfaced 6 years later as the front man for the soft rock group Bread.

41. **Fun Fun Fun** was a Beach Boys hit written by Brian Wilson and Mike Love. Mike Love sang lead on this great cruisin' hit from '64 which was backed on the single with their version of 'Why Do Fools Fall In Love'.

42. **Love Me with All Your Heart** was a big hit for the Ray Charles Singers, an easy listening group who also backed up Perry Como on many of his hits. He's the 'other Ray Charles', not to be confused with the legendary blind singer.

43 **Bits and Pieces** by The Dave Clark Five was their 2nd hit. Lead singer/ keyboardist Mike Smith died in February of 2008, one month before they were finally inducted into the Rock And Roll Hall Of Fame.

44. **We'll Sing in The Sunshine** was the only hit for singer/actress/writer Gale Garnett, who was born in New Zealand and later made Canada her home.

45. **Surfin' Bird** by The Trashmen was a novelty hit which was a combination of two songs, - 'The Bird Is the Word' and 'Papa oom Mow Mow' which was a hit for The Rivingtons.

46. **Forget Him** was the final top 10 hit for Philadelphia's Bobby Rydell, best known for early 60's hits like 'Wild One', 'Volare' and 'The Cha-Cha-Cha'.

47. **Don't Let the Sun Catch You Crying** was Gerry And The Pacemakers first and biggest hit in North America. Lead singer Gerry Marsden wrote this heartfelt ballad.

48. **Glad All Over** was the first hit for The Dave Clark Five from Tottenham, England led by their namesake producer/drummer and songwriter.

49. **G.T.O**. was a hit for hot rod rock group Ronny & the Daytonas. They were actually a group of session musicians who included Bobby Russell and Chips Moman. Bill Justis, who had a big hit with 'Raunchy', was the producer of this top ten hit.

50. **Out Of Limits** was a popular hit for instrumental surf group The Marketts from Hollywood. This tune was their take on 'Outer Limits', a popular sci-fi TV show at the time.

51. **Have I the Right** was an energetic hit by the British group The Honeycombs featuring one of rock's first female drummers, Ann 'Honey' Lantree.

52. **Hey Little Cobra** was a hot rod hit by The Rip Chords, a California duo consisting of Bruce Johnston in his pre-Beach Boys days and Terry Melcher, Doris Day's son, who became a producer of other groups including Paul Revere & The Raiders.

53. **People** from the Broadway musical 'Funny Girl' was Barbara Streisand's first hit.

54. **Java** by Trumpeter Al Hirt, from New Orleans, was one of the top instrumental hits of the year.

55. **California Sun** was the only hit for a teenage band from Indiana known as The Rivieras. It was a classic upbeat, goodtime hit.

56. **Shoop Shoop Song (It's In His Kiss)** was the biggest solo hit of Betty Everett, who also had a major duet hit in 1964 with Jerry Butler with 'Let It Be Me'.

57. **Can't You See That She's Mine** was one of eight singles The Dave Clark Five released in their debut year on the charts. Seven of the eight reached the top 20 on the charts.

58. **The Girl from Ipanema** by Stan Getz and Astrud Gilberto won The Grammy Award for Record of the Year in 1965. The song was inspired by the real girl from Ipanema who was 15 at the time and would stroll by their café everyday on her way to buy cigarettes for her mother.

59. **Wishin' and Hopin'** by Dusty Springfield is a Burt Bacharach/Hal David composition which was originally recorded by Dionne Warwick in 1963, but failed to chart.

60. **C'mon and Swim** was a hit by San Francisco R & B singer Bobby Freeman about one of the hottest dances of the year. This top ten hit was actually written and produced by a then-unknown Sylvester Stewart, better known as Sly Stone of The Family Stone.

61. **Remember (Walkin' in The Sand)** was the second most popular hit for the girl group The Shangri-las. Their biggest hit 'Leader of The Pack' was also from 1964.

62. **Goin' Out Of My Head** was a top ten hit by Little Anthony & The Imperials co-written by Teddy Randazzo, who also co-wrote their next hit, 'Hurt So Bad'. Coincidentally, both were later released as singles by The Lettermen.

63. **Time Is on My Side** by The Rolling Stones was actually their first top ten hit in North America. They performed this song on their first appearance on The Ed Sullivan Show. Mick Jagger was 21 at the time.

64. **Um Um Um Um Um Um** was a soulful, catchy song by Chicago's Major Lance, written by Curtis Mayfield of The Impressions.

65. **Walk on By** was one of Dionne Warwick's first major hits written by Burt Bacharach/Hal David, who composed all of her notable hits of the 60's.

66. **Navy Blue** was a hit for 17 year old Diane Renay from Philadelphia. This song was written by Bob Crewe, Bud Rehak and Eddie Rambeau. Her follow up was the similar sounding 'Kiss Me Sailor'.

67. **Don't Let The Rain Come Down (Crooked Little Man)** was a top ten hit by the pop-folk group, Serendipity Singers, a nine member group organized at The University of Colorado.

68. **It Hurts to Be in Love** by Gene Pitney was originally planned to be recorded by Neil Sedaka, but he turned it down. It turned out to be one of Pitney's biggest hits. He was inducted into the Rock And Roll Hall Of Fame in 2002.

69. **Just like Romeo and Juliet** was the only notable hit for The Reflections, a pop rock group out of Detroit, Michigan featuring Tony Micale on lead vocals.

70. **All My Loving** by The Beatles was a much bigger hit in Britain and Canada than it was in the U.S. where it failed to reach the top 40. Paul wrote and sang lead on this hit from the year of Beatlemania.

71. **Little Children** was a hit for Billy J. Kramer who was also from Liverpool and managed by Brian Epstein. It was John Lennon who suggested he add the 'J' to distinguish himself by adding a 'tougher edge'.

72. **Little Honda** was a hit by a Southern California studio group The Hondells written by The Beach Boys' Brian Wilson. The song was a tribute to the Honda Motorcycle.

73. **You Really Got Me** by The Kinks has one of the greatest guitar riffs of all time. It's believed by many that session player Jimmy Page played guitar on this track, but that is not true. Ray Davies' brother Dave Davies was the featured guitarist on this rock classic.

74. **Dance Dance Dance** was a Beach Boys hit which featured session player Glen Campbell on guitar. This upbeat single was featured on 'The Beach Boys Today' album.

75. **For You** by Rick Nelson was his final top ten hit until 8 years later when 'Garden Party' reached number six. Rick died in a plane crash New Years Eve in 1985 at the age of 45.

76. **A Summer Song** was a soothing, harmonizing song for a perfect day by Chad Stuart and Jeremy Clyde, better known as simply Chad and Jeremy. This was the most successful hit in North America for this British folk duo of the 60's.

77. **Mountain of Love** was one of many remake hits for Johnny Rivers during the 60's. This song was originally a hit for Harold Dorman in 1960.

78. **Dang Me** was Roger Miller's first hit on the pop charts. This hit was number one for six weeks on the Country charts. His follow up was 'Chug A Lug' which was very similar in style and humor.

79. **The Door Is Still Open to My Heart** was another big hit for Dean Martin. The song was a remake of an R & B hit from the 50's by The Cardinals. This was Dean's follow up to 'Everybody Loves Somebody'.

80. **Ronnie** by The Four Seasons was one of seven singles The Four Seasons released in 1964. Other girl's names in Four Seasons' hits include 'Sherry', Dawn', Marlena', and (C'mon) Marianne'.

81. **Deadman's Curve** by Jan and Dean was an actual strip of a road in Los Angeles, California where eerily Jan Barry would crash his Corvette two years later. He received severe head injuries, resulting in brain damage and partial paralysis. The 'B' side of the single was 'The New Girl in School'.

82. **Amen** by R & B group The Impressions was featured in the film 'Lilies of The Field' starring Sidney Poitier. Curtis Mayfield was the lead singer on this top ten hit.

83. **Anyone Who Had a Heart** was Dionne Warwick's first hit to reach the top ten. The singer from East Orange, New Jersey began singing in church choir from age six.

84. **How Do You Do it** was a hit by Gerry & The Pacemakers produced by George Martin and written by Mitch Murray, who also wrote their hit 'I Like It'. Mitch Murray later co-wrote hits like 'Hitchin' a Ride', 'Billy Don't Be a Hero' and 'The Night Chicago Died'.

85. **Chug a Lug** was another humorous pop country hit from Roger Miller in his debut year on the pop charts. This was his follow up to 'Dang Me'.

86. **White on White** was a wedding song hit by African-born Danny Williams who moved to England when he was 18 in 1960. This was his only hit.

87. **Bad to Me** was one of Billy J. Kramer's hits written by Lennon and McCartney. Since Brian Epstein also managed Billy, he had the opportunity to record some of the songs the Beatles passed on.

88. **Stop and Think It Over** was one of two major hits for Dale And Grace, a duo from Louisiana whose full names were Dale Houston and Grace Broussard. Their biggest hit was 'I'm Leaving It up To You' which was number one when J.F.K. was assassinated in November of 1963.

89. **Baby I Need Your Lovin'** was the first hit by The Four Tops and despite the popularity of this hit, it failed to reach the top ten. This classic Motown hit featuring Levi Stubbs on lead vocals remains a staple on radio today.

90. **It's Over** by Roy Orbison was a hit a few months before his biggest hit of all time 'Oh Pretty Woman' reached number one.

91. **Walk Don't Run '64** by The Ventures was an updated electrified version of their own original version from four years earlier in 1960. Their new version in 1964 also reached the top ten.

92. **I'm Gonna Be Strong** by Gene Pitney was written by Barry Mann and Cynthia Weil. It was a much bigger hit in the U.K. (where it peaked at number two), than it was in North America.

93. **No Particular Place to Go** by the legendary Chuck Berry was a remake of his own song 'School Day', from 1957, with different lyrics.

94. **The Nitty Gritty** by Shirley Ellis was one of three notable novelty hits. She wrote them with her Manager/Producer Lincoln Chase.

95. **When I Grow Up (To Be A Man)** by The Beach Boys was written by Brian Wilson and Mike Love, who shared lead vocals on this cut from their 'Beach Boys Today' album.

96. **What Kind Of Fool (Do You Think I Am)** was the only hit for The Tams, an R & B quintet from Atlanta. Bill Deal & the Rhondells remade this song in 1969.

97. **I'm The One** by Gerry & The Pacemakers was a major hit in England and Canada, but only a minor hit in the U.S.

98. **See the Funny Little Clown** was Bobby Goldsboro's first major hit. From '62 to '64 he toured with Roy Orbison.

99. **The Way You Do the Things You Do** by The Temptations featured Eddie Kendricks on lead vocals. This hit was produced and co-written by Smokey Robinson of The Miracles.

100. **And I Love Her/ If I Fell** was a double-sided hit single of ballads by The Beatles. They were both included in the film and album 'A Hard Day's Night'.

101. **Viva Las Vegas** by Elvis Presley was the title song of the Elvis movie of the same which co-starred Ann- Margret.

102. **I'm Into Something Good** was the very first hit for Britain's Herman's Hermits featuring a then-16 year old Peter Noone on lead vocals. Carole King and Gerry Goffin wrote this feel good hit from '64.

103. **Needles and Pins** by The British band The Searchers was co-written by Sonny Bono of Sonny & Cher fame. It was originally released by Jackie DeShannon in 1963, but failed to crack the Top 40.

104. **Maybe I Know** by Lesley Gore was the first and biggest of four hits from her album 'Girl Talk'. This singer raised in Tenafly, New Jersey was discovered by Quincy Jones while singing at a hotel in Manhattan.

105. **The Wedding** was the only notable hit for British singer Julie Rogers, despite the fact that she toured successfully for many years afterwards.

106. **I Only Want To Be With You** was the very first solo hit for Dusty Springfield after leaving the folk trio The Springfields. This song became a hit for The Bay City Rollers the following decade.

107. **Maybelline** was Johnny Rivers' second hit and the first two were both written by Chuck Berry. His first was a remake of Chuck Berry's classic 'Memphis'.

108. **Hippy Hippy Shake** was the biggest hit for Liverpool, England's Swinging Blue Jeans. Terry Sylvester, who later joined the Hollies to replace Graham Nash was a member of this British rock band.

109. **I Like It** by Gerry & The Pacemakers was one of almost half a dozen hits they had in 1964 alone. They were signed in 1962 by Beatles Manager Brian Epstein.

110. **Saturday Night at The Movies** by The Drifters was their final top 40 hit. This goodtime hit, which featured Johnny Moore on lead vocals, was written by Barry Mann and Cynthia Weil.

111. **Diane** was the first and biggest hit for The Bachelors, a pop vocal trio from Dublin, Ireland. This song dates back to 1928 when it was a major hit for the Nat Shilkret Orchestra.

112. **(You Don't Know) How Glad I Am** was the most successful hit for jazz-oriented singer Nancy Wilson, not to be confused with the member of Heart, popular a decade later.

113. **Do You Love Me** was Dave Clark Five's remake of the Contours hit from two years earlier.

114. **From a Window** was the third of three 1964 hits in a row by Billy J. Kramer written by John Lennon and Paul McCartney.

115. **Save It for Me** by The Four Seasons was their follow up to their number one hit 'Rag Doll' just two months earlier.

116. **I Wanna Love Him So Bad** was the only hit for The Jellybeans, a girl group quintet from Jersey City which included two sisters.

117. **I Love You More and More Every Day** was among Al Martino's three biggest hits of the 60's. The other two were 'Spanish Eyes' and 'I Love You Because'.

118. **Tobacco Road** was the only hit for the British group the Nashville Teens. This rock classic was written by John D. Loudermilk, who wrote hits which included 'Indian Reservation', 'Norman' and 'Ebony Eyes'.

119. **Nobody I Know** by Peter and Gordon was the second of three 1964 hits with songwriting credits to John Lennon and Paul McCartney.

120. **You Never Can Tell** by Chuck Berry was later made famous in the dance scene of the movie 'Pulp Fiction' with John Travolta and Uma Thurman.

121. **You're A Wonderful One** was an upbeat feel good song by Motown's Marvin Gaye. Although it failed to reach the top ten, it is considered to be a Motown classic.

122. **Such a Night** by Elvis Presley was written by Lincoln Chase in 1954 and became a hit for Johnny Ray. Elvis recorded it on his 1960 album 'Elvis Is Back', but the single didn't chart until four years later.

123. **In The Misty Moonlight** was a hit for singer/guitarist Jerry Wallace, whose biggest hit was 'Primrose Lane' in 1959.

124. **Farmer John** was a hit for The Premiers, a Latin Rock band from California. They recorded their only hit 'live' at The Rhythm Room in Fullerton, California.

125. **You're My World** was a hit for Liverpool's Cilla Black, whose real name was Priscilla White. She was discovered by Beatles' manager Brian Epstein while she was working as a coat check/singer at Liverpool's Cavern Club.

126. **The French Song** was a major hit in Canada for Quebec singer Lucille Starr.

127. **A Fool Never Learns** was an upbeat hit by Andy Williams written by Sonny Curtis, one of Buddy Holly's Crickets who went on to become a successful country artist and songwriter. The 'B' side of this single was 'Charade', the title song of the movie which starred Cary Grant and Audrey Hepburn.

128. **Drag City** was one of many hot rod or surfin' hits by California's Jan and Dean during their heyday in the early 60's.

129. **Whispering** by brother and sister duo Nino Tempo and April Stevens from Niagara Falls, New York was their follow up to their number one hit 'Deep Purple'. 'Whispering' was also a remake, this time from 1920, originally by Paul Whiteman & His orchestra.

130. **Anyway You Want it** was a fast paced rock hit by The Dave Clark Five complete with a great 'echo' effect.

131. **Don't Throw Your Love Away** was the second of five hits charted by British act The Searchers in 1964. Like The Beatles, Gerry & the Pacemakers and Billy J. Kramer, they also hailed from Liverpool, England.

132. **Stay** by The Four Seasons gave us their trademark harmonies and Frankie Valli's falsetto voice on this previous success by Maurice Williams & The Zodiacs.

133. **Abigail Beecher** was a fun song by Freddy 'Boom Boom' Cannon about the history teacher. It was his first hit with Warner Brothers and his second last hit of the 60's.

134. **Yesterday's Gone** was the first hit from the British folk/rock duo Chad & Jeremy. 1964 - 65 were their only years in the top 20 in North America.

135. **Sidewalk Surfin'** by Jan and Dean used the music of the Beach Boys 'Catch A Wave' with new lyrics for this hit about skateboarding.

136. **It's All in the Game** was a hit by Cliff Richard which was much more popular in Britain and Canada than in the U.S. This was a remake of the Tommy Edwards hit from 1958.

137. **Slow Down/Matchbox** was a double sided hit single by The Beatles of two non-original songs. 'Slow Down' was written by Larry Williams and 'Matchbox' was a Carl Perkins song.

138. **Hey Jean, Hey Dean** was a party hit by Dean And Jean, who were actually Welton Young and Brenda Lee Jones from Dayton, Ohio.

139. **Kiss Me Quick** by Elvis Presley was an underrated song written by Doc Pomus and Mort Shuman. The flip side of this single was 'Suspicion' which became a top ten hit for Elvis sound-a-like Terry Stafford.

140. **When You Walk In the Room** was written by Jackie DeShannon and made popular by both the Searchers, and the songwriter.

141. **My Heart Belongs to Only You** by Bobby Vinton was originally a hit for June Christy in 1953.

142. **That's The Way Boys Are** was one of many consecutive hits for Lesley Gore in 1963 - '64, all of which were produced by the legendary Quincy Jones.

143. **Haunted House** was a hit for Tupelo, Mississippi-born Jumpin' Gene Simmons, not to be confused with the Kiss front man. This hit popular during Halloween was this singer's only hit.

144. **Good News** was a hit for Sam Cooke the same year we heard the bad news that he was shot and killed by a Motel owner under mysterious circumstances.

145. **Right or Wrong** was one of the first hits for Ronnie Dove. This song was a Country hit for Wanda Jackson three years earlier in 1961.

146. **Shangrila** was an instrumental hit for Robert Maxwell, his Harp and Orchestra. Robert Maxwell co-wrote this tune back in 1946.

147. **Everybody Knows** was a hit by The Dave Clark Five. Coincidentally, in late 1967 they also released a single titled 'Everybody Knows' which was an entirely different song.

148. **Ask Me/Ain't That Loving You Baby** was a double-sided hit single by Elvis Presley. 'Ain't That Loving You Baby' written by Clyde Otis and Ivory Joe Hunter was actually recorded in 1958, 6 years before it became a hit.

149. **I Don't Want To See You Again** by Peter and Gordon was another of their hits written by Paul McCartney and credited to Lennon/McCartney. McCartney wrote a total of four of their charted hits.

150. **The Shelter of Your Arms** by Sammy Davis Jr. was written by Jerry Samuels who later recorded under the name Napoleon 14th on the novelty million seller 'They're Coming To Take Me Away Ha Ha'.

151. **Hooka Tooka** was Chubby Checker's final top 20 hit of the 60's. He had a total of 15 from 1960 to 1964.

152. **Penetration** was an instrumental hit for the California surf band The Pyramids who performed in the movie 'Bikini Beach' starring Frankie Avalon and Annette Funicello.

153. **Tell Me (You're Coming Back)** was one of the first hits in North America for The Rolling Stones. This was also the first original composition 'A' side hit by Jagger/Richards for The Rolling Stones.

154. **Baby I Love You** was a Phil Spector production by his girl group The Ronettes. Veronica Bennett (Ronnie Spector) was married to Phil Spector from 1968 to 1974.

155. **It's All Over Now** was a The Rolling Stones hit which was originally a hit for The Valentinos featuring Bobby Womack, who co-wrote this song. The Stones recorded this at the Chess studios in Chicago.

156. **Tra La La La Suzy** by Dean and Jean was one of two top 40 hits they achieved and both were popular in 1964.

157. **Rip Van Winkle** was a fun, novelty hit by one hit wonder The Devotions. It was released in 1962 and by the time it became a hit in 1964, the group had already broken up.

158. **Wendy** was a Beach Boys hit which failed to crack the top 40. It was the single between 'When I Grow Up' and 'Dance Dance Dance'. The 'B' side was the original version of 'Little Honda' which The Hondells had a hit with that same year.

159. **Leader Of The Laundromat** was a parody of 'Leader Of The Pack' by The Detergents. This one hit wonder trio from New York featured Ron Dante, lead singer on the Archies' 'Sugar Sugar' and The Cuff Links' hit 'Tracy'.

160. **Nadine (Is That You)** was a moderate hit for one of the pioneers of Rock And Roll, Chuck Berry. He still managed to have three top 40 hits in 1964, the year of the British Music Invasion, headed by The Beatles.

More Hits of 1964

Hi-Heel Sneakers was the only notable hit for Springfield, Ohio's Tommy Tucker. Sadly, he died in 1982 at the age of 48 from inhaling carbon tetrachloride while refinishing the hardwood floors of his home.

Forever by Pete Drake featured his innovative talking steel guitar on this easy listening hit. He was one of Nashville's top steel guitar session men and played on hits like 'Stand By Your Man', 'Lay Lady Lay', 'Rose Garden' and 'Behind Closed Doors'.

Not Fade Away/I Wanna Be Your Man was a double-sided hit single by The Rolling Stones. This was their first single and both sides were non-originals. 'Not Fade Away' was a Buddy Holly tune and 'I Wanna Be Your Man' was written by Lennon and McCartney.

Keep on Pushing was a hit for the soul group The Impressions, who were inducted into the Rock And Roll Hall Of Fame in 1991.

Selfish One was the only notable hit for American soul singer Jackie Ross.

Sha La La was Manfred Mann's follow up to 'Do Wah Diddy Diddy' from earlier in '64.

As Usual by Brenda Lee was one of 30 top 40 hits during the 60's for the singer known as 'Little Miss Dynamite'.

Kissin' Cousins was the title song of the movie in which Elvis Presley played two parts. He had to wear a strawberry blonde wig for the part of his look-a-like hillbilly cousin in the film which co-starred Jack Albertson and Arthur O'Connell.

People Say was The Dixie Cups follow up hit to 'Chapel Of Love' which reached number one. This girl group trio from New Orleans was discovered by Joe Jones of 'You Talk Too Much' fame.

Every Little Bit Hurts was the first and biggest hit for California soul singer Brenda Holloway, who later became a backup singer for Joe Cocker. Five years later, Blood, Sweat & Tears had a hit with a song she co-wrote and recorded in 1967, 'You've Made Me So Very Happy'.

Tell Me Why was a Bobby Vinton hit originally popularized by The Four Aces in 1952.

Cotton Candy was one of three instrumental hits Al Hirt charted in his most successful year, 1964. This was his follow up to his signature hit 'Java'.

Daisy Petal Pickin' by Jimmy Gilmer & the Fireballs was very similar in sound to their previous hit 'Sugar Shack' which stayed at number one longer than any other hit in 1963.

Southtown U.S.A. was a hit by The Dixiebelles, a female trio from New Orleans. They were backed by Jerry Smith's piano.

Ride the Wild Surf by Jan & Dean was the title song from the movie which starred Fabian and Tab Hunter.

Today by American folk group The New Christy Minstrels was from the movie 'Advance to the Rear' starring Glenn Ford. This group had much success with their Christmas albums during the 60's.

Sugar And Spice by The Searchers was a fast-paced hit which did much better in Britain and Canada than in the U.S. The group 'The Cryin' Shames' had a minor hit with it in 1966.

Invisible Tears was a popular easy listening hit for Ray Coniff and The Singers. It was also a Country hit for Ned Miller in 1964.

TOP 16 ALBUMS OF 1964

1. A Hard Day's Night - The Beatles
2. Meet The Beatles - The Beatles
3. The Singing Nun - Singing Nun
4. Hello Dolly - Louis Armstrong
5. The Beatles Second Album - The Beatles
6. People - Barbara Streisand
7. Beach Boys Concert - The Beach Boys
8. Hello Dolly - Original Soundtrack
9. Introducing… The Beatles - The Beatles
10. Funny Girl - Original Cast
11. Everybody Loves Somebody - Dean Martin
12. Little Deuce Coupe - The Beach Boys
13. Something New - The Beatles
14. Call Me Irresponsible & Other Hit Songs - Andy Williams
15. Stan Getz & Jose Gilberto - Getz/Gilberto
16. Honey In The Horn - Al Hirt

TOP 16 COUNTRY HITS OF 1964

1. Once A Day - Connie Smith
2. My Heart Skips A Beat - Buck Owens
3. I Guess I'm Crazy - Jim Reeves
4. Dang Me - Roger Miller
5. Understand Your Man - Johnny Cash
6. Saginaw, Michigan - Lefty Frizzell
7. I Don't Care - Buck Owens
8. Begging To You - Marty Robbins
9. Together Again - Buck Owens
10. B.J. The D.J. - Stonewall Jackson
11. The Race Is On - George Jones
12. Chug A Lug - Roger Miller
13. 500 Miles Away From Home - Bobby Bare
14. The Ballad of Ira Hayes - Johnny Cash
15. Forever - Pete Drake
16. Four Strong Winds - Bobby Bare

TOP 16 ONE HIT WONDERS OF 1964

1. J. Frank Wilson - Last Kiss
2. The Honeycombs - Have I The Right?
3. Gale Garnett - We'll Sing In The Sunshine
4. The Rivieras - California Sun
5. The Reflections - Just Like Romeo & Juliet
6. Danny Williams - White On White
7. The Hondells - Little Honda
8. Julie Rogers - The Wedding
9. Joey Powers - Midnight Mary
10. Nashville Teens - Tobacco Road
11. Pyramids - Penetration
12. The Premiers - Farmer John
13. The Jelly Beans - I Wanna Love Him So Bad
14. Jumpin' Gene Simmons - Haunted House
15. The Devotions - Rip Van Winkle
16. Tommy Tucker - Hi Heel Sneakers

16 GREAT 'LOST 45'S FROM 1964

1. Such A Night - Elvis Presley
2. Saturday Night At The Movies - The Drifters
3. Farmer John - The Premiers
4. Don't Throw Your Love Away - The Searchers
5. A Fool Never Learns - Andy Williams
6. Right Or Wrong - Ronnie Dove
7. Yesterday's Gone - Chad & Jeremy
8. Penetration - The Pyramids
9. How Glad I Am - Nancy Wilson
10. Abigail Beecher - Freddy Cannon
11. Kiss Me Quick - Elvis Presley
12. The Wedding - Julie Rogers
13. Um Um Um Um Um Um - Major Lance
14. Whispering - Nino Tempo & April Stevens
15. Hey Dean, Hey Jean - Dean & Jean
16. Forever - Pete Drake & His Talking Guitar

TOP 16 R & B/SOUL HITS OF 1964

1. Baby Love - The Supremes
2. My Guy - Mary Wells
3. Where Did Our Love Go - The Supremes
4. Come See About Me - The Supremes
5. Dancing In The Street - Martha & The Vandellas
6. Amen - The Impressions
7. Baby I Need Your Lovin' - Four Tops
8. The Way You Do The Things You Do - The Temptations
9. You're A Wonderful One - Marvin Gaye
10. Good News - Sam Cooke
11. Keep On Pushing - The Impressions
12. Selfish One - Jackie Ross
13. Every Little Bit Hurts - Brenda Holloway
14. You Must Believe Me - The Impressions
15. Try It Baby - Marvin Gaye
16. Wish Someone Would Care - Irma Thomas

TOP 16 DANCE/PARTY HITS OF 1964

1. Pretty Woman - Roy Orbison
2. Twist And Shout - The Beatles
3. Do Wah Diddy Diddy - Manfred Mann
4. Dancing In The Street - Martha & The Vandellas
5. I Want To Hold Your Hand/I Saw Her Standing... - The Beatles
6. Memphis - Johnny Rivers
7. Fun Fun Fun - The Beach Boys
8. Glad All Over - Dave Clark Five
9. Baby Love - The Supremes
10. I Get Around - The Beach Boys
11. Have I The Right? - The Honeycombs
12. C'mon And Swim - Bobby Freeman
13. You Really Got Me - The Kinks
14. Hippy Hippy Shake - Swinging Blue Jeans
15. Do You Love Me - Dave Clark Five
16. You Never Can Tell - Chuck Berry

60's NUMBER ONES THE DAY TODAY'S STARS WERE BORN!

Paula Abdul - June 19 1962 - I Can't Stop Loving You - Ray Charles
Pamela Anderson - July 1 1967 - Windy - The Association
Jennifer Aniston - Feb 11 1969 - Crimson & Clover - Tommy James
Marc Anthony - Sept 16 1968 - People Got To Be Free - The Rascals
Antonio Banderas - Aug 10 1960 - Itsy Bitsy Teenie…Bikini - Brian Hyland
Halle Berry - Aug 14 1966 - Summer In The City - Lovin' Spoonful
Jack Black - Aug 28 1969 - Honky Tonk Women - Rolling Stones
Cate Blanchett - May 14 1969 - Aquarius/Sunshine In - 5th Dimension
Bono - May 10 1960 - Stuck On You - Elvis Presley
Toni Braxton - Oct. 7 1968 - Hey Jude - Beatles
Mathew Broderick - Mar 21 1962 - Soldier Boy - Shirelles
Garth Brooks - Feb 7 1962 - Peppermint Twist - Joey Dee
Bobby Brown - Feb 5 1969 - Crimson & Clover - Tommy James
Sandra Bullock - July 26 1964 - Rag Doll - Four Seasons
Nicolas Cage - Jan 7 1964 - There I've Said It Again - Bobby Vinton
Jim Carrey - Jan 17 1962 - The Twist - Chubby Checker
Kenny Chesney - Mar. 26 1968 - Dock Of The Bay - Otis Redding
George Clooney - May 6 1961 - Runaway - Del Shannon
Cindy Crawford - Feb. 20 1966 - Lightning Strikes - Lou Christie
Courtney Cox - June 15 1964 - Chapel Of Love - Dixie Cups
Sheryl Crow - Feb. 11 1962 - Peppermint Twist - Joey Dee
Russell Crowe - Apr. 7 1964 - Can't Buy Me Love - Beatles
Tom Cruise - July 3 1962 - I Can't Stop Loving You - Ray Charles
John Cusack - June 28 1966 - Paperback Writer - Beatles
Billy Ray Cyrus - Aug. 25 1961 - Tossin' & Turnin' - Bobby Lewis
Patrick Dempsey - Jan. 13 1966 - We Can Work It Out - Beatles
Johnny Depp - June 9 1963 - It's My Party - Lesley Gore
Celine Dion - Mar. 30 1968 - Dock Of The Bay - Otis Redding
Rosie O'donnell - Mar. 21 1962 - Hey Baby - Bruce Channel
Robert Downey Jr. - Apr. 4 1965 - Stop In The Name Of Love - Supremes
David Duchovny - Aug. 7 1960 - I'm Sorry - Brenda Lee
Emilio Estevez - May 12 1962 - Soldier Boy - Shirelles
Will Ferrell - July 16 1967 - Windy - The Association
Calista Flockhart - Nov. 11 1964 - Baby Love - Supremes
Jodie Foster - Nov. 19 1962 - Big Girls Don't Cry - Four Seasons
Matthew Fox - July 14 1966 - Strangers In The Night - Frank Sinatra
Michael J. Fox - June 9 1961 - Running Scared - Roy Orbison
Brendan Fraser - Dec. 3 1968 - Love Child - Supremes
Cuba Gooding Jr. - Jan. 2 1968 - Hello Goodbye - Beatles
Hugh Grant - Sept. 9 1960 - Michael (Row The Boat…) - Highwayman
Teri Hatcher - Dec. 8 1964 - Ringo - Lorne Greene

Salam Hayek - Sept. 2 1966 - Summer In The City - Lovin' Spoonful
Faith Hill - Sept. 21 1967 - Ode To Billie Joe - Bobbie Gentry
Whitney Houston - Aug. 9 1963 - So Much In Love - Tymes
Elizabeth Hurley - June 10 1965 - Help Me Rhonda - Beach Boys
Hugh Jackman - Oct. 12 1968 - Hey Jude - Beatles
Janet Jackson - May 16 1966 - Monday Monday - Mamas & Papas
Jon Bon Jovi - Mar. 2 1962 - Duke Of Earl - Gene Chandler
Michael Jordan - Feb. 17 1963 - Hey Paula - Paul & Paula
Ashley Judd - Apr. 19 1968 - Honey - Bobby Goldsboro
Toby Keith - July 8 1961 - Quarter To Three - Gary U.S. Bonds
Nicole Kidman - June 20 1967 - Respect - Aretha Franklin
Lenny Kravitz - May 26 1964 - My Guy - Mary Wells
Lisa Kudrow - July 30 1963 - Surf City - Jan & Dean
Diane Lane - July 22 1965 - I Feel Fine - Beatles
Matt Leblanc - July 25 1967 - Windy - The Association
Lucy Liu - Dec. 2 1968 - Love Child - Supremes
Heather Locklear - Sept. 25 1961 - Take Good Care Of My Baby - Bobby Vee
Jennifer Lopez - July 24 1969 - In The Year 2525 - Zager & Evans
Julia Louis-Dreyfuss Jan. 13 1961 - Wonderland By Night - Bert Kaempfert
Courtney Love - July 9 1964 - I Get Around - Beach Boys
Rob Lowe - Mar. 17 1964 - I Want To Hold Your Hand Beatles
Marilyn Manson - Jan. 5 1969 - I Heard It ...Grapevine - Marvin Gaye
Martina Mcbride - July 29 1966 - Hanky Panky - Tommy James
Matthew Mcconaughey Nov. 4 1969 - Suspicious Minds - Elvis Presley
Dylan Mcdermott - Oct. 26 1961 - Runaround Sue - Dion
Tim Mcgraw - May 1 1967 - Somethin' Stupid - Nancy/Frank Sinatra
Kylie Minogue - May 28 1968 - Tighten Up - Archie Bell
Demi Moore - Nov. 11 1962 - He's A Rebel - Crystals
Julianne Moore - Dec. 3 1960 - Are You Lonesome Tonight - Elvis Presley
Eddie Murphy - Apr. 3 1961 - Ponytime - Chubby Checker
Mike Myers - May 25 1963 - If You Wanna Be Happy - Jimmy Soul
Ed Norton - Aug. 18 1969 - In The Year 2525 - Zager & Evans
Clive Owen - Oct. 3 1964 - Pretty Woman - Roy Orbison
Sarah Jessica Parker Mar. 25 1965 - Eight Days A Week - Beatles
Sean Penn - Aug. 17 1960 - A Summer Place - Percy Faith
Matthew Perry - Aug. 19 1969 - In The Year 2525 - Zager & Evans
Luke Perry - Oct. 11 1965 - Yesterday - Beatles
Brad Pitt - Dec. 18 1963 - Dominique - Singing Nun
Lisa Marie Presley - Feb. 1 1968 - Judy In Disguise - John Fred
Jason Priestley - Aug. 28 1969 - Honky Tonk Women - Rolling Stones
Keanu Reeves - Sept. 2 1964 - Where Did Our Love Go - Supremes
Molly Ringwald - Feb. 18 1968 - Love Is Blue - Paul Mauriat
Guy Ritchie - Sept. 10 1968 - People Got To Be Free - Rascals
Julia Roberts - Oct. 28 1967 - To Sir With Love - Lulu
Chris Rock - Feb. 7 1965 - You've Lost ...Feelin' - Righteous Bros.
Axl Rose - Feb. 6 1962 - Peppermint Twist - Joey Dee
Meg Ryan - Nov. 19 1961 - Big Bad John - Jimmy Dean
Adam Sandler - Sept. 9 1966 - Sunshine Superman - Donovan

David Schwimmer - Nov. 12 1966 - Poor Side Of Town - Johnny Rivers
Charlie Sheen - Sept. 3 1965 - I Got You Babe - Sonny & Cher
Nicolette Sheridan Nov 21 1963 - Deep Purple - Nino T & Apr S.
Brooke Shields - May 31 1965 - Help Me Rhonda - Beach Boys
Christian Slater - Aug. 18 1969 - In The Year 2525 - Zager & Evans
Will Smith - Sept. 25 1968 - Harper Valley P.T.A. - Jeannie C. Riley
Wesley Snipes - July 31 1962 - Roses Are Red (My Love) - Bobby Vinton
David Spade - July 22 1964 - Rag Doll - Four Seasons
John Stamos - Aug. 19 1963 - Fingertips Part 2 - Stevie Wonder
Gwen Stefani - Oct. 3 1969 - Sugar Sugar - Archies
Ben Stiller - Nov. 30 1965 - I Hear A Symphony - Supremes
Keifer Sutherland - Dec. 21 1966 - Good Vibrations - Beach Boys
Quentin Tarantino - Mar. 27 1963 - Our Day Will Come - Ruby & the Romantics.
Shania Twain - Aug. 28 1965 - I Got You Babe - Sonny & Cher
Keith Urban - Oct. 26 1967 - To Sir With Love - Lulu
Jean-Claude Van Damme - Oct. 18 1960 - Save The Last Dance For Me - Drifters
Naomi Watts - Sept. 28 1968 - Hey Jude - Beatles
Owen Wilson - Nov. 18 1968 - Hey Jude - Beatles
Trisha Yearwood - Sept. 16 1964 - House Of The Rising Sun - Animals
Catherine Zeta-Jones Sept. 25 1969 - Sugar Sugar - Archies
Renee Zellweger - Apr. 25 1969 - Aquarius/Sunshine In - 5th Dimension
Rob Zombie - Jan. 12 1965 - I Feel Fine - Beatles

♫ The Beach Boys' Brian Wilson wrote this number one Jan & Dean hit!

♫ The F.B.I. investigated the lyrics of this song because it was believed to be obscene!

♫ This Number one song was popular originally in 1939 and a Hard Rock group took their name from the title!

♫ Carole King co-wrote no less than 6 top ten hits of 1963!

♫ Phil Spector produced many hits of 1963, including a song from a 1947 Disney movie!

♫ The lead singer of two Drifters' hits in 1963 died suddenly of a heart attack at age 27.

FIND OUT THAT...and MUCH MORE...INSIDE...1963!

60'S 1963 Hits and Trivia

1. **Sugar Shack** gave Jimmy Gilmer & The Fireballs the sweet smell of success with the hit that topped all others in 1963. This group from New Mexico had only one other top ten hit when 'Bottle of Wine' (as simply 'The Fireballs') celebrated such an accomplishment in 1968.

2. **He's So Fine** was a huge hit for a female group from the Bronx known as The Chiffons. This hit was produced by the group The Tokens. In a 1976 court ruling, this song written by Ronnie Mack found George Harrison guilty of 'subconcious plagiarism of writing the song 'My Sweet Lord'.

3. **Blue Velvet** was a multi-week number one hit for Bobby Vinton and immediately followed another 'blue' song, 'Blue on Blue'. This hit featured session musicians Floyd Cramer, Boots Randolph, Grady Martin and Charlie McCoy. Tony Bennett had the original hit with 'Blue Velvet' back in 1951.

4. **Hey Paula** by Paul and Paula was one of the most popular sweetheart songs of the 60's. Paul was Ray Hildebrand and Paula was Jill Jackson. Before the year was over, Ray decided that show business was not a future he wanted, and left to pursue other interests.

5. **Dominique** by The Singing Nun was the surprise hit of 1963, topping the charts for a full month. The Singing Nun, who recorded under the name Soeur Sourire committed suicide in 1985 at the age of 52.

6. **Walk Like a Man** was the third consecutive number one hit by The Four Seasons featuring Frankie Valli. The first two were 'Sherry' and 'Big Girls Don't Cry'.

7. **My Boyfriend's Back** was a hit for The Angels, the first white girl group of the 60's to have a number one hit. 1963 was a big year for girl groups which included The Chiffons, The Ronettes, The Crystals, The Shirelles, The Supremes and others.

8. **Sukiyaki** was a big hit for Kyu Sakamoto, the first music artist from Japan to have a hit record in North America. Kyu Sakamoto died tragically in 1985 at 43 as one of 520 people who perished in the Japan Airlines 747 that crashed into the side of a mountain.

9. **I Will Follow Him** was a number one hit for 15 year old Little Peggy March. Her real name was Margaret Battavio, but record producers Hugo Perotti and Luigi Creatore gave the March -born singer a new name.

10. **It's My Party** was Lesley Gore's first and biggest hit. She was discovered by Producer Quincy Jones, who selected this song which Lesley recorded when she was 16 years old.

11. **Go Away Little Girl** was a number one hit for Brooklyn, New York born Steve Lawrence, whose real name is Sidney Leibowitz. This hit was one of many 1963 hits written by Carole King and Gerry Goffin who placed hits like 'One Fine Day', 'Up On The Roof', and 'Hey Girl' into the top 20 that year.

12. **Fingertips Part 2** was Little Stevie Wonder's claim to fame. Stevie Wonder was only 12 years old when he recorded this 'live' performance singing and playing harmonica and bongos. It became the second number one hit for Berry Gordy's Motown label.

13. **Surf City** was Jan & Dean's only official number one hit and it was co-written by Brian Wilson, who also sang backup. Brian Wilson and The Beach Boys became friends with Jan & Dean when they played together at shows in Southern California.

14. **If You Wanna Be Happy** by Jimmy Soul was based on a calypso melody titled 'Ugly Woman'. Producer/Songwriter Frank Guida teamed up with his wife Carmela and a friend Joseph Royster to come up with 'If You Wanna Be Happy', which went all the way to number one.

15. **I'm Leaving It up To You** was a number one hit for Dale And Grace when President John F. Kennedy was assassinated. Coincidentally, Dale & Grace were on tour with Dick Clark's Caravan of Stars at the time and stood on the steps of their hotel and watched as the President's Motorcade passed by them in Dallas, Texas. Three blocks later, the tragedy happened.

16. **Deep Purple** was the biggest hit for Nino Tempo and April Stevens, a brother and sister duo from Niagara Falls, New York. This song was a remake of a hit Larry Clinton & His Orchestra had a number one hit with in 1939. A few years later, the British rock group Deep Purple took their name from this song.

17. **Louie, Louie** by The Kingsmen was one of the classic garage band hits of the 60's.It was the subject of an F.B.I. investigation for its non-existent obscene lyrics. The song was written in 1955 by Richard Berry and recorded by many music artists through the years.

18. **Walk Right In** by the folk trio The Rooftop Singers was a reworking of a song recorded in 1929 by Gus Cannon's Jug Stompers.

19. **So Much in Love** was a hit for the Philadelphia quintet known as The Tymes. Their sound was similar to that of Johnny Mathis and this romantic song was embellished by the sounds of the seashore, birds chirping and fingers snapping. Originally this song was to be called 'As We Stroll Along'.

20. **Easier Said than Done** was a hit for The Essex, 2 guys and a girl who were serving their country in The United States Marine Corps when this hit went to number one. Anita Humes was the lead singer of this trio, whose only other hit was the similar-sounding 'A Walkin' Miracle'.

21. **Our Day Will Come** by Ruby & the Romantics was recorded with a Bossa Nova rhythm. The group consisted of Ruby Nash and four guys who were originally known as The Supremes, but had to change their name. This number one hit was their only hit to reach the top ten.

22. **Wipeout** by the teenage surf band from California known as The Surfaris was a drummer's delight. Back then, if someone knew you were a drummer, the next question was 'Can you play "Wipeout"? This high energy instrumental re-charted in 1966.

23. **The End of The World** was the biggest hit of Skeeter Davis' career. She was a Country singer from Kentucky who had another pop hit in 1963 with the bright and bouncy 'I Can't Stay Mad at You' written by Carole King and Gerry Goffin.

24. **Be My Baby** was the first and biggest hit for The Ronettes, Phil Spector's main girl group of the 60's and a perfect example of his 'Wall of Sound'. The song was written by Phil Spector, Jeff Barry and Ellie Greenwich.

25. **Ruby Baby** was a hit for Dion, seven years after The Drifters had a hit with this Leiber/Stoller classic. This was Dion's first hit on the Columbia record label.

26. **Hello Muddah, Hello Faddah** was a comedy hit about a letter from camp as delivered by Allan Sherman. He was a comedy writer for Jackie Gleason before having a successful career of his own. In 1963, he had three number one albums all beginning with the title 'My Son The…".

27. **Blowin' in The Wind** by folk trio Peter, Paul & Mary was written by Bob Dylan. It has been described as the anthem of the 1960's civil rights movement. Mary Travers died Sept 16th 2009 at the age of 72.

28. **Sally Go Round the Roses** by The Jaynetts was a haunting song from this female group from the Bronx. Their only hit was arranged by Artie Butler, who used his talents on 'Society's Child' and 'Indian Reservation' to name just two.

29. **Rhythm of The Rain** was a big hit for the soft pop group The Cascades from San Diego. It was their only hit to reach the top 40.

30. **Surfin' U.S.A.** by The Beach Boys was originally credited as a Brian Wilson composition, but later was credited to Chuck Berry due to the similarity of his song 'Sweet Little Sixteen'. The flip side of this single was the car song 'Shut Down'.

31. **Washington Square** was a major instrumental hit for the Dixieland-styled Village Stompers from Greenwich Village, New York. The banjo was a prominent instrument in this hit which reached number one on the Adult Contemporary charts.

32. **Puff the Magic Dragon** by Peter, Paul & Mary was a story for children, although many believed it was drug-related. This was one of three top ten folk hits they achieved in 1963.

33. **The Night Has a 1000 Eyes** was a hit by Bobby Vee backed by The Johnny Mann Singers. Bobby Vee was one of many of the Bobby singers of the early 60's which included Bobby Vinton, Rydell, and Darin.

34. **I Love You Because** was Al Martino's first and biggest hit. It was originally recorded by Country singer Leon Payne in 1950.

35. **Everybody** was a goodtime, party hit from Atlanta, Georgia's Tommy Roe. He had a respectable string of hits during the 60's including 'Sheila', 'Sweet Pea' and 'Dizzy'.

36. **If I Had a Hammer** by Trini Lopez was an upbeat version of the hit Peter, Paul & Mary had a hit with in 1962. As an actor, Trini Lopez portrayed Pedro Jimenez in the movie The Dirty Dozen.

37. **You're the Reason I'm Living** by Bobby Darin was popular the same year he was nominated for an Academy Award for his performance in the film 'Captain Newman M.D.'

38. **Heatwave** by Martha & The Vandellas with its 'Charleston intro' was the first top ten hit for this popular Motown group inducted into The Rock And Roll Hall Of Fame in 1995.

39. **You Can't Sit Down** was one of two top ten hits for the Dovells, a Philadelphia vocal group lead by Leonard Borisoff, better known as Len Barry of '1,2,3, fame'.

40. **Da Do Ron Ron** by The Crystals was one of the most popular Phil Spector productions. He co-wrote this top ten hit with Jeff Barry and Ellie Greenwich. Cher was a background singer on this 'wall of sound' girl group classic.

41. **Blue on Blue** was a hit for Bobby Vinton, born Stanley Robert Vintula in Canonsburg, Pennsylvania. He was the only child to bandleader Stan Vinton. He had two big 'blue' hits in 1963 with 'Blue Velvet' being the other.

42. **Hello Stranger** was the first major hit for Michigan-born R & B singer Barbara Lewis. The Dells supplied the backing vocals on this top ten hit.

43. **(You're the) Devil in Disguise** by Elvis Presley was popular back when he made between two and three movies a year. In 1963 he starred in 'It Happened at The World's Fair' and 'Fun in Acapulco'.

44. **Candy Girl** by The Four Seasons was written by Larry Santos and produced by Bob Crewe. The 'B' side of this single was 'Marlena' which was a moderate hit.

45. **You Don't Have To Be a Baby to Cry** was a top ten hit for the one hit wonder English duo The Caravelles. The song was a top ten country hit for Ernest Tubb back in 1950.

46. **One Fine Day** by The Chiffons was not only co-written by Carole King, but also featured her playing piano on this classic girl group hit.

47. **South Street** by the Philadelphia R & B group The Orlons was their third of three consecutive top 5 hits. It's interesting to note the use of the word 'hippy' in this song, years before the term became popular.

48. **Tie Me Kangaroo Down ,Sport** was a big novelty hit for Perth, Australia-born Rolf Harris. He offered four unknown backing musicians 10% of the royalties from this song rather than a fee, but instead, they decided on the recording fee of 28 pounds between them.

49. **Since I Fell For You** by Lenny Welch was a silky smooth ballad by this singer from Ashbury Park, New Jersey. The song itself was originally a hit in 1947 for Paul Gayten.

50. **Pipeline** was an instrumental by the one hit wonder teenage surf/rock group known as The Chantays. The term 'pipeline' is a surfing term for the curl of the wave before it breaks.

51. **Tell Him** was a hit for The Exciters, an R & B vocal quartet from Jamaica, New York. This top 5 hit was produced by Jerry Leiber & Mike Stoller.

52. **Cry Baby** was the only major hit for Garnet Mimms, an R & B singer from West Virginia with a powerful voice. This song was number one on the R & B charts for several weeks.

53. **Up on the Roof** is a timeless tune by The Drifters written by Carole King and her then-husband Gerry Goffin. Rudy Lewis sang lead on this hit and 'On Broadway', also from 1963.

54. **Hotel Happiness** was a top ten hit for Brook Benton, whose real name was Benjamin Franklin Peay. His deep, smooth voice was perfect on this and other ballads like 'It's Just a Matter of Time' and 'Rainy Night In Georgia'.

55. **Its All Right** by The Impressions featured lead singer and songwriter Curtis Mayfield upfront. This was their biggest chart success as a group. Curtis Mayfield left in 1970 for a solo career.

56. **Busted** by Ray Charles was written by Harlan Howard, who wrote country hits like 'I Fall to Pieces' for Patsy Cline and 'Heartaches By The Number' by Guy Mitchell. This hit by Ray Charles won the Best R & B Grammy Award.

57. **Loop De Loop** was the only hit for Florida-born R & B singer Johnny Thunder. This was one of the great party hits of 1963.

58. **Foolish Little Girl** by The Shirelles was one of several hit songs in the early 60's by this girl group from Passaic, New Jersey.

59. **She's a Fool** by Lesley Gore was the third of four top ten hits in her first and biggest year on the charts, 1963.

60. **Then He Kissed Me** by The Crystals was produced by Phil Spector. He also co-wrote this hit with Jeff Barry & Ellie Greenwich. La La Brooks sang lead on this and 'Da Do Ron Ron, also from 1963.

61. **Memphis** by Lonnie Mack was a popular instrumental version of a tune Chuck Berry originated in 1959. Johnny Rivers had a vocal hit with it in 1964.

62. **Baby Workout** was a hit for Jackie Wilson, one of pop music's most charismatic singers. Sadly, he collapsed on stage while performing on stage in 1975 and spent the rest of his life in hospitals until he died in 1984.

63. **Judy's Turn to Cry** was Lesley Gore's sequel to 'Its My Party'. Lesley's most successful songs were all produced by Quincy Jones.

64. **Mean Woman Blues** by Roy Orbison was previously a hit for Elvis Presley in 1957 from the movie 'Loving You'.

65. **From a Jack to a King** was Ned Miller's most famous hit. This Country singer from Rains, Utah also wrote the Gale Storm and Bonnie Guitar hit 'Dark Moon'.

66. **Those Lazy, Hazy, Crazy, Days of Summer** was a goodtime song from Nat 'King' Cole in the summer of '63. He died of lung cancer two years later in 1965 at the age of 47.

67. **Be True To Your School/In My Room** was a double-sided hit single by The Beach Boys. Be True To Your School featured Mike Love on lead vocals

194

with cheerleading by The Honeys. The 'B' side ballad 'In My Room' was written by Brian Wilson and Gary Usher.

68. **My Dad** by Paul Peterson was a top ten hit while he starred as Jeff Stone in the 'Donna Reed Show'. He co-starred opposite Shelly Fabares, who also had a hit in the early 60's with 'Johnny Angel'.

69. **Two Faces Have I** was the biggest of Lou Christie's two 1963 hits. The other was his very first hit, 'The Gypsy Cried'.

70. **Pepino the Italian Mouse** was a novelty hit for Lou Monte, an Italian-American born in Lyndhurst, New Jersey. The Joe Reisman Orchestra backed the singer on this million seller.

71. **Maria Elena** was a popular instrumental hit for Los Indios Tabajaras. The act consisting of two Brazilian/Indian brothers recorded this tune five years before it became a hit. It was originally recorded by The Jimmy Dorsey Orchestra who had a number one hit with it in 1941.

72. **It's Up To You** was a top ten hit for teen idol and TV star Rick Nelson, who was starring in TV's 'The Adventures Of Ozzie & Harriet' at the time of his hits from 1957 to 1964.

73. **Donna the Prima Donna** was Dion's first of two hit singles which were listed as 'Dion DiMucci'. The other was 'Drip Drop'. Both featured the backing of the Del Satins.

74. **Losing You** by Brenda Lee was the only top ten hit of the 6 singles she released in 1963.She's regarded by many as the number one female singer of the 60's.

75. **Surfer Girl/Little Deuce Coupe** was a double-sided hit single by The Beach Boys. The title song of the 'Surfer Girl' album was written and produced by Brian Wilson who was inspired by the song 'When You Wish Upon a Star'. The 'B' side became one of their most popular hot rod hits.

76. **Mockingbird** was a top ten hit by Charlie & Inez Foxx, a brother and sister duo from Greensboro, North Carolina. It was their only hit on the pop charts.

77. **In Dreams** by Roy Orbison was revived in 1986 when movie producer David Lynch included 'In Dreams' in a key scene in his compelling, oddball mystery movie 'Blue Velvet', which also featured Bobby Vinton's 1963 hit of the same name.

78. **Blame It on The Bossa Nova** by Eydie Gorme was written by Barry Mann & Cynthia Weil. The Brazilian dance the Bossa Nova was quite popular in 1963 and was also featured in titles 'Bossa Nova Baby' by Elvis Presley and 'Fly Me to the Moon- Bossa Nova' by Joe Harnell.

79. **Another Saturday Night** was one of many great songs written and recorded by Sam Cooke. He was inducted into the Rock And Roll Hall Of Fame in 1986, 22 years after his death.

80. **Wild Weekend** by the (Rockin') Rebels was Buffalo, New York DJ Tom Shannon's theme song and he brought in The Rebels to record it. This 'saxy' hit became one of the greatest instrumentals of the 60's.

81. **Don't Say Nothin' Bad about My Baby** by The Cookies was written by Carole King and Gerry Goffin, who also wrote their hit 'Chains'.

82. **I Can't Stay Mad at You** by Skeeter Davis was yet another song written by the husband and wife team of Carole King and Gerry Goffin. This was quite a change of pace from her other hit from 1963, 'The End of The World'.

83. **Wonderful, Wonderful** was a hit by The Tymes two months after their number one hit 'So Much in Love'. Since the group's style was often compared to that of Johnny Mathis, it was decided that they re-do his first hit 'Wonderful Wonderful'. The Tymes brought it into the top ten again.

84. **On Broadway** by The Drifters featured Phil Spector on guitar. Rudy Lewis, who died in 1964, sang lead on this and their other top ten hit of '63, 'Up on The Roof'. This song was written by Barry Mann, Cynthia Weil, Jerry Leiber and Mike Stoller.

85. **Talk Back Trembling Lips** by Johnny Tillotson was also a number one Country hit that year for Ernest Ashworth.

86. **You've Really Got a Hold on Me** was The Miracles' second Million Seller behind their debut hit 'Shop Around'. Smokey Robinson wrote and sang lead on this classic Motown favorite.

87. **More** was an instrument hit for Kai Winding a jazz trombonist who was with Benny Goodman and Stan Kenton in the 1940's. This tune was the theme from the movie 'Mondo Cane'.

88. **The Monkey Time** was the first major hit by Major Lance. This song was written by Curtis Mayfield of The Impressions. Major Lance spent three years in prison from 1978 to 1981 and died of heart disease in 1994.

89. **Mickey's Monkey** by The Miracles was another song about one of 1963's most popular dances. This was one of the few Miracles hits not written by lead singer Smokey Robinson. This top ten hit was composed by the Motown main writers Holland/Dozier/Holland.

90. **Still** by Bill Anderson was an even bigger hit on the Country charts where it remained at number one for almost two months!

91. **Zip-A-Dee Doo-Dah** by Bob B. Soxx & the Blue Jeans was produced by Phil Spector and recorded on his 'Philles' record label. This song was introduced in the Disney movie 'Song of The South' and was the Academy Award winning song in 1947.

92. **Quicksand** by Martha & The Vandellas was their very similar-sounding follow up to 'Heatwave'. 'Quicksand' was written and produced by Motown's legendary Holland/Dozier/Holland.

93. **Denise** by Randy & The Rainbows was a goodtime top 10 hit from this white doo-wop group from Queens, New York.

94. **Young Lovers** was Paul & Paula's only other major hit besides their signature 'Hey Paula' from earlier in the year.

95. **Just One Look** was Doris Troy's only major hit, although she performed on stage and was signed to the Beatles' 'Apple' label in the early 70's. She also was a backing vocalist on Pink Floyd's album 'Dark Side of The Moon'.

96. **Bossa Nova Baby** was a top ten hit for Elvis Presley from the movie 'Fun in Acapulco' which co-starred Ursula Andress.

97. **Walking the Dog** was the most famous hit for Mississippi soul man Rufus Thomas who recorded on the legendary Stax label during the 60's and 70's.

98. **Midnight Mary** was the only hit for Joey Powers, a singer from Canonsburg, Pennsylvania. It was co-written by Artie Wayne.

99. **Hey Girl** was the only major hit for singer Freddie Scott from Providence, Rhode Island. This classic hit was written by Carole King and Gerry Goffin.

100. **Pride and Joy** by Marvin Gaye featured Motown label mates Martha & The Vandellas on backing vocals

101. **Two Lovers** was Mary Wells' third consecutive top ten hit the year before her biggest hit 'My Guy' arrived.

102. **Reverand Mr. Black** was The Kingston Trio's final top ten hit. The lyrics were written by Billy Edd Wheeler, Jerry Leiber & Mike Stoller and the chorus came from the traditional folk song 'Lonesome Valley' by The Carter family in 1931.

103. **Take These Chains from My Heart** by Ray Charles featured the Jack Halloran Singers on backing vocals. This song was a Country hit for Hank Williams in 1953.

104. **Our Winter Love** was an easy listening instrumental by California pianist Bill Purcell.

105. **Down at Papa Joe's** was a top ten party song by a black trio from Memphis known as The Dixiebelles. The prominent piano was played by Jerry Smith of Cornbread and Jerry.

106. **What Will Mary Say** was the final top ten hit of the 60's for Johnny Mathis. He didn't have his next notable hit until 15 years later with 'Too Much, Too Little, Too Late'.

107. **Don't Think Twice, It's All Right** was a hit by folk trio Peter, Paul & Mary written by Bob Dylan. It followed their other Dylan-penned hit 'Blowin' in The Wind'.

108. **500 Miles Away From Home** was one of two pop country hits for Bobby Bare in 1963.The other was 'Detroit City'. In the late 50's, Bobby Bare had a big hit with 'The All American Boy' recorded under the name Bill Parsons.

109. **Watermelon Man** was a mostly-instrumental hit by Cuban Bandleader Mongo Santamaria written by Herbie Hancock.

110. **18 Yellow Roses** by Bobby Darin was a song he wrote inspired by the flowers he sent to Sandra Dee while they were courting. They were married from 1960 to 1967.

111. **Talk to Me** was the only hit for Sunny & the Sunglows, a group from San Antonio, Texas who formed in 1959. This song was a remake of Little Willie John's hit from 1958.

112. **One Broken Heart for Sale** by Elvis Presley was from his movie 'It Happened at the World's Fair' which co-starred a young kid played by Kurt Russell. Coincidentally, years later, Kurt Russell would play Elvis in a made-for-TV film of the same name.

113. **Danke Schoen** was Wayne Newton's claim to fame and was recorded when he was only 21 years old. The music was composed by Bert Kaempfert of 'Wonderland By Night' fame. 'Danke Schoen is German for the equivalent of 'thank you very much' in English.

114. **Mr. Bass Man** was a hit for Johnny Cymbal, who recorded under the name 'Derek' five years later when he had a big hit with 'Cinnamon'. By the way, the bass singer on 'Mr. Bass Man' was Ronnie Bright who was a member of The Valentines.

115. **Ring Of Fire** was the song most identified with Johnny Cash as his biggest hit of all time. Although it didn't even reach the top ten on the pop charts, it was a multi-week number one hit on the Country charts.

116. **Twenty Four Hours from Tulsa** by Gene Pitney was one of two 1963 hits written by Burt Bacharach and Hal David. The other was 'True Love Never Runs Smooth'.

117. **He's Sure the Boy I Love** by The Crystals was actually The Blossoms with Darlene Love on lead vocals. This was another Phil Spector creation.

118. **Hot Pastrami** by one hit wonder California group The Dartells had very few words other than 'yeah' in this hit that almost made the top ten.

119. **Honolulu Lulu** was Jan & Dean's follow up to their biggest hit 'Surf City' which went all the way to number one. This song was co-written by Los Angeles DJ Roger Christian, who co-wrote a handful of early 60's hits with both Jan & Dean and Brian Wilson.

120. **Mecca** by Gene Pitney opened with the unusual Indian fakir flute instrument. It was one of 5 hits from his album 'Only Love Can Break A Heart'.

121. **Loddy Lo** by Chubby Checker was written for his wife, Dutch born Catharina Loddlers, Miss World 1962.

122. **That Summer, That Sunday** was the hit which followed 'Those Lazy, Hazy, Crazy Days of Summer' by Nat 'King' Cole. This was his final hit to reach the top 20 in his lifetime. He died of lung cancer two years later in 1965.

123. **Fools Rush In** by Rick Nelson was originally a number one hit for Glenn Miller in 1940.Brook Benton had a hit with it in 1960.

124. **Green Green** by The New Christy Minstrels featured Barry McGuire on lead vocals two years before he had a number one solo hit with 'Eve Of Destruction'.

125. **I Saw Linda Yesterday** was a bright and bouncy hit for Dickey Lee, whose real name was Dickey Lipscomb. He first recorded for Sun Records in 1957 and later became a Country singer.

126. **Wonderful Summer** was a wonderful song by Robin Ward. This song was similar in style to that of Lesley Gore in the early 60's.Although this was Robin Ward's only hit, she has been a very successful session singer as 'Jackie Ward' on many popular jingles and songs through the years. She also sang the 'la la la' in Pat Boone's hit 'Speedy Gonzales'.

127. **On Top Of Spaghetti** was a fun novelty hit by Tom Glazer. It was a great kid's campfire song which was a parody of 'On Top Of Old Smokey'.

128. **Do the Bird** was a song about a popular dance at the time. It was Dee Dee Sharp's 5th and final consecutive top ten hit. This Philadelphia born singer married record producer and writer Kenny Gamble in 1967.

129. **A Walkin' Miracle** was the very similar-sounding follow up to the only other hit by The Essex, 'Easier Said Than Done' which went to number one.

130. **Half Heaven Half Heartache** was one of four 1963 hits for Rock And Roll Hall of Famer Gene Pitney.

131. **Little Town Flirt** was one of many early 60's hits for Del Shannon, who died of a self-inflicted gunshot wound in 1990.

132. **Hey Little Girl** by Major Lance was a fun song co-written by the legendary Otis Blackwell who wrote 'Great Balls Of Fire' for Jerry Lee Lewis and 'Don't Be Cruel' , 'All Shook Up' and other classic pop/rock songs.

133. **Wives and Lovers** by Jack Jones was inspired by the movie starring Janet Leigh. The lyrics of this song may be considered demeaning to women in today's world. Jack Jones was also known as the singer of 'The Love Boat' TV theme.

134. **Mama Didn't Lie** was the only hit for Mississippi soul singer Jan Bradley. In the mid 70's she left music for a career as a social worker.

135. **All I Have to Do Is Dream** was Richard Chamberlain's remake of this classic Everly Brothers hit from the 1958. He was starring in the top rated TV show 'Dr. Kildare' when this was a hit.

136. **Abilene** by George Hamilton 1V was number one on the Country charts for a full month in 1963. His biggest pop hit was 'A Rose and A Baby Ruth' from 1956.

137. **Martian Hop** was a one hit wonder novelty hit by The Randells, two brothers and a cousin from New Jersey.

138. **Killer Joe** was a catchy one hit wonder hit by a father and his four sons from the Philippines known as The Rocky Fellers.

139. **Detroit City** was one of two notable hits by Bobby Bare. This hit was written by Mel Tillis.

140. **The Kind Of Boy You Can't Forget** was a hit for The Raindrops, who were actually songwriters and producers Jeff Barry and Ellie Greenwich. Together they wrote dozens of big hits for others during the 60's.

141. **Greenback Dollar** by The Kingston Trio was written by Hoyt Axton, who later wrote hits like 'Joy To the World' and 'Never Been To Spain' for 3 Dog Night and the 'No No Song' for Ringo Starr. In 2008, two of the members of The Kingston Trio Nick Reynolds and John Stewart died.

142. **I Wonder What She's Doing Tonight** is not to be confused with the 1968 hit by Tommy Boyce and Bobby Hart. This title was a hit for Barry & The Tamerlanes, a one hit wonder California trio led by Barry DeVorzon who later had a top ten hit with 'Nadia's Theme' in 1976. Perry Botkin Jr., who arranged this 1963 hit, also collaborated with Barry on that popular 70's instrumental.

143. **Can I Get a Witness** was a gospel-influenced Motown hit by Marvin Gaye which featured backing vocals by The Supremes. It's interesting to note that Marvin Gaye played piano on this Holland/Dozier/Holland composition and production.

144. **Only In America** by Jay & The Americans was written by Barry Mann, Cynthia Weil, Jerry Leiber and Mike Stoller. It was originally recorded by The Drifters, although they never had a hit with it. It was also originally a song about racism with lyrics 'Only in America, land of opportunity can they save a seat in the back of the bus for me', but it was changed to a song about patriotism.

145. **Yakety Sax** by Boots Randolph is one of those instrumental hits that you instantly recognize. Boots Randolph was one of the most successful Nashville saxophone session players. He was inspired to do 'Yakety Sax' by the sax solo by King Curtis in the Coasters' 1957 hit 'Yakety Yak'. This tune later became the theme to the 'Benny Hill Show'.

146. **Birdland** was one of several early 60's dance hits by the King of the Twist, Chubby Checker. Some of Checker's other dance hits included The Limbo, The Hucklebuck, The Pony, The Fly, and The Popeye.

147. **Not Me** was a hit for the Philadelphia group The Orlons featuring 3 girls and one guy singing bass.

148. **Fly Me to the Moon - Bossa Nova** by Joe Harnell was an updated version of this tune which has been recorded many times, including the first time by Kaye Ballard in 1954.

149. **Painted, Tainted Rose** by Al Martino was one of three hits he charted in 1963, his best year on the pop charts.

150. **Harry the Hairy Ape** was a hit for Ray Stevens, the number one novelty recording artist of the 60's. Some of his other wacky 60's hits include 'Ahab the Arab', Gitarzan' and 'Along Came Jones'.

151. **El Watusi** was a hit for Ray Baretto, the godfather of Latin Jazz. He recorded this hit in 1961, but it took two years before it became a hit.

152. **Wildwood Days** was a fun, nostalgic song by one of the boys of Bandstand, Philadelphia's Bobby Rydell.

153. **I'm Gonna Be Warm This Winter** by Connie Francis was a song about meeting at a ski lodge and falling in love by the fireplace. This feel good hit was one of Connie's final hits.

154. **Till Then** was a great song by a one hit wonder group from Brooklyn, New York known as The Classics. This song was originally popular in 1944 by The Mills Brothers and again ten years later in 1954 by The Hilltoppers.

155. **The Gypsy Cried** was the first hit for the falsetto-voiced Lou Christie who turned 20 when this hit was riding up the charts.

156. **Remember Then** was the only hit for The Earls, a white doo-wop vocal group from the Bronx.

157. **My Summer Love** was a moderate hit for Ruby & the Romantics, who were exclusive to 1963 on the charts. 'Our Day Will Come' was their signature hit reaching number one near the beginning of the year.

158. **Young and in Love** was a sweetheart song by Dick and Deedee, a duo that formed while in High School at Santa Monica.

159. **Alice in Wonderland** was a Neil Sedaka hit inspired by the classic children's story.

160. **Linda** by Jan & Dean was actually written for a then-five year old Linda Eastman, who later became Paul McCartney's wife. Jack Lawrence wrote this song in 1947 to help pay a legal fee to Lee Eastman, who wanted him to write him a song for his daughter, Linda.

More hits from 1963!

The Boy Next Door was the only hit for the girl group from Cleveland known as The Secrets. This upbeat hit was very typical in sound to the girl groups of that period.

Have You Heard was the fourth and final hit by the Italian/American vocal quartet The Duprees. All of their hits charted in 1962 and '63.

Let's Limbo Some More was Chubby Checker's sequel to 'Limbo Rock'.

My Coloring Book was a hit for Sandy Stewart, a singer from Philadelphia who was a regular on the Perry Como and Eddie Fisher TV Shows back then. Kitty Kallen also had a hit with this song in 1963.

Don't Make Me Over was Dionne's Warwick's very first hit and the beginning of a long association with the songwriting team of Burt Bacharach and Hal David.

Little Band of Gold was a real gem that's almost forgotten by Mississippi singer James Gilreath. This was his only notable hit.

Shutters and Boards by Jerry Wallace was co-written by movie star and World War 2 hero Audie Murphy.

The Cinnamon Cinder (It's A Very Nice Dance) was a party hit by The Pastel Six, a young group aged 18 to 21 from California. They took the song title from the club in North Hollywood where they headlined, - The Cinnamon Cinder Club.

Hitch Hike was Marvin Gaye's very first hit and it featured Martha & The Vandellas on backing vocals.

Swinging on a Star was a 1963 hit by Big Dee Irwin with Little Eva. This song was originally a number one hit for Bing Crosby in 1944 and featured in the movie 'Going My Way'.

Hootenanny was a fun folk music hit for The Glencoves who consisted of three teenagers who formed at Chaminade High School in Minneola, Long Island, New York.

TOP 16 ALBUMS OF 1963

1. Days Of Wine And Roses - Andy Williams
2. The First Family - Vaughn Meader
3. My Son, The Nut - Allan Sherman
4. In The Wind - Peter, Paul & Mary
5. Songs I Sing On The Jackie Gleason Show - Frank Fontaine
6. Little Stevie Wonder - Stevie Wonder
7. My Son, The Celebrity - Allan Sherman
8. Jazz Samba - Stan Getz/Charlie Byrd
9. Moving - Peter, Paul & Mary
10. Trini Lopez At PJ's - Trini Lopez
11. The Singing Nun - The Singing Nun
12. West Side Story - Soundtrack
13. Peter, Paul & Mary - Peter, Paul & Mary
14. Fly Me To The Moon - Joe Harnell & The Bossa Nova Pops
15. My Son, The Folk Singer - Allan Sherman
16. Ingredients In A Recipe For Soul - Ray Charles

TOP 16 COUNTRY HITS OF 1963

1. Don't Let Me Cross Over - Carl Butler
2. Love's Gonna Live Here - Buck Owens
3. Still - Bill Anderson
4. Ring Of Fire - Johnny Cash
5. Act Naturally - Buck Owens
6. Lonesome 7 - 7203 - Hankshaw Hawkins
7. Abilene - George Hamilton 1V
8. The Ballad Of Jed Clampet - Flatt & Scruggs
9. Talk Back Trembling Lips - Ernest Ashworth
10. Ruby Ann - Marty Robbins
11. Six Days On The Road - Dave Dudley
12. The End Of The World - Skeeter Davis
13. From A Jack To A King - Ned Miller
14. Detroit City - Bobby Bare
15. 8 X 10 - Bill Anderson
16. Sweet Dreams (Of You) - Patsy Cline

TOP 16 ONE HIT WONDERS OF 1963

1. Kyu Sakamoto - Sukiyaki
2. The Singing Nun - Dominique
3. The Village Stompers - Washington Square
4. The Jaynetts - Sally Go Round The Roses
5. The Chantays - Pipeline
6. The Exciters - Tell Him
7. Johnny Thunder - Loop De Loop
8. Randy & The Rainbows - Denise
9. Kai Winding - More
10. The Murmaids - Popsicles & Icicles
11. Joey Powers - Midnight Mary
12. Sunny & The Sunglows - Talk To Me
13. Jan Bradley - Mama Didn't Lie
14. Rocky Fellers - Killer Joe
15. The Randells - Martian Hop
16. The Secrets - The Boy Next Door

16 GREAT 'LOST 45's' FROM 1963

1. Wonderful Summer - Robin Ward
2. I Wonder What She's Doing Tonight - Barry & The Tamerlanes
3. Killer Joe - Rocky Fellers
4. Alice In Wonderland - Neil Sedaka
5. Little Band Of Gold - James Gilreath
6. The Boy Next Door - The Secrets
7. Mr. Bass Man - Johnny Cymbal
8. Till Then - Classics
9. True Love Never Runs Smooth - Gene Pitney
10. Have You Heard - Duprees
11. The Kind Of Boy You Can't Forget - Raindrops
12. The Cinnamon Cinder - Pastel Six
13. El Watusi - Ray Barreto
14. Remember Then - Earls
15. Swinging On A Star - Big D. Irwin
16. Hootenanny - Glencoves

TOP 16 R & B/SOUL HITS OF 1963

1. Fingertips part 2 - Stevie Wonder
2. Hello Stranger - Barbara Lewis
3. Heatwave - Martha & The Vandellas
4. It's All Right - The Impressions
5. Baby Workout - Jackie Wilson
6. You've Really Got A Hold On Me - Miracles
7. Mickey's Monkey - Miracles
8. The Monkey Time - Major Lance
9. Quicksand - Martha & The Vandellas
10. Walking The Dog - Rufus Thomas
11. Pride & Joy - Marvin Gaye
12. Prisoner Of Love - James Brown
13. Can I Get A Witness - Marvin Gaye
14. Laughing Boy - Mary Wells
15. Part Time Love - Little Johnny Taylor
16. Hitch Hike - Marvin Gaye

TOP 16 DANCE/PARTY HITS OF 1963

1. Louie, Louie - The Kingsmen
2. Wipeout - Surfaris
3. It's My Party - Lesley Gore
4. If You Wanna Be Happy - Jimmy Soul
5. Surfin' U.S.A. - Beach Boys
6. Fingertips part 2 - Stevie Wonder
7. South Street - Orlons
8. Heatwave - Martha & The Vandellas
9. Everybody - Tommy Roe
10. Loop De Loop - Johnny Thunder
11. Baby Workout - Jackie Wilson
12. Wild Weekend - The Rockin' Rebels
13. The Monkey Time - Major Lance
14. Bossa Nova Baby - Elvis Presley
15. Loddy Lo - Chubby Checker
16. Mickey's Monkey – Miracles

THE TOP 60 60's REMAKES OF HITS IN THE 60's

| Title | Original 60's Artist & Year | Remake | & | Year. |

1. The Twist - Hank Ballard - 1960 - Chubby Checker - 1960
2. I Heard It...Grapevine - Gladys Knight - 1967 - Marvin Gaye - 1969
3. Light My Fire - The Doors - 1967 - Jose Feliciano - 1968
4. You Keep Me Hangin' On - Supremes - 1966 - Vanilla Fudge - 1968
5. Will You Love Me Tomorrow-Shirelles - 1961 - Four Seasons - 1968
6. Respect - Otis Redding - 1965 - Aretha Franklin - 1967
7. You've Lost...Feeling - Righteous Bros - 1965 - Dionne Warwick - 1969
8. Hey Jude - Beatles - 1968 - Wilson Pickett - 1969
9. Go Away Little Girl - Steve Lawrence - 1963 - Happenings - 1966
10. Twist And Shout - Isley Bros. - 1962 - Beatles - 1964
11. Dedicated To One. . Love - Shirelles - 1961 - Mamas & Papas - 1967
12. Barbara Ann - Regents - 1961 - Beach Boys - 1966
13. Do You Love Me - Contours - 1962 - Dave Clark Five - 1964
14. This Guy's In Love... - Herb Alpert - 1968 - Dionne Warwick - 1969
15. Grazing In The Grass - Hugh Masekela - 1968 - Friends Of Distinction - 1969
16. This Magic Moment - Drifters - 1960 - Jay & The Americans - 1969
17. Stand By Me - Ben E. King - 1961 - Spyder Turner - 1967
18. I Say A Little Prayer - Dionne Warwick - 1967 - Aretha Franklin - 1968
19. Stay - Maurice Williams - 1960 - Four Seasons - 1964
20. Theme from A Summer Place-Percy Faith - 1960 - Lettermen - 1965
21. Blowin' In The Wind - Bob Dylan/P. P & M - 1963 - Stevie Wonder - 1966
22. Baby I Need Your Lovin' - Four Tops - 1964 - Johnny Rivers - 1967
23. Let It Be Me - Everly Bros. - 1960 - Jerry Butler/Betty E. - 1964
24. Baby I Love You - Ronettes - 1964 - Andy Kim - 1969
25. Tracks Of My Tears - Miracles - 1965 - Johnny Rivers - 1967
26. Wonderful World - Sam Cooke - 1960 - Herman's Hermits - 1965
27. If I Had A Hammer - Peter, Paul & Mary - 1962 - Trini Lopez - 1963
28. Walk Away Renee - Left Banke - 1966 - Four Tops - 1968
29. How Sweet It Is - Marvin Gaye - 1964 - Jr. Walker & All Stars - 1966
30. (My Girl)Hang On Sloopy - Vibrations - 1964 - McCoys - 1965
31. Release Me - Little Esther Phillips - 1962 - Englebert Humperdinck 1967
32. Wooden Heart - Elvis Presley - 1960 - Joe Dowell - 1961
33. Can't Take My Eyes... - Frankie Valli - 1967 - Lettermen - 1968
34. I'm Gonna Make You... - Madeline Bell - 1968 - Supremes/Temptations 1969
35. Just One Look - Doris Troy - 1963 - Hollies - 1964
36. Please Love Me Forever - Cathy Jean & Roomates 1961 Bobby Vinton - 1967
37. Turn Around Look At Me - Glen Campbell - 1961 - Vogues - 1968
38. Yesterday - Beatles - 1965 - Ray Charles - 1967
39. You Got What It Takes - Marv Johnson - 1960 - Dave Clark Five - 1967
40. I Love How You Love Me - Paris Sisters - 1961 - Bobby Vinton - 1968
41. If I Were A Carpenter - Bobby Darin - 1966 - Four Tops - 1968
42. Bring It On Home To Me - Sam Cooke - 1962 - Animals/65 Eddie Floyd/69

43. Hush - Billy Joe Royal - 1967 - Deep Purple - 1968
44. I Like It Like That - Chris Kenner - 1961 - Dave Clark Five - 1965
45. Lemon Tree - Peter, Paul & Mary - 1962 - Trini Lopez - 1965
46. Mountain Of Love - Harold Dorman - 1960 - Johnny Rivers - 1964
47. Eleanor Rigby - Beatles - 1966 - Ray C/68 Aretha F - 1969
48. Amen - Impressions - 1965 - Otis Redding - 1968
49. Hurt So Bad - Little Anthony - 1965 - Lettermen - 1969
50. Fools Rush In - Brook Benton - 1960 - Rick Nelson - 1963
51. Love Letters - Ketty Lester - 1962 - Elvis Presley - 1966
52. Needles And Pins - Jackie DeShannon - 1963 - Searchers - 1964
53. Shake A Tail Feather - Five Du-Tones - 1963 - James & Bobby Purify 1967
54. Don't Think Twice - Peter, Paul & Mary - 1963 - Wonder Who? - 1965
55. Alfie - Cher - 1966 - Dionne Warwick - 1967
56. Mercy Mercy Mercy - Cannonball Adderley - 1967 - Buckinghams - 1967
57. I Can Hear Music - Ronettes - 1966 - Beach Boys - 1969
58. The River Is Wide - Forum - 1967 - Grassroots - 1969
59. Halfway To Paradise - Tony Orlando - 1961 - Bobby Vinton - 1968
60. Frankie And Johnny - Brook Benton - 1961 - Elvis Presley – 1966

♫ The Harmonica player on this number one hit taught John Lennon how to play the instrument!

♫ The singer of this number one hit also starred in 2 popular TV series and 3 Elvis movies!

♫ The man who would later become host of The Gong Show wrote this popular 1962 hit!

♫ This top 10 hit by Pat Boone inspired Elton John's Crocodile Rock!

♫ Gene Pitney wrote this number one girl group hit produced by Phil Spector!

♫ There were 6 different Twist hits in the top ten in 1962, including the only hit to reach number one twice!

FIND OUT THAT...and MUCH MORE...INSIDE...1962!

1. **I Can't Stop Loving You** was a huge hit for the legendary Ray Charles written by Country singer/songwriter Don Gibson in a house trailer in Tennessee in 1958. Ray Charles recorded songs in many genres including Soul, Rock, Blues and Country And Western.

2. **Big Girls Don't Cry** by The Four Seasons was a multi-week number one hit co-written by Bob Crewe. The Four Seasons producer and co-writer was inspired to write it after watching a dreadful late night movie in which the star, John Payne, slapped the blonde bombshell in the face and she replied with 'Big Girls Don't Cry'.

3. **Sherry** by The Four Seasons was the very first hit for this New Jersey vocal group led by lead singer Frankie Valli. Keyboardist Bob Gaudio, formerly of The Royal Teens (of 'Short Shorts' fame) wrote this million seller produced by Bob Crewe.

4. **Roses Are Red (My Love)** was Bobby Vinton's first hit, and one of his biggest. This song was co-written by Paul Evans, who had hits of his own including 'Seven Little Girls Sittin' in The Back Seat' which reached the top ten in 1959.

5. **Hey Baby** by Bruce Channel featured Delbert McClinton on harmonica. Back then when on tour with the Beatles on the same bill, backstage, John Lennon asked Delbert to show him how to play it. Lennon then played the harmonica on 'Love Me Do' and other hits by the Fab Four.

6. **The Twist** by Chubby Checker was number one in 1960 and again in 1962 when there was a renewed interest in the dance. There were no less than a dozen 'Twist' hits on the charts in 1962.

7. **Peppermint Twist** was a number one hit for Joey Dee & The Starliters,

the house band at the hottest place to dance, - The Peppermint Lounge. His backup band later became known on their own as 'The Young Rascals'.

8. **Sheila** was a Buddy Holly-influenced song written by Tommy Roe when he was only 14 years old. This was the first of several hits for Atlanta, Georgia born Tommy Roe who topped the charts with this one.

9. **Telstar** was a million selling instrumental by The Tornados. They were the first British group to have a number one hit in North America. The writer and producer of this classic hit, Joe Meek committed suicide by shooting himself at his studio on February 3, 1967.

10. **Duke of Earl** was a number one hit by Gene Chandler, who was born Eugene Dixon in Chicago. On stage he took on the identity of the Duke by dressing up in a cape, top hat and monocle.

11. **Breaking Up is Hard To Do** was Neil Sedaka's signature hit and a number one hit he would remake and have a hit with again over a dozen years later. He co-wrote this hit with his songwriting partner Howard Greenfield, a neighbor he met when he was 13 years old.

12. **Good Luck Charm** was Elvis Presley's 16th number one hit. It was to be his last number one song until 'Suspicious Minds' in 1969.

13. **Soldier Boy** by The Shirelles was recorded in one take with five minutes of studio time left at the end of a session. It became their biggest hit of all, surpassing 'Will You Love Me Tomorrow', their previous number one hit.

14. **Johnny Angel** by Shelley Fabares reached number one when she was starring as Mary Stone in The Donna Reed Show'. She later co-starred in three Elvis Presley movies and in 1964 married record producer Lou Adler, best known for his work with Jan and Dean and the Mamas & Papas.

15. **Stranger on The Shore** was a number one hit instrumental by Mr. Acker Bilk. In the same year The Tornados became the first British group to have a number one hit in North America, he was the first British single music artist to achieve this milestone.

16. **He's a Rebel** by The Crystals was produced by Phil Spector and written by Gene Pitney. Because the real group The Crystals were on tour at the time and Phil Spector wanted to rush release this song, he had Darlene Love and The Blossoms record this song as the Crystals. The original Crystals were shocked at the news.

17. **Monster Mash** by Bobby 'Boris' Pickett was a number one hit in 1962 and top ten again in 1973. He was encouraged to record the song after doing his impersonation of Boris Karloff to the song 'Little Darlin'. The response was great and Bobby and group member Leonard Capizzi wrote this novelty hit which became an instant smash hit.

214

18. **The Locomotion** was a song and dance by Little Eva written by Carole King and Gerry Goffin. Little Eva babysat for Carole and Gerry and they knew she could sing, so they asked if she would like to sing on the demo. They liked the result so much, they released her version and it went to number one.

19. **The Stripper** was composed by Orchestra leader David Rose four years before it became a number one hit. He also wrote the music for the TV show 'Bonanza' and later 'Little House On The Prairie'. He was married to actresses' Martha Raye and Judy Garland.

20. **Can't Help Falling in Love** by Elvis Presley was from his movie 'Blue Hawaii'. Although this song is considered to be one of Elvis Presley's most popular hits, it surprisingly did not reach number one.

21. **Don't Break the Heart That Loves You** was a number one hit for Connie Francis at a time when she was starring in films while recording songs. She later said that it was clear that acting would never replace her singing career.

22. **Do You Love Me** was the only notable hit for the Motown group The Contours. This1962 million seller was a hit again after it was featured in the movie 'Dirty Dancing' in 1988.

23. **Return to Sender** by Elvis Presley from his film 'Girls! Girls! Girls! was co-written by legendary songwriter Otis Blackwell, who wrote many hits during the 50's and 60's.

24. **Ramblin' Rose** was one of Nat 'King' Cole's biggest hits. It was number one on the easy listening charts for over a month and was nominated for a Grammy Award in the Record of The Year category.

25. **Only Love Can Break a Heart** was Gene Pitney's biggest charting hit. This Burt Bacharach/Hal David composition by Gene Pitney was number two at the time 'He's A Rebel', written by Gene Pitney for The Crystals, was number one.

26. **Palisades Park** by Freddy Cannon was written by Chuck Barris who would later become the host of 'The Gong' Show' in the late 70's.

27. **Limbo Rock** was one of several 'dance' hits for Chubby Checker during the early 60's. The 'B' side of this single 'Popeye the Hitchhiker' was also a top ten hit.

28. **The Wanderer** by Dion was originally the 'B' side of 'The Majestic'. Radio DJ's preferred 'The Wanderer' and it became one of Dion's biggest hits.

29. **Green Onions** was Booker T. & the MG's most popular hit. This great instrumental featured talents which included Steve Cropper, Donald 'Duck'

Dunn and of course, Booker T. Jones on the organ. The MG's played on many of the Stax and Atlantic record label recordings during the 60's.

30. **Mashed Potato Time** was Dee Dee Sharp's signature hit and was followed by 'Gravy' (for my mashed potatoes).This popular dance was referred to in other hits of the 60's including 'Do You Love Me' by The Contours, 'Let's Dance' by Chris Montez', 'Harry The Hairy Ape' by Ray Stevens and 'Land of 1000 Dances' by Wilson Pickett.

31. **The Wah Watusi** was the first and biggest hit for the Philadelphia R & B vocal group The Orlons. The Watusi was another of the many popular dances during the early 60's.

32. **Sealed with a Kiss** was a major hit for Brian Hyland in the summer of 1962. This song was also a hit in the summer of '68 by Gary Lewis & The Playboys, then a third time by Bobby Vinton in the summer of '72.

33. **You Don't Know Me** by Ray Charles was originally a hit in 1956 by Eddy Arnold on the Country charts. Although this song has been recorded by many artists through the years, including Elvis Presley, Mickey Gilley, Kenny Loggins and Michael Buble, this is the most famous hit version of this beautiful ballad.

34. **I Know (You Don't Love Me No More)** was the only hit for New Orleans R & B singer Barbara George.

35. **Bobby's Girl** was a top 5 hit for Marcie Blane, a singer from Brooklyn, New York. Marcie was 18 years old when she had her one and only top 40 hit.

36. **Norman** by Sue Thompson was written by John D. Loudermilk, who also composed her three other hits. While many pop female singers were in their teens or early 20's, Sue Thompson was 37 when she had a hit with 'Norman' She was born in Nevada, Missouri, July 19th, 1925.

37. **All Alone Am I** was Brenda Lee's final hit to reach the top five on the pop charts. She had more hits in the 60's than any other female singer and by the time she was 19 years old, she had already charted 17 top 40 hits.

38. **Midnight in Moscow** was a major instrumental hit by Kenny Ball & His Jazzman. He was the leader of this English Dixieland Jazz band formed in 1958.The original Russian title is 'Padmeskoveeye Vietcera'.

39. **Dream Baby** was one of Roy Orbison's greatest hits. He was inducted into the Rock And Roll Hall of Fame in 1987 and he died of a heart attack in 1988.

40. **Things** was a summer of 1962 top ten hit for Bobby Darin, born Walden Robert Cassotto in the Bronx. He died of heart failure in December 1973 at the age of 37.

216

41. **(The Man Who Shot) Liberty Valance** by Gene Pitney was written for the movie of the same name, but not used in the soundtrack. This Burt Bacharach/Hal David composition was inspired by the film that starred John Wayne and James Stewart.

42. **It Keeps Right On-A Hurtin'** by Johnny Tillotson was a country-flavored hit nominated for a Grammy Award. This Florida born and raised performer also sang the theme for the TV show 'Gidget' starring Sally Field in 1965.

43. **Let's Dance** was the first and biggest hit by Los Angeles-born Chris Montez, a protégé of Ritchie Valens. His late 60's hits that followed were all easy listening songs like 'Call Me', The More I See You' and 'Time After Time'.

44. **Slow Twistin'** was another Twist song by the man who made it famous, Chubby Checker. The Mashed Potato Time singer Dee Dee Sharp sang backup on this hit.

45. **Lovers Who Wander** was Dion's follow up to 'The Wanderer'. He charted four top ten hits in 1962.

46. **Let Me In** by one hit wonder Philadelphia R & B group The Sensations was first recorded in 1956. It took six years before it became a hit.

47. **I Remember You** by British singer Frank Ifield was a hit for Jimmy Dorsey back in 1942. This hit reached number one in Britain.

48. **Don't Hang Up** was the second big hit by the Philadelphia vocal group the Orlons, consisting of 3 girls and a bass singing guy. Two of the three ladies are now deceased, including Shirley Brickley who was shot and killed by an intruder in her home in Philadelphia in October of 1977.

49. **Break It to Me Gently** was another big hit for Little Miss Dynamite, Brenda Lee. She was born Brenda Lee Tarpley in Lithonia, Georgia December 11, 1944.

50. **Party Lights** was the only hit for Macon, Georgia's Claudine Clark who also wrote this top 5 hit popular in the summer of '62.

51. **Wolverton Mountain** was a legendary Country hit by Claude King. 'Wolverton Mountain' is an actual place in Arkansas where Clifton Clowers lived. He died in the summer of 1994 at the age of 102.

52. **Love Letters** was the only hit for singer/actress Ketty Lester. This song was originally popular in 1945 by Dick Haymes. Elvis Presley had a moderate hit with this song in 1966.

53. **She Cried** was the very first hit for Jay & The Americans. This hit featured Jay Traynor on lead vocals, while Jay Black was the front man for all their hits that followed.

54. **Teenage Idol** was a true-to-life song for Rick Nelson. He was the first teenage idol to utilize TV to promote records and it all began in 1957 when he was 17 years old.

55. **Old Rivers** by Walter Brennan was one of the surprise hits of 1962. He was a beloved 69 year old character actor when he had a top 5 hit with this song. He was starring as Grandpa on the 'Real McCoys' TV Show at the time of this hit.

56. **Next Door To An Angel** was Neil Sedaka's follow up to the similar-sounding 'Breaking Up is Hard to Do'. He attended the Julliard School of classical piano and began his string of hits in early 1959 with 'The Diary'.

57. **She's not You** by Elvis Presley was written by Jerry Leiber, Mike Stoller and Doc Pomus. This prime cut from the album 'Elvis' Golden Records Vol.3' was a number one hit in Britain for 3 weeks in '62.

58. **Young World** by Rick Nelson was written by Jerry Fuller who wrote 23 of Rick's recordings, including 'Travelin' Man', 'A Wonder Like You' and 'It's Up To You'.

59. **Ahab the Arab** was the first top ten hit for funnyman Ray Stevens, whose real name was Ray Ragsdale. This novelty hit was hilarious with Ray's fast talking random list of objects and his vocalization of 'Clyde' the camel. By the way, Ray Stevens' publishing Company is Ahab Music Inc.

60. **Shout, Shout Knock Yourself Out** was Ernie Maresca's only hit as a singer, but he wrote two of Dion's biggest hits. He co-wrote 'The Wanderer' and 'Runaround Sue', the later of which was mentioned in this fast-paced party song.

61. **The Lonely Bull** was the first of a long string of very successful instrumental hits for Herb Alpert & the Tijuana Brass. The crowd noises on this hit were actually dubbed in from a bullring in Tijuana, Mexico.

62. **Venus in Blue Jeans** was the final hit for Jimmy Clanton, a singer from Baton Rouge, Louisiana who started his career with the hit 'Go Jimmy Go' in 1958. This hit was co-written by Neil Sedaka.

63. **Al Di La** by Emilio Pericoli was one of the surprise hits of 1962. This hit was featured in the film 'Rome' starring Troy Donahue.

64. **Patches** by Dickey Lee was a teen tragedy song co-written by Barry Mann. In this same year George Jones had a number one hit with 'She Thinks I Still Care' which was written by Dickey Lee.

65. **Speedy Gonzales** by Pat Boone had a la la la la la section that Elton John later copied for his number one 1973 hit 'Crocodile Rock'. Robin Ward of 'Wonderful Summer' fame was the female voice and the man of a thousand voices, Mel Blanc did the voice of 'Speedy Gonzales'.

66. **Crying in The Rain** by The Everly Brothers was written by Carole King and Howard Greenfield.

67. **Alley Cat** was a very popular instrumental by Bent Fabric, a Danish pianist who was the founder and Head of Metronome Records in Denmark.

68. **Johnny Get Angry** was Joannie Somers' only top ten hit. She was born in Buffalo, New York and moved to California. She was the singer of the popular 'Come Alive, You're In the Pepsi Generation' jingle.

69. **Playboy** was a top ten hit for Motown's first female group, The Marvelettes. This was their second hit, following Beechwood 4-5789.

70. **Lover Please** was a solo hit for Clyde McPhatter, the first lead singer of the Drifters. This song was written by a then-unknown teenaged Billy Swan, who had a number one hit of his own in 1974 with 'I Can Help'.

71. **Ride** was the third consecutive top ten hit in 1962 for Dee Dee Sharp, whose real name is Dione La Rue.

72. **Baby it's You** by The Shirelles was written by Burt Bacharach and Hal David. The Beatles also covered this song and in 1969 the group 'Smith' had a top ten hit with it, produced by Del Shannon.

73. **You'll Lose a Good Thing** was a hit for Barbara Lynn, an R & B singer/guitarist from Beaumont, Texas. She played piano as a child before switching to guitar.

74. **Twistin' the Night Away** by Sam Cooke was another song about the most popular dance of the year and the decade.

75. **Vacation** was the final top ten hit for Connie Francis. It was a fun summertime hit which also referred to one of the big dances of the year, the Mashed Potato.

76. **That's Old Fashioned** was the final top ten hit of the 60's for The Everly Brothers. They were inducted into the Rock And Roll Hall Of Fame in 1986.

77. **Shout** was Joey Dee & The Starliter's remake of the classic Isley Brothers party song. This version was featured in the film 'Hey, Let's Twist' starring Joey Dee.

78. **When I Fall In Love** was a top ten hit for the Lettermen, known for their harmonizing easy listening pop songs during the 60's. This song was originally a hit for Doris Day 10 years earlier in 1952.

79. **What's Your Name** was the only hit for the duo Don and Juan from New York City. Their real names were Roland Trone and Claude Johnson, who was formerly a member of the Genies.

80. **You Belong to Me** was the first and most popular hit for The Duprees, a vocal quintet from Jersey City. This classic song was a remake of Jo Stafford's number one hit in 1952.

81. **Her Royal Majesty** was a hit for singer/actor James Darren, who played the part of 'Moondoggy' in the popular 'Gidget' movies. He later starred in the TV series 'The Time Tunnel' and 'T.J. Hooker'.

82. **Snap Your Fingers** was the only notable hit for Mississippi-born R & B singer Joe Henderson. He died two years later at the age of 26.

83. **Release Me** was a top ten hit for Little Esther Phillips, a powerful R & B singer from Texas. This song was originally a country hit in the early 50's and remade in the late 60's by Engelbert Humperdinck. Esther Phillips died in 1984 after years of drug addiction which led to liver and kidney failure.

84. **Dear Lady Twist** by Gary U.S. Bonds was one of over half a dozen Twist hits in 1962. Gary Anderson from Jacksonville, Florida was 'Gary U.S. Bonds', who had 5 top 10 hits from 1960 to 1962.

85. **The One Who Really Loves You** was the first top ten hit for Motown's Mary Wells. This song was written by Smokey Robinson.

86. **Gina** by Johnny Mathis was co-written by Paul Vance, who also wrote Johnny's next and last top ten hit of the 60's, 'What Will Mary Say'. Paul Vance also co-wrote the hits 'Catch a Falling Star', Itsy Bitsy Teenie Weenie Yellow Polka Dot Bikini', 'Tracy' and 'Playground In My Mind'.

87. **If I Had a Hammer** was the first top ten hit for Peter, Paul & Mary. It was co-written by Pete Seeger in 1949 and was a hit originally for The Weavers.

88. **Second Hand Love** was the second of three top ten hits in 1962 for Connie Francis. Her real name is Concetta Rosa Maria Franconera, and she was born in Newark, New Jersey.

89. **Theme from Dr. Kildare (Three Stars Will Shine Tonight)** by Richard Chamberlain was the biggest of his early 60's hits. He played Dr. Kildare in the top rated TV series of the same name from 1961 to 1966. He also starred in film, theatre and some very popular TV miniseries.

90. **Rinky Dink** was a big instrumental hit for Dave 'Baby' Cortez, and was especially popular at roller skating rinks back then. His real name is Dave Cortez Clowney, and his biggest hit was the number one instrumental hit 'The Happy Organ' in 1959.

91. **A Little Bitty Tear** was a hit for Academy Award winning actor, writer and acclaimed folk singer, Burl Ives. He had a sound of his own, and had a very soothing voice.

92. **Town Without Pity** was a hit by Gene Pitney from the movie of the same name which starred Kirk Douglas. Gene was the first pop singer to perform at The Academy Awards in 1962. Although this song was nominated for best song, it lost to 'Moon River' by Henry Mancini.

93. **Cindy's Birthday** was the biggest hit for then-16 year old Johnny Crawford. He played Mark, the son of Lucas McCain, played by Chuck Connors in the TV series 'The Rifleman' from 1958 to 1963.

94. **Chip Chip** was one of a handful of early 60's hits for Kansas City's Gene McDaniels. He also starred in the film 'It's Trad Dad' in 1962. His other hits included 'A Hundred Pounds of Clay', 'Tower Of Strength', and 'Point Of No Return'.

95. **P.T. 109** by Jimmy Dean was also a biographical movie which shows the events of John F. Kennedy's actions in Motor Torpedo Boat P.T. 109 as an officer of the U.S. Navy during World War Two.

96. **Little Diane** was a hit for Dion, who co-wrote this hit with Ernie Maresca , the man responsible for giving Dion his two biggest hits, - 'The Wanderer' and 'Runaround Sue'. This hit prominently features a kazoo as a main instrument.

97. **You Beat Me to The Punch** by Mary Wells was another top ten hit written and produced by Smokey Robinson. This hit reached number one on the R & B charts.

98. **Close to Cathy** was the only hit for Los Angeles born singer/actor Mike Clifford. In the 70's he starred in the Broadway production of 'Grease'.

99. **Dear One** was the only hit for New York City born Larry Finnegan. He died of a brain tumor in 1973 at the age of 34.

100. **Surfin' Safari** was the Beach Boys first hit single. David Marks was in the group when they recorded this hit, but was replaced by Al Jardine shortly after.

101. **Twist, Twist Senora** was Gary U.S Bonds' final top ten hit of the 60's. This song was inspired by the calypso song 'Shake Shake Shake Senora' (Jump in the Line).Gary U.S. Bonds made a comeback with 'This Little Girl', produced by Bruce Springsteen in 1981.

102. **(Dance With the) Guitar Man** was one of Duane Eddy's few hits which wasn't a total instrumental. This hit was written by Lee Hazelwood and featured singing by Darlene Love & the Blossoms as The Rebelettes.

103. **Love Me Warm and Tender** was the first of three top 20 hits for Paul Anka in 1962. He was 16 years old when his first hit, 'Diana', was number one in 1957.

104. **Bring It on Home To Me/Having A Party** was a double-sided hit single by singer/songwriter Sam Cooke. 'Bring It on Home To Me' featured a then-unknown Lou Rawls accompanying Cooke on vocals. This Sam Cooke original was later remade by The Animals and Eddie Floyd, who both charted this song in the 60's. 'Having A Party' was a fun, upbeat Sam Cooke original which makes reference to some of the top hits of the day.

105. **Girls, Girls, Girls (Made to Love)** was a hit for Eddie Hodges who played Frank Sinatra's son in the movie 'A Hole In The Head'. He also sang with ol' blue eyes on the hit 'High Hopes'. This hit was written by Phil Everly of the Everly Brothers.

106. **Please Don't Ask About Barbara** was a Bobby Vee ballad co-written by Jack Keller, who also was responsible for co-composing hits like 'Run To Him' by Bobby Vee and 'Everybody's Somebody's Fool' for Connie Francis.

107. **Twist and Shout** by The Isley Brothers was the original version of the hit The Beatles made famous two years later.

108. **Chains** was a hit by The Cookies written by Carole King and Gerry Goffin. This song was later recorded by The Beatles.

109. **Beechwood - 4-5789** was a hit for Motown's Marvelettes. Wilson Pickett later borrowed the number on his phone hit 634-5789. Marvin Gaye co-wrote this hit.

110. **I Left My Heart in San Francisco** became the signature hit for Tony Bennett, one of the top jazz vocalists of all time. New lyrics for this song were written in 1954. This Queens, New York born singer's real name is Anthony Dominick Benedetto.

111. **Let's Go** was an upbeat hit for the one hit wonder group The Routers. This hit was an instrumental with the exception of the 'Let's Go' shouts during this cheerleader favorite.

112. **Silver Threads & Golden Needles** was a hit for the British folk trio The Springfields, featuring Dusty Springfield. After leaving this group, she began her successful string of solo hits.

113. **My Boomerang Won't Come Back** by British singer/comedian Charlie Drake was a fun novelty hit which was more successful in Britain and Canada than in the United States.

114. **A Wonderful Dream** was a wonderful Doo Wop song by The Majors, a Philadelphia R & B group which featured the falsetto-voiced Ricky Cordo on lead vocals.

115. **Gravy (For My Mashed Potatoes)** was Dee Dee Sharp's top ten follow up to her signature hit, the million selling 'Mashed Potato Time' from earlier in the year.

116. **Percolator** by Billy Joe & The Checkmates was an instrumental hit based on the perking Maxwell House coffee commercial from the early 60's.

117. **Don't Play That Song** was a hit for Ben E. King co-written by Ahmet Ertegun, co-founder and Executive of Atlantic Records. He was also the Chairman of The Rock And Roll Hall Of Fame and Museum. Aretha Franklin had a hit with this song in 1970.

118. **Uptown** was a hit for the teenaged girl group from Brooklyn known as the Crystals, produced by Phil Spector. Barbara Alston was the lead singer on this top 20 hit.

119. **Irresistible You /Multiplication** was a double-side hit single for Bobby Darin. 'Multiplication' was from the movie 'Come September' which he starred with his actress wife Sandra Dee. They were married from 1960 to 1967.

120. **Devil Woman** was a hit for country/pop singer songwriter Marty Robbins, who was born Martin David Robinson in Glendale, Arizona. He died of a heart attack in 1982 at the age of 57.

121. **Point Of No Return** by Gene McDaniels was written by Carole King & Gerry Goffin. The Johnny Mann singers backed McDaniels on all of his early 60's hits.

122. **It Might As Well Rain Until September** was Carole King's first hit as a singer. After this song, she concentrated on writing dozens of hit songs for others. It wasn't until nine years later that she got back to singing her songs when she released The Tapestry album with 'It's Too Late' in 1971, both of which reached number one.

123. **The Cha-Cha-Cha** by Bobby Rydell had a melody and arrangement very similar to the instrumental 'Rinky Dink' by Dave 'Baby' Cortez from earlier in '62.

124. **Keep Your Hands off My Baby** by Little Eva was another hit written by Carole King and Gerry Goffin. The Beatles recorded a version of this song in 1963 for a BBC Special.

125. **Dancin' Party** by Chubby Checker was another dance hit from the twist king in the year his hit 'The Twist' hit number one, two years after its first run at the top of the charts.

126. **A Swingin' Safari** was the final top 40 hit for orchestra leader Billy Vaughn, who was the music director for Dot Records. This very familiar instrumental hit was written by Bert Kaempfert.

127. **A Steel Guitar and a Glass Of Wine** by Paul Anka was one of three top 20 hits from 1962 by the singer/songwriter born in the Capitol Of Canada, Ottawa, Ontario.

128. **Your Nose Is Gonna Grow** was one of three 1962 hits for singer/actor Johnny Crawford. He was starring in 'The Rifleman' at the time his hits from the early 60's were all popular.

129. **I Wish That We Were Married** was the only hit for Ronnie & The Hi-Lites, an R & B quintet from Jersey City. The lead singer Ronnie Goodson was only 13 years old when he sang his only hit. He died of a brain tumor in 1980.

130. **James (Hold the Ladder Steady)** by Sue Thompson was a lighthearted look at eloping. All of her four notable hits from the early 60's were written by John B. Loudermilk.

131. **Send Me the Pillow You Dream On** by Johnny Tillotson was a major country hit for Hank Locklin in 1958 and a top 40 hit for Dean Martin in 1965.

132. **She Can't Find Her Keys** was Paul Petersen's first hit. At the time, he was starring as Jeff Stone in the Donna Reed Show. Petersen later became an author of over a dozen Adventure books.

133. **Shadrack** by Brook Benton was a great soul and gospel-flavored hit. It was written in 1931 as 'Shadrack, Meshack, Abednigo'.

134. **Eso Beso (That Kiss)** by Paul Anka was popular the same year he appeared in the movie 'The Longest Day'.

135. **Torture** was a hit for one hit wonder Kris Jensen, a pop/country singer from New Haven, Connecticut. This song was written by renowned composer John D. Loudermilk.

136. **Pop Pop Pop Pie** was a fun, upbeat hit by the one hit wonder girl group The Sherrys. They were a Philadelphia group formed by Joe Cook and included his young daughters Dinell & Delphine. Joe Cook had his own hit in

1957 with 'Peanuts' as Little Joe & The Thrillers.

137. **Love Came to Me** was the fourth of 4 1962 top ten hits for Dion. The Del Satins provided backup vocals on this upbeat hit by this singer from the Bronx. Dion was inducted into the Rock And Roll Hall of Fame in 1989.

138. **Funny Way of Laughing** by Burl Ives was one of four notable hits he achieved in his most successful year on the pop charts, 1962.

139. **Conscience** was singer/actor James Darren's final early 60s hit. He concentrated more on his acting career in the 60's through the 80's.

140. **Smokey Places** was a hit for the Corsairs, an R & B quartet from North Carolina who had a sound similar to The Drifters. This group consisted of 3 brothers and a cousin.

141. **What's A Matter Baby** was a hit for Chicago-born Timi Yuro who was born Rosemarie Timothy Aurro Yuro. She was one of the first blue- eyed soul singers of the Rock era. She was diagnosed with throat cancer in the 80's and had her larynx removed. Sadly, she died of cancer in 2004 at the age of 63.

142. **Rain Rain Go Away** by Bobby Vinton was inspired by the children's nursery rhyme which they usually sing on rainy days. This was popular the same year as his first hit 'Roses Are Red' (My Love), which was also inspired by a poem.

143. **Rumors** was the third and final top 20 hit for Johnny Crawford from his most successful year on the pop charts.

144. **Cottonfields** by the folk quintet The Highwaymen was a traditional American ballad which originated in 1850.

145. **Lie to Me** was one of three top 20 hits in 1962 for Brook Benton, a smooth sounding R & B singer/songwriter from Camden, South Carolina. He died in 1988 of complications from spinal meningitis.

146. **My Own True Love** by The Duprees was Tara's Theme from the movie 'Gone with the Wind' starring Clark Gable and Vivian Leigh.

147. **I Sold My Heart to the Junkman** by The Blue- belles, led by Patti Labelle, was actually recorded by The Starlets due to contractual problems. The Blue- belles are only listed on the record label.

148. **Cinderella** was a hilarious spoken word tale by Jack Ross. In this novelty hit, he twisted the words to 'Cinderella lived in a big hark douse with her mean old mepstother and her two sisty uglers'. This comedic version was recorded 'live' in front of an audience.

149. **Tuff** was an instrumental hit for Mississippi born Sax man Ace Cannon, who played and toured with Bill Black's Combo for many years.

150. **What Kind of Fool Am I** by Sammy Davis Jr. was a song from the musical 'Stop the World, I Want to Get Off', starring Anthony Newley. Newley later co-wrote Sammy's number one hit 'The Candy Man'.

151. **Soul Twist** was King Curtis' contribution to the Twist craze in 1962. R & B Sax man King Curtis not only had a hit career of his own, but played on many of the hits of others including Aretha Franklin, Nat King Cole and Bobby Darin, to name just a few. Sadly he was stabbed to death in New York City in 1971.

152. **Don't go Near the Indians** was a pop/country hit for Rex Allen. He starred in many western movies in the 50's and narrated many documentaries for Walt Disney during the 60's and 70's.

153. **I've Got Bonnie** was one of many early 60's hits for one of the boys of Bandstand, Bobby Rydell. In both the Broadway musical and movie 'Grease', the high school was named 'Rydell High', after Bobby Rydell.

154. **I'm Blue** was a hit for The Ikettes, an R & B trio assembled to back up Ike and Tina Turner. Tina Turner sang backup on this hit.

155. **Ginny Come Lately** was Brian Hyland's hit just before his classic 'Sealed with a Kiss'.

156. **There's No Other (Like My Baby)** was the first hit by The Crystals and was produced and co-written by Phil Spector. Barbara Alston sang lead on this top 20 hit. The Beach Boys covered this song in 1965 on 'The Beach Boys Party' album.

157. **So This Is Love** was a hit for the California quartet The Castells. Two of the group's members later joined The Hondells.

158. **If You Gotta Make a Fool of Somebody** was a hit for James Ray, who was discovered living on the street. This singer from Washington, D.C. died soon after his success as a singer.

159. **Nut Rocker** by B. Bumble & the Stingers was a rockin' instrumental hit which was an adaption of Tchaikovsky's "The Nutcracker Ballet'.

160. **I Need Your Lovin'** was a high energy Soul hit by the Philadelphia R & B duo Don Gardner & Dee Dee Ford.

MORE HITS FROM 1962

Letter Full of Tears was one of the earliest hits for Gladys Knight & The Pips. They would have to wait 5 more years until their next notable hit, 'I Heard It Through the Grapevine'.

Call Me Mr. In-Between by Burl Ives was his final hit of the 60's and his third top 20 hit of 1962.

I've Got a Woman was an instrumental hit for Jimmy McGriff, a Jazz R & B organist/multi-instrumentalist from Philadelphia. Ray Charles had a vocal hit with this upbeat tune.

Make It Easy on Yourself by Jerry Butler was originally intended for Dionne Warwick, but songwriters Burt Bacharach & Hal David offered it to Butler instead. Three years later, The Walker Brothers had a hit with this song.

Where Have All the Flowers Gone by The Kingston Trio, was written by folk legend Pete Seeger.

Johnny Jingo was a hit for British actress Hayley Mills, the star of Disney movies back in the early 60's. Her father was actor Sir John Mills.

Small Sad Sam was a parody of 'Big Bad John' by Detroit radio DJ Phil McLean. It was his only hit.

Love Me Tender was Richard Chamberlain's remake of the song Elvis Presley recorded in the 50's. The song was adapted from the 1861 song 'Aura Lee'.

Funny How Time Slips Away by Jimmy Elledge was written by Willie Nelson. Elledge was discovered in Nashville by Chet Atkins, who also produced this hit.

West of the Wall was the last of Miss Toni Fisher's top 40 hits. This song was inspired by the Berlin Wall crisis of 1961.

Fortune Teller was a hit for Canadian teen idol Bobby Curtola who had a string of hits in Canada during the early 60's.

1. West Side Story - Soundtrack
2. Breakfast At Tiffany's - Henry Mancini
3. Modern Sounds in Country & Western Music - Ray Charles
4. Peter, Paul & Mary - Peter, Paul & Mary
5. The Music Man - Soundtrack
6. Blue Hawaii - Elvis Presley
7. College Concert - Kingston Trio
8. My Son The Folk Singer - Allan Sherman
9. Your Twist Party - Chubby Checker
10. Stranger On The Shore - Mr. Acker Bilk
11. Ramblin' Rose - Nat 'King' Cole
12. The Sound Of Music - Original Cast
13. Camelot - Original Cast
14. Joan Baez Vol. 2 - Joan Baez
15. Judy At Carnegie Hall - Judy Garland
16. Time Out - Dave Brubeck Quartet

TOP 16 COUNTRY HITS OF 1962

1. Wolverton Mountain - Claude King
2. Devil Woman - Marty Robbins
3. Mama Sang A Song - Bill Anderson
4. She Thinks I Still Care - George Jones
5. She's Got You - Patsy Cline
6. I've Been Everywhere - Hank Snow
7. Charlie's Shoes - Billy Walker
8. Misery Loves Company - Porter Wagoner
9. That's My Pa - Sheb Wooley
10. Old Rivers - Walter Brennan
11. Crazy - Patsy Cline
12. A Little Bitty Tear - Burl Ives
13. It Keeps Right On A-Hurtin'- Johnny Tillotson
14. Adios Amigo - Jim Reeves
15. A Girl I Used To Know - George Jones
16. Lonesome Number One - Don Gibson

TOP 16 ONE HIT WONDERS OF 1962

1. Bruce Channel - Hey Baby
2. Tornadoes - Telstar
3. Mr. Acker Bilk - Stranger On The Shore
4. Marcie Blane - Bobby 's Girl
5. Barbara George - I Know (You Don't Love Me No More)
6. Contours - Do You Love Me
7. Sensations - Let Me In
8. Ernie Maresca - Shout, Shout Knock Yourself Out
9. Claudine Clark - Party Lights
10. Don & Juan - What's Your Name
11. Mike Clifford - Close To Cathy
12. Larry Finnegan - Dear One
13. Routers - Let's Go
14. Kris Jensen - Torture
15. Ronnie & The Hi-Lites - I Wish That We Were Married
16. Barbara Lynn - You'll Lose A Good Thing

16 GREAT 'LOST' 45's FROM 1962

1. I Need Your Loving - Don Gardner & Dee Dee Ford
2. Shadrack - Brook Benton
3. Ginny Come Lately - Brian Hyland
4. Please Don't Ask About Barbara - Bobby Vee
5. Point Of No Return - Gene McDaniels
6. Close To Cathy - Mike Clifford
7. James (Hold The Ladder Steady) - Sue Thompson
8. Dear One - Larry Finnegan
9. Smokey Places - The Corsairs
10. Silver Threads & Golden Needles - The Springfields
11. Girls Girls Girls (Made To Love) - Eddie Hodges
12. A Wonderful Dream - The Majors
13. West Of The Wall - Toni Fisher
14. Pop Pop Pop-Pie - The Sherrys
15. Multiplication - Bobby Darin
16. Little Red Rented Rowboat - Joe Dowell

1. Do You Love Me - The Contours
2. Playboy - The Marvelettes
3. You'll Lose A Good Thing - Barbara Lynn
4. Twistin' The Night Away - Sam Cooke
5. Snap Your Fingers - Joe Henderson
6. The One Who Really Loves You - Mary Wells
7. You Beat Me To The Punch - Mary Wells
8. Release Me - Little Esther Phillips
9. Smokey Places - Corsairs
10. Don't Play That Song - Ben E. King
11. I Sold My Heart To The Junkman - Blue-belles
12. Twist & Shout - Isley Brothers
13. Letter Full Of Tears - Gladys Knight & The Pips
14. Any Day Now - Chuck Jackson
15. Night Train - James Brown
16. I'll Try Something New - Miracles

TOP 16 DANCE/PARTY HITS OF 1962

1. The Twist - Chubby Checker
2. Peppermint Twist - Joey Dee & The Starliters
3. Monster Mash - Bobby 'Boris' Pickett
4. The Locomotion - Little Eva
5. Do You Love Me - The Contours
6. Limbo Rock - Chubby Checker
7. Palisades Park - Freddy Cannon
8. Mashed Potato Time - Dee Dee Sharp
9. The Wah Watusi - Orlons
10. Let's Dance - Chris Montez
11. Let Me In - Sensations
12. Party Light - Claudine Clark
13. Shout, Shout Knock Yourself Out - Ernie Maresca
14. Twistin' The Night Away - Sam Cooke
15. Shout - Joey Dee & The Starliters
16. Dear Lady Twist - Gary U.S. Bonds

Top 16 Hits from the Summer of 1960

1. It's Now Or Never - Elvis Presley
2. I'm Sorry - Brenda Lee
3. Everybody's Somebody's Fool - Connie Francis
4. Itsy Bitsy Teenie Weenie Yellow Polka Dot Bikini - Brian Hyland
5. Alley Oop - Hollywood Argyles
6. Only The Lonely - Roy Orbison
7. Walk Don't Run - Ventures
8. Because They're Young - Duane Eddy
9. Burning Bridges - Jack Scott
10. Mule Skinner Blues - Fendermen
11. Paper Roses - Anita Bryant
12. Walking To New Orleans - Fats Domino
13. Image Of A Girl - Safaris
14. Swingin' School - Bobby Rydell
15. Finger Poppin' Time - Hank Ballard & Midniters
16. Tell Laura I Love Her - Ray Petersen

Top 16 Hits from the Summer of 1961

1. Tossin' And Turnin' - Bobby Lewis
2. Quarter To Three - Gary U.S. Bonds
3. Running Scared - Roy Orbison
4. Wooden Heart - Joe Dowell
5. Moody River - Pat Boone
6. The Boll Weevil Song - Brook Benton
7. I Like It Like That - Chris Kenner
8. Raindrops - Dee Clark
9. Stand By Me - Ben E. King
10. Hats Off To Larry - Del Shannon
11. Dum Dum - Brenda Lee
12. Let's Twist Again - Chubby Checker
13. The Writing On The Wall - Adam Wade
14. I Feel So Bad - Elvis Presley
15. Every Beat Of My Heart - The Pips
16. Pretty Little Angel Eyes - Curtis Lee

Top 16 Hits from the Summer of 1962

1. I Can't Stop Loving You - Ray Charles
2. Roses Are Red (My Love) - Bobby Vinton
3. Breaking Up Is Hard To Do - Neil Sedaka
4. The Locomotion - Little Eva
5. The Stripper - David Rose
6. Palisades Park - Freddy Cannon
7. The Wah-Watusi - Orlons
8. Sealed With A Kiss - Brian Hyland
9. Things - Bobby Darin
10. Liberty Valence - Gene Pitney
11. It Keeps Right On A-Hurtin' - Johnny Tillotson
12. Lovers Who Wander - Dion & The Belmonts
13. Wolverton Mountain - Claude King
14. Ahab The Arab - Ray Stevens
15. Al Di La - Emilio Pericoli
16. Speedy Gonzales - Pat Boone

Top 16 Hits from the Summer of 1963

1. My Boyfriend's Back - The Angels
2. Sukiyaki - Kyu Sakamoto
3. It's My Party - Lesley Gore
4. Fingertips Part 2 - Stevie Wonder
5. Surf City - Jan & Dean
6. So Much In Love - Tymes
7. Easier Said Than Done - Essex
8. Wipeout - Surfaris
9. Hello Muddah, Hello Faddah - Allan Sherman
10. Blowin' In The Wind - Peter, Paul & Mary
11. You Can't Sit Down - Dovells
12. Blue On Blue - Bobby Vinton
13. Hello Stranger - Barbara Lewis
14. (You're The) Devil In Disguise - Elvis Presley
15. I Love You Because - Al Martino
16. Candy Girl - Four Seasons

Top 16 Hits from the Summer of 1964

1. Chapel Of Love - Dixie Cups
2. A Hard Day's Night - Beatles
3. I Get Around - Beach Boys
4. Rag Doll - Four Seasons
5. Where Did Our Love Go - Supremes
6. Everybody Loves Somebody - Dean Martin
7. A World Without Love - Peter & Gordon
8. Memphis - Johnny Rivers
9. My Boy Lollipop - Millie Small
10. Little Old Lady From Pasadena - Jan & Dean
11. Love Me With All Your Heart - Ray Charles Singers
12. Don't Let The Sun Catch You Crying - Gerry & The Pacemakers
13. Under The Boardwalk - Drifters

14. People - Barbara Streisand
15. Can't You See That She's Mine - Dave Clark Five
16. Wishin' And Hopin' - Dusty Springfield

Top 16 Hits from the Summer of 1965

1. Satisfaction - Rolling Stones
2. I Got You Babe - Sonny & Cher
3. Unchained Melody - Righteous Brothers
4. I Can't Help Myself - Four Tops
5. Mr. Tambourine Man - Byrds
6. California Girls - Beach Boys
7. I'm Henry The Eighth I Am - Herman's Hermits
8. Wooly Bully - Sam The Sham & The Pharoahs
9. Back In My Arms Again - Supremes
10. Crying In The Chapel - Elvis Presley
11. Save Your Heart For Me - Gary Lewis & The Playboys
12. What's New Pussycat - Tom Jones
13. Cara Mia - Jay & The Americans
14. Wonderful World - Herman's Hermits
15. It's The Same Old Song - Four Tops
16. Yes, I'm Ready - Barbara Mason

Top 16 Hits from the Summer of 1966

1. Summer In The City - Lovin' Spoonful
2. Wild Thing - Troggs
3. Paint It Black - Rolling Stones
4. Paperback Writer - Beatles
5. Strangers In The Night - Frank Sinatra
6. Hanky Panky - Tommy James & The Shondells
7. Sunny - Bobby Hebb
8. Lil Red Riding Hood - Sam The Sham & The Pharoahs
9. Red Rubber Ball - Cyrkle
10. Did You Ever Have To Make Up Your Mind - Lovin' Spoonful
11. See You In September - Happenings
12. I Am A Rock - Simon & Garfunkel
13. The Pied Piper - Crispian St. Peters
14. They're Coming To Take Me Away - Napoleon 14th
15. You Don't Have To Say You Love Me - Dusty Springfield
16. Sweet Pea - Tommy Roe

Top 16 Hits from the Summer of 1967

1. Ode To Billie Joe - Bobbie Gentry
2. All You Need Is Love - Beatles
3. Windy - Association
4. Light My Fire - Doors
5. Respect - Aretha Franklin
6. Can't Take My Eyes Off You - Frankie Valli
7. Little Bit O' Soul - Music Explosion
8. A Whiter Shade Of Pale - Procol Harum
9. I Was Made To Love Her - Stevie Wonder
10. She'd Rather Be With Me - Turtles
11. Pleasant Valley Sunday - Monkees
12. San Francisco - Scott McKenzie
13. Somebody To Love - Jefferson Airplane
14. Mercy Mercy Mercy - Buckinghams
15. Up, Up And Away - 5th Dimension
16. Don't Sleep In The Subway - Petula Clark

Top 16 Hits from the Summer of 1968

1. Mrs. Robinson - Simon & Garfunkel
2. People Got To Be Free - Rascals
3. This Guy's In Love With You - Herb Alpert
4. Born To Be Wild - Steppenwolf
5. Hello I Love You - Doors
6. Lady Willpower - Gary Puckett & The Union Gap
7. Grazing In The Grass - Hugh Masekela
8. MacArthur Park - Richard Harris
9. Jumpin' Jack Flash - Rolling Stones
10. Classical Gas - Mason Williams
11. The Horse - Cliff Nobles & Co
12. The Good, The Bad & The Ugly - Hugo Montenegro
13. Stoned Soul Picnic - 5th Dimension
14. Yummy Yummy Yummy - Ohio Express
15. Angel Of The Morning - Merilee Rush
16. Hurdy Gurdy Man - Donovan

Top 16 Hits from the Summer of 1969

1. In The Year 2525 - Zager & Evans
2. Honky Tonk Women - Rolling Stones
3. Crystal Blue Persuasion - Tommy James & The Shondells
4. Spinning Wheel - Blood, Sweat & Tears
5. Bad Moon Rising - C.C.R.
6. A Boy Named Sue - Johnny Cash
7. Love Theme From Romeo & Juliet - Henry Mancini
8. Sweet Caroline - Neil Diamond
9. In The Ghetto - Elvis Presley
10. Grazing In The Grass - Friends Of Distinction
11. Put A Little Love In Your Heart - Jackie DeShannon
12. My Cherie Amour - Stevie Wonder
13. Good Morning Starshine - Oliver
14. What Does It Take - Jr. Walker & The All-Stars
15. Too Busy Thinkin' 'Bout My Baby - Marvin Gaye
16. One - 3 Dog Night

♫ This singer grew up in an orphanage and had the number one song of the year!

♫ Del Shannon wrote his biggest hit while working part time at a carpet store!

♫ This girl group delivered the first number one hit for Motown in 1961!

♫ This number one Elvis Presley hit was based on an Italian song written in the early 1900's!

♫ This number one hit was based on a South African Zulu song!

♫ Rodgers and Hart wrote this hit in 1934 and it became a number one hit in 1961 for this Doo Wop group!

FIND OUT THAT...and MUCH MORE...INSIDE...1961!

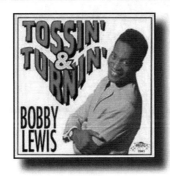

1. **Tossin' and Turnin** was a huge hit for Bobby Lewis, an R & B singer from Indianapolis. He grew up in an orphanage and was then adopted by a family in Detroit at the age of 12.

2. **Big Bad John** by Jimmy Dean was written in a little over an hour on a plane ride to Nashville by this Pop/Country singer from Texas. Jimmy Dean later launched successful businesses with a restaurant chain and a line of pork sausage.

3. **Runaway** by Del Shannon was a hit he wrote while working part time at a carpet store. His friend Max Crook contributed to writing this multi-week number one million seller and added the unusual Musitron organ to this catchy classic. Sadly, Del Shannon died of a self-inflicted gunshot wound on February 8th, 1990.

4. **The Lion Sleeps Tonight** by The Tokens was based on a South African Zulu song titled 'Wimoweh'. Group member Jay Siegal sang lead on this multi-million seller which was revived later in Disney's 'The Lion King'.

5. **Blue Moon** by the doo-wop group the Marcels was written in 1934 by the famous songwriting team of Rodgers and Hart. In 1935, there were three hit versions of this song. The Marcels, a quintet from Pittsburgh brought it to number one, where it remained for almost a month.

6. **Take Good Care Of My Baby** by Bobby Vee was written by Carole King and Gerry Goffin and was produced by Snuff Garrett. The song was originally recorded by Dion, but was not released. The introductory line 'My tears are falling, 'cause you've taken her away..." was added by Carole and producer Snuff, just before Bobby Vee recorded it.

7. **Wonderland By Night** by Bert Kaempfert was one of the top instrumentals of the 60's. Bert had connections with the careers of Frank

243

Sinatra, Elvis Presley and The Beatles. He co-wrote Sinatra's hit 'Strangers In The Night' and Elvis Presley's 'Wooden Heart' from the movie 'G.'I. Blues and produced Tony Sheridan and The Beatles early recording of 'My Bonnie' and 'When The Saints Go Marching In'.

8. **Will You Love Me Tomorrow** by The Shirelles was the first major hit written by Carole King and Gerry Goffin. The Shirelles were the very first girl group to have a number one hit and this song (which featured Carole King on kettle drums) was the one to do it.

9. **Pony Time** was a number one hit for the Twist king, Chubby Checker. Born Ernest Evans, he was discovered at a local poultry shop where he was a chicken plucker. He often sang for the customers and the shop owner was so impressed that he introduced him to Kal Mann and Dave Appell, producers at Philadelphia's Cameo-Parkway records.

10. **Travelin' Man/Hello Mary Lou** was a double-sided hit single by teen idol Rick Nelson. Travelin' Man was written by Jerry Fuller, who wrote many of Nelson's hits as well as 'Young Girl', 'Lady Willpower' and 'Over You' for Gary Puckett & the Union Gap. The 'B' side of this 45 was 'Hello Mary Lou', was written by Gene Pitney. It featured a guitar solo by legendary guitarist James Burton.

11. **Hit the Road Jack** by Ray Charles was a song presented to him by his friend Percy Mayfield, an R & B songwriter. Ray thought the song was cute and liked the 'call and response' that was also featured in his first big hit 'What'd I'd Say'.

12. **Surrender** by Elvis Presley, was a song based on the Italian song 'Torna a Sorrento' written in the early 1900's. It became Elvis Presley's 15th number one hit.

13. **Quarter to Three** by Gary U.S. Bonds was recorded 'live' in the studio and was written in just a few minutes. Bruce Springsteen would perform this song as an encore before he became a superstar, and in the 80's helped re-launch Gary's career.

14. **Michael (Row the Boat Ashore)** by the folk group The Highwaymen was a traditional folk song sung in the 19th century by slaves who lived on the islands off the coast of Georgia and traveled to work on the mainland each day by boat.

15. **Runaround Sue** was Dion's biggest hit, and one he co-wrote with Ernie Maresca. Although Dion married a girl named Sue, this song wasn't about her. The Del Satins were the uncredited backup vocal group on this number one hit.

16. **Calcutta** was the fifth title of this number one instrumental by Lawrence Welk. The harpsichord was one of the main instruments featured in this tune

by the man who had his own long-running music show on television for many years. Lawrence Welk died in 1992 at the age of 89.

17. **Running Scared** by Roy Orbison really demonstrated the power of his clear, full voice. This song, written by Roy Orbison and Joe Melson became this legendary singer's first official number one hit. 'Love Hurts', which later became a hit for Nazareth was the 'B' side of this single.

18. **Please Mr. Postman** was the Marvelettes' debut hit and the first number one for Motown. Gladys Horton sang lead on this hit which also reached number one for The Carpenters 14 years later. The Beatles recorded it two years after this original version.

19. **Wooden Heart** by Joe Dowell was inspired by the Elvis movie 'G.I. Blues' when producer Shelby Singleton heard the king perform it in the movie. This part- English, part- German song was recorded by Elvis, but was a hit for Joe Dowell, who took it to number one.

20. **Mother-In-Law** was a number one hit for Ernie K. Doe which he found in songwriter Allen Toussaint's trash. It was a song he had written and thrown away. Ernie was having marital problems at the time and asked Toussaint if he could record it. The rest as they say is history.

21. **Moody River** was Pat Boone's final number one hit. While Pat Boone's movie and TV careers were doing well, he had not had a number one hit since 1957 with 'April Love'.

22. **Shop Around** by the Miracles was Motown's first million seller. It was produced by Motown Founder and President Berry Gordy Jr. and written by Gordy and Smokey Robinson. Berry Gordy Jr. also played piano on this Motown first.

23. **The Boll Weevil Song** was Brook Benton's highest ranking hit, even though it was a novelty hit. The song was an adaption of a traditional American folk song. The Mike Stewart singers supplied the backing vocals.

24. **Bristol Stomp** by The Dovells featured Len Barry on lead vocals. 'Bristol' was a town near Philadelphia where this vocal group formed. Len Barry later went on to have solo success with hits that included '1 2 3'.

25. **I Like It Like That** was a hit for Chris Kenner, an R & B singer from Louisiana. The Dave Clark Five had a hit with this song 3 years later. Chris Kenner also did the original version of 'Land of 1000 Dances, which became a soul classic for Wilson Pickett.

26. **Raindrops** was a million seller for Dee Clark, an R & B singer who was born in Arkansas and raised in Chicago. The song featured the sounds of rain and thunder along with Clark's powerful voice. He died in 1990 at age 52 of a heart attack.

27. **Exodus** by Ferrante and Teicher was the theme of the Otto Preminger film starring Paul Newman, Eve Marie Saint and Ralph Richardson.

28. **Apache** was a very popular instrumental by Jorgen Ingmann and his guitar. It was the only notable hit for this instrumentalist from Copenhagen, Denmark.

29. **The Mountain's High** was the most successful hit for the duo Dick and Deedee, who formed while they were students in high school in Santa Monica, California.

30. **Crying** was written by Roy Orbison after seeing a girlfriend he had broken up with, walking by while he was in a barber shop. 'Candy Man' was the 'B' side of this single.

31. **Run To Him** by Bobby Vee was written by Gerry Goffin and Jack Keller, and was originally intended for The Everly Brothers to record. The flip side was 'Walkin' with My Angel', which was written Gerry Goffin and Carole King.

32. **Daddy's Home** by Shep & the Limelites was actually an answer song to the similar-sounding 'A Thousand Miles Away' by The Heartbeats. Lead singer James 'Shep' Shephard was found shot to death in his car on the Long Island Expressway in 1970.

33. **A Hundred Pounds of Clay** was the first and biggest of Gene McDaniel's half a dozen top 40 hits from '61 and '62. The Johnny Mann Singers provided backing vocals on them all. Over a dozen years later, as Eugene McDaniels, he wrote the number one hit 'Feel like Makin' Love' for Roberta Flack.

34. **I've Told Every Little Star** was a hit by a then-15 year old Linda Scott from Queens, New York. The song was originally popular in 1933 in the Broadway musical 'Music in the Air'.

35. **Stand by Me** was a hit for Ben E. King the year after he left his position as lead singer of The Drifters. Ben E. King wrote this song with Jerry Leiber and Mike Stoller. It was revived in 1988 after it became the title of the Stephen King film of the same name.

36. **Goodbye Cruel World** was the biggest hit for singer/actor James Darren. In the year this hit was big, he had a role in the World War 2 film 'The Guns of Navarone'.

37. **Dedicated to the One I Love** by The Shirelles was originally released in 1959, with unsuccessful results. When it was re released after their number one hit 'Will You Love Me Tomorrow', it reached the top five on the pop charts. The Mamas & Papas had a major hit with this song in 1967.

38. **Calendar Girl** featured Neil Sedaka going through every month of the year in this happy-go-lucky hit. Before his successful string of hits began, Sedaka attended the Julliard School for classical piano.

39. **My True Story** was the only hit for The Jive Five, an R & B vocal group from Brooklyn, New York. The lead singer, Eugene Pitt was formerly with The Genies.

40. **Wheels** was a catchy, upbeat instrumental by The String-A-Longs. This tune also charted in 1961 by Billy Vaughn.

41. **Last Night** by The Mar-Keys, was an instrumental hit which has been used in many trailers for movies through the years. This Memphis group formed in 1958 and featured Steve Cropper and Donald 'Duck' Dunn, two future members of Booker T. & the MG's. This was the only top 40 hit for The Mar-Keys.

42. **There's a Moon out Tonight** was by one hit wonder group The Capris from Queens, New York. The song was originally released two years earlier without much success and when it was reissued in 1961, the group re-formed after splitting up in 1959.

43. **(Marie's The Name) His Latest Flame/Little Sister** was a double-sided hit single by Elvis Presley. Both songs were written by Mort Shuman and Doc Pomus, who composed over two dozen songs recorded by Elvis.

44. **Fool #1** was another big hit for Little Miss Dynamite, Brenda Lee. She was born Brenda Mae Tarpley on December 11, 1944 in Lithonia, Georgia. She was a teenager during all her top ten hits.

45. **(I Don't Know Why) But I Do** was the biggest hit by Louisiana's Clarence 'Frogman' Henry. His other notable hit in 1961 was 'You Always Hurt the One You Love'. In 1964, he opened many concerts in North America for The Beatles.

46. **Where the Boys Are** was the title song from the movie of the same name which starred Connie Francis and George Hamilton, among others. The song was written by Neil Sedaka and Howard Greenfield.

47. **Don't Worry** by Marty Robbins was number one on the Country charts for over two months. This hit is famous for its 'fuzz-bass' guitar, which was a new sound back then.

48. **On the Rebound** was an upbeat instrumental by pianist Floyd Cramer, one of Nashville's top session pianists. He played on dozens of big hits in the 50's and 60's including Elvis Presley's first major hit 'Heartbreak Hotel'. Floyd Cramer died in 1997 as a result of lung cancer at the age of 64.

49. **You Don't Know What You've Got** was the biggest of two Elvis sound-a-like hits Ral Donner had hits with in 1961.This Chicago-born singer died of cancer in 1984 at the age of 41.

50. **Hats Off to Larry** was Del Shannon's follow up to his biggest hit 'Runaway'. 'Hats Off to Larry' was his second biggest hit in his most successful year on the charts, 1961.

51. **Walk on By** was Leroy Van Dyke's signature hit and the number one Country hit of the entire year in 1961. His first major hit was 'The Auctioneer'.

52. **I Love How You Love Me** by The Paris Sisters was one of Phil Spector's earliest productions. Albeth, Priscilla and Sherrell Paris hailed from San Francisco.

53. **Happy Birthday Sweet Sixteen** by Neil Sedaka, was written for his then close friend, Annette Funicello. Neil Sedaka wrote the music while Howard Greenfield wrote the lyrics.

54. **Mama Said** was the Shirelles third consecutive hit of 1961.The girls formed in Junior High School as the Poquellos.

55. **Hurt** was the biggest hit by Timi Yuro and was originally an R & B hit in 1955 for Roy Hamilton. Elvis Presley later recorded this song and performed it regularly in concert.

56. **Who Put the Bomp** was the only hit as a singer for Barry Mann, but he went on to become one of the most successful songwriters of our time with his wife Cynthia Weil. It's interesting that this song is a thank you to songwriters, before he became one of the best.

57. **Angel Baby** was the only hit for Rosie & The Originals. This San Diego vocal group was fronted by Rosie Hamlin, who wrote the lyrics of this song as a poem when she was 14 years old.

58. **Rubber Ball** was a bouncy little number by Bobby Vee, co-written by Gene Pitney under his mother's name, Ann Orlowski. Aaron Schroeder, who co-wrote the song with Pitney, also wrote several hits for Elvis Presley, including the number one hits 'It's Now or Never' and 'Stuck On You'.

59. **Dum Dum** was one of four top 10 hits in 1961 for Brenda Lee. This song was written by Jackie DeShannon.

60. **Does Your Chewing Gum Lose Its Flavor** was a novelty hit for Lonnie Donegan, Britain's 'King of Skiffle'. This song was originally a hit in 1924 for Ernest Hare and Billy Jones as 'Does Your Spearmint Lose Its Flavor on the Bedpost Overnight'.

61. **Tower of Strength** by Gene McDaniels, was co-written by Burt Bacharach without his longtime collaborator, Hal David. Gene McDaniels can be heard playing the trombone on the opening of this top ten hit.

62. **Let's Twist Again** was a great follow up to his original Twist hit. Chubby Checker, whose real name is Ernest Evans was given his new name by Dick Clark's then-wife Bobbie. She thought he had a resemblance to Fats Domino and came up with 'Chubby' for Fats and 'Checker' for Domino.

63. **Sad Movies (Make Me Cry)** was the first of four notable hits for Sue Thompson. She was born in Nevada, Missouri as Eva Sue McKee.

64. **You Must Have Been a Beautiful Baby** by Bobby Darin was originally a big hit for Bing Crosby in 1938. Bobby Darin was married to Sandra Dee at the time this song was popular.

65. **School Is Out** by Gary U.S. Bonds had the same 'live' party feel as his other big 1961 hit 'Quarter To Three'.

66. **This Time** was the only top 40 hit for Troy Shondell, a pop/country singer from Fort Wayne, Indiana.

67. **Baby Sittin' Boogie** was a fun novelty hit by Buzz Clifford which featured baby sounds delivered in a hilarious manner. Illinois-born Buzz Clifford went on the write songs for other music artists, mostly in the country music field.

68. **Yellow Bird** was a hit for Hawaiian instrumentalist Arthur Lyman. He played the vibraphone, guitar, piano and drums. This tune was adapted from a West Indian folk song.

69. **Crazy** by Patsy Cline became her signature hit and was written by the legendary Willie Nelson.

70. **Walk Right In/Ebony Eyes** was a double-sided hit single by The Everly Brothers. 'Walk Right In' was written by Sonny Curtis, a former member of Buddy Holly's Crickets. 'Ebony Eyes' was a tearjerker song about a young man losing his fiancee in an airplane crash. This song was written by John D. Loudermilk.

71. **The Writing on the Wall** was the biggest of Adam Wade's three top ten hits, all popular in 1961.

72. **I Feel So Bad** by Elvis Presley was originally a top ten R & B hit for Chuck Willis in 1954. The 'B' side of this single was 'Wild in the Country', the title song of the movie starring Elvis.

73. **Let There Be Drums** was an instrumental hit by drummer Sandy

Nelson, born in Santa Monica, California. As a session drummer, he played on many hits including 'To Know Him Is To Love Him' by The Teddy Bears, 'Alley Oop' by the Hollywood Argyles, and 'A Thousand Stars' by Kathy Young.

74. **Mexico** was an instrumental by Bob Moore, a one hit wonder on his own. As a session bass player, he played on recordings by Elvis Presley, and performed with many music artists including Frank Sinatra, Bob Dylan, Andy Williams, Connie Francis, Wayne Newton and many others.

75. **Ya Ya** was the first notable hit for Lee Dorsey, a former prizefighter in the early 50's. He was born in New Orleans, but moved to Portland, Oregon when he was ten years old. He was born on Christmas Eve in 1924 and died of emphysema on December 1 1986 at the age of 61.

76. **Every Beat of My Heart** was the very first hit for Gladys Knight & The Pips, listed as simply 'The Pips.' Gladys Knight had just turned 17 when this hit reached the top ten.

77. **Without You** was a top ten hit by a then- 22 year old Johnny Tillotson. He had one top ten hit per year from 1960 to 1963.

78. **Pretty Little Angel Eyes** was a great doo-wop hit by Curtis Lee, featuring backing vocals by The Halos. Curtis Lee co-wrote this song with Tommy Boyce (of Boyce and Hart fame) which was produced by Phil Spector.

79. **Moon River** by Henry Mancini, was the Academy Award Winning Song from the movie 'Breakfast At Tiffany's', which starred Audrey Hepburn and George Peppard.

80. **The Fly** was one of five top 40 hits Chubby Checker achieved in 1961 alone. His hits were mostly about dances of the day with The Twist leading the way.

81. **Take Good Care of Her** was the first top ten hit for Pittsburgh-born Adam Wade. He later hosted the TV game show 'Musical Chairs' and became a talk show host in Los Angeles in the 1980's.

82. **You Can Depend on Me** by Brenda Lee was originally a big hit for Louis Armstrong in 1932.Brenda Lee was only 13 when she recorded 'Rockin' Round the Christmas Tree' in 1958.

83. **Spanish Harlem** was Ben E. King's first solo hit after leaving The Drifters. This song was written by Jerry Leiber and Phil Spector and became a hit again when Aretha Franklin covered it in 1971.

84. **Tonight** by Ferrante and Teicher was an instrumental hit from 'West Side Story'. The film won 10 Academy Awards, including Best Picture.

85. **Corinna, Corinna** was a major hit for Ray Peterson, who started singing in his early teens while being treated for polio at a Texas hospital. Phil Spector produced this top ten hit from 1961. Ray Peterson died of cancer in 2005.

86. **Breakin' in a Brand New Broken Heart/Together** by Connie Francis was a double sided hit single and one of seven singles she released in 1961. 'Breakin' in a Brand New Broken Heart' was written by Neil Sedaka's songwriting partner Howard Greenfield with Jack Keller. 'Together' was a hit for Paul Whiteman back in 1928.

87. **Heartaches** by the Marcels, was delivered in the same style as their biggest hit 'Blue Moon'. Like 'Blue Moon', this song was also a classic revived. 'Heartaches' was a hit for Guy Lombardo in 1931 and a number one hit in 1947 for Ted Weams.

88. **Emotions** was another top ten hit for Brenda Lee, who began singing professionally at the age of six, and signed with Decca records in 1956 when she was only 12 years old.

89. **Asia Minor** was an energetic instrumental hit by one hit wonder act Kokomo. The group was actually Jimmy 'Wiz' Wisner, a pianist who had to release this top ten tune with his own money, because the 10 labels he approached all turned him down.

90. **Those Oldies But Goodies (Remind Me of You)** was the only hit to reach the top 40 for the Los Angeles-based quintet, Little Caesar & The Romans.

91. **Let's Get Together** was the first and biggest hit for Hayley Mills. She played twin sisters in the Disney film 'The Parent Trap' which featured this top ten hit.

92. **One Mint Julep** was one of seven singles Ray Charles released in 1961 alone. This song was previously a hit on the R & B charts for The Clovers in 1952.

93. **Portrait of My Love** was a hit for Steve Lawrence, whose real name is Sidney Leibowitz. He married Eydie Gorme in 1957 and have been together as a married couple for over 50 years.

94. **I Understand (Just How You Feel)** was a hit for the G-Clefs, which featured the tune of Auld Lang Syne'. This group from Roxbury, Massachusetts featured three brothers and two friends.

95. **Dance on Little Girl** was another hit for Canadian born teen idol Paul Anka, who wrote most of the hits he recorded.

96. **You're the Reason** was a pop/country hit for Bobby Edwards, whose real name is Robert Moncrief. A vocal group known as 'Four Young Men' supplied the backing vocals. His next hit was titled 'What's The Reason'.

97. **Don't Bet Money Honey** was one of three hits Linda Scott charted in her first and biggest year, 1961. She was still in high school at the time she recorded her only 3 top 40 hits.

98. **San Antonio Rose** was Floyd Cramer's third consecutive top ten hit. This instrumental hit was written by Bob Willis in 1938. Floyd Cramer's greatest success came as a much sought after piano session player.

99. **Good Time Baby** was one of many goodtime hits for Philadelphia's Bobby Rydell. Back in the late 50's, he was the drummer with Rocco & the Saints, which included Frankie Avalon.

100. **Little Devil** was Neil Sedaka's follow up to 'Calendar Girl', his biggest hit of 1961.

101. **My Empty Arms** was a hit by the legendary Jackie Wilson. This song was based on 'Vesti La Giubba' from the opera 'I Pagliacci'. Jackie Wilson was posthumously inducted into the Rock And Roll Hall Of Fame in 1987. He died in 1984.

102. **I Fall to Pieces** by Patsy Cline was her first number one hit on the Country charts, and her second hit to chart on the Pop charts. She was killed in a plane crash two years later, in 1963, near Camden, Tennessee.

103. **Unchain My Heart** was a hit by Ray Charles, backed by the Raelettes. The song was written by Bob Sharp, who was a drug addict at the time who sold the song for $50. to Teddy Powell, who demanded half of the songwriting credits.

104. **I'm Gonna Knock on Your Door** was the first and biggest hit for Eddie Hodges, who was 14 years old when he released this hit. He starred as Frank Sinatra's son in the movie 'A Hole in the Head'.

105. **Please Love Me Forever** by Cathy Jean & The Roommates was a one hit wonder group from Brooklyn, New York. Bobby Vinton had a hit with this song in the late 60's.

106. **You Always Hurt the One You Love** was one of two successful hits for Clarence 'Frogman' Henry in 1961. This song was a number one hit in 1944 for the Mills Brothers.

107. **Let the Four Winds Blow** was Fats Domino's final hit to reach the top 20. Believe it or not, he never had an official number one hit, even with the classic 'Blueberry Hill'.

108. **Sweets for My Sweets** was a hit for the Drifters, and later the Searchers. This hit was written by Mort Shuman and Doc Pomus, who wrote many hits for others including several for Elvis Presley.

109. **A Wonder like You/Everlovin'** was one of many double-sided hit singles for TV and music star Rick Nelson. His real name was Eric Hilliard Nelson and he was born May 8 1940 in Teaneck, New Jersey.

110. **Cupid** was a song written and recorded by Sam Cooke, which later became a hit for both Johnny Nash in the late 60's, Tony Orlando & Dawn in the 70's and the Spinners in the 80's.

111. **Gee Whiz (Look at His Eyes)** was the first and biggest hit for Carla Thomas, the daughter of Rufus Thomas. Carla was born in Memphis and later recorded duets with Otis Redding including 'Tramp' in 1967.

112. **When We Get Married** was a hit for the Dreamlovers, a group that took their name from the Bobby Darin hit of the same name. This group backed up Chubby Checker on many of his hits.

113. **As If I Didn't Know** was Adam Wade's final top ten hit of his three in 1961, his only year in the top ten.

114. **Wings of A Dove** was a hit for Country singer/songwriter/guitarist Ferlin Husky. This song was number one for an incredible 10 weeks on the Country charts.

115. **Hello Walls** was the biggest hit for Faron Young, a Country singer/ songwriter born in Shreveport, Louisiana. This song was written by Willie Nelson.

116. **You Can Have Her** was a powerful hit by Roy Hamilton. This R & B singer from Leesburg, Georgia died of a stroke in 1969 at the age of 40.

117. **A Little Bit of Soap** was a hit for The Jarmels, an R & B vocal group named from a street in Harlem. The group was from Richmond, Virginia and had only one hit.

118. **Rama Lama Ding Dong** was the only notable hit for the R & B Quintet the Edsels, from Youngstown, Ohio. The song was released in 1958 as 'Lama Rama Ding Dong'.

119. **Bumble Boogie** was an instrumental hit by B. Bumble & The Stingers, which was actually an assemblage of Los Angeles session men. Ernie Freeman was the piano player known as 'B. Bumble'. This energetic classic was an adaption of 'Flight of the Bumble Bee'.

120. **One Track Mind** was the only other hit for Bobby Lewis, who achieved the number one song of the entire year with 'Tossin' And Turnin'.

121. **When the Boy in Your Arms (Is The Boy In Your Heart)** was the seventh single of 1961 by Connie Francis, and it was the year she starred in the film 'Where The Boys Are'.

122. **Tragedy** was a hit for the group The Fleetwoods, who had two major hits in the late 50's with 'Come Softly To Me' and 'Mr. Blue', both of which reached number one.

123. **Once in Awhile** was a hit for the Chimes, a vocal quintet from Brooklyn, New York. This song was a number one hit for Tommy Dorsey in 1937.

124. **Moon River** was a vocal hit version by Jerry Butler the same year Henry Mancini won the Best Original Song Academy Award with his version from 'Breakfast at Tiffany's'.

125. **Think Twice** by Brook Benton, was another of his string of hits during the early 60's. After 'Hotel Happiness' in 1962, Brook Benton didn't have another top ten hit again until 1970 when 'Rainy Night in Georgia' (written by Tony Joe White), reached the top 5 on the pop charts.

126. **I Don't Know Why** by Linda Scott was her third and final top 40 hit. Linda Scott was born Linda Joy Sampson in Queens, New York. This song was a remake of a hit which Wayne King charted in 1931.

127. **Baby Blue** was a hit for the soft pop trio the Echoes from Brooklyn, New York. This was their only top 20 hit, and not to be confused with the Badfinger title of the same name.

128. **I'll be There** was the biggest hit for Damita Jo, a singer from Austin, Texas. This song was the answer song to Ben E. King's 'Stand by Me'.

129. **The Way You Look Tonight** was the first of many easy listening hits for the Lettermen, who had many hit albums during the 60's. This song was a number one hit for Fred Astaire in 1936 from the film 'Swing Time'.

130. **Never on Sunday** was the final hit for The Chordettes, who were known for their close harmony and hits like 'Mr. Sandman' and 'Lollipop'. 'Never On Sunday' was a vocal version of the theme from the movie of the same name.

131. **Tonight My Love, Tonight** was a hit for teen idol Paul Anka. He has five daughters with first names all beginning with the letter 'A', Amelia, Anthea, Alicia, Amanda and Alexandra.

132. **Barbara Ann** by the Regents was the original version of the song the Beach Boys made famous five years later. The short-lived Regents had already split up by the time this song hit the charts.

133. **It's Gonna Work out Fine** was one of the earliest hits by Ike and Tina Turner. Mickey & Sylvia of 'Love Is Strange' fame provided backing vocals on this hit.

134. **'Til** was the debut hit of the Angels, a female trio from Orange, New Jersey. Their biggest hit arrived two years later with 'My Boyfriend's Back'.

135. **Please Stay** by the Drifters featured their new lead singer Rudy Lewis. This song was written by Burt Bacharach and Bob Hilliard and featured background vocals by future stars Dionne Warwick and Doris Troy.

136. **Look in My Eyes** was a hit for The Chantels, an R & B group from the Bronx which formed in high school. They took their name from a rival school, St. Francis de Chantelle.

137. **Lazy River** was the first of four singles Bobby Darin released in 1961. This song was originally a hit for Hoagy Carmichael back in 1932.

138. **Flaming Star** by Elvis Presley, was the title song from the movie of the same name in which he starred. Barbara Eden co-starred in this Elvis Western film.

139. **Tonight I Fell In Love** was the first hit by the harmonizing group, The Tokens. Their next hit that year was their biggest, - 'The Lion Sleeps Tonight'. Group member Hank Medress later formed his own label B.T.Puppy, and produced the hits of the Happenings. In the 70's he produced Tony Orlando and Dawn's biggest hits.

140. **Bless You** was one of two 1961 solo hits for Tony Orlando. The other was 'Halfway to Paradise', written by Carole King and Gerry Goffin. With the exception of singing lead on Wind's hit 'Make Believe', Tony Orlando would have to wait nine years before his next hit, 'Candida' with Dawn, in 1970.

141. **Revenge** was a hit for Brook Benton, one of the smoothest soul singers of the 60's. He was not only a talented singer, but he also wrote many of his biggest hits.

142. **The Story of My Love** by Paul Anka was the first of five hits he charted in 1961. His first hit 'Diana' reached number one in 1957 as he was about to turn 16 years old.

143. **I Just Don't Understand** was a moderate hit by singer/actress Ann-Margret. She starred in many movies including 'Viva Las Vegas' with Elvis Presley. The Beatles later covered this song.

144. **I Count the Tears** was the final hit by the Drifters to feature Ben E. King on lead vocals. He began his solo career with hits 'Spanish Harlem' and 'Stand By Me' in the same year, 1961. 'I Count the Tears' was similar to the Grassroots 1967 hit 'Let's Live For Today' in the chorus.

145. **My Kind Of Girl** was a hit by British singer Matt Monroe, who had a huge following in many parts of the world. He sold more than 100 million records during his lifetime. He died of liver cancer in 1985 at the age of 54.

146. **Heart and Soul** was a hit by the doo-wop group the Cleftones from Queens, New York. The song was a number one hit in 1938 by Larry Clinton.

147. **Girl of My Best Friend** was a hit for Ral Donner, whose voice resembled that of Elvis Presley, who recorded this song in 1960 on his 'Elvis Is Back' album. It was never a hit for Elvis.

148. **Bonanza** by Al Caiola and his orchestra was the instrumental title tune from the top rated TV series of the same name. Al Caiola also did the theme for 'The Magnificent Seven' starring Yul Brynner that year.

149. **Gypsy Woman** by the Impressions featured Curtis Mayfield on lead vocals. Brian Hyland had a hit with this song nine years later in 1970.

150. **Sacred** was a hit for the Santa Rosa, California quartet, the Castells. Two of the group's members later joined the Hondells, best known for their hit 'Little Honda'.

151. **I Dreamed of Hill-Billy Heaven** was a hit for Tex Ritter, the father of actor John Ritter. It was a remake of a hit originally popular in 1955 on the Country charts for Eddie Dean.

152. **Angel on My Shoulder** was a soft ballad by Shelby Flint, a singer born in 1939 in North Hollywood, California, who later became a voice actress.

153. **C'est Si Bon (It's So Good)** was a hit for Country/Pop singer Conway Twitty. His real name was Harold Jenkins and he changed his name by looking on a map and picking Conway, from Arkansas and Twitty, from Texas.

154. **A Scottish Soldier** was a hit for Scottish singer Andy Stewart. This hit stayed on the UK charts for 36 weeks in 1961 and reached number one in some major cities in Canada that year.

155. **Take Five** was a signature hit of the Dave Brubeck Quartet, one of the most popular jazz acts of our time.

156. **Heart and Soul** was a hit for Jan & Dean the same year The Cleftones revived this classic from 1938.

157. **Tonight (Could Be The Night)** was the only top 40 hit for the Velvets, an R & B doo-wop quintet from Odessa, Texas.

158. **Right or Wrong** was a hit for Wanda Jackson, a Country singer/songwriter/guitarist. Three years later, it was a hit for Ronnie Dove. Wanda Jackson, who was born in Maud, Oklahoma, did much better with this song on the Country charts, where it reached top ten.

159. **Ghost Riders in the Sky** was an instrumental hit in 1961 for the group the Ramrods from Connecticut. There have been many versions of this tune through the years, but Vaughn Monroe's 1949 rendition was the most popular.

160. **Johnny Willow** was a story song by Fred Darian, a singer/songwriter/producer from Detroit. He wrote and sang backup on the hit 'Mr. Custer' by Larry Verne and produced the early hits of Dobie Gray including 'The 'In' Crowd.

MORE HITS FROM 1961

Donald, Where's Your Trousers was a comedy hit for Scotland's Andy Stewart, who was quite the performer and impressionist. He died at the age of 60 in 1993.

(He's my) Dreamboat - was one of six hits Connie Francis charted in 1961 and only one of two that didn't reach the top ten.

Little Boy Sad was a hit for Johnny Burnette, who had a boy who later had a hit of his own, Rocky Burnette who hit top ten with 'Tired of Toeing the Line' in 1980. His cousin, Billy Burnette became a member of Fleetwood Mac.

Pepe by the King of the 'twangy' guitar, Duane Eddy, was the title tune of the movie which starred Cantinflas.

Tell Me Why was a hit for Dion's backup vocal group The Belmonts. Dion went solo the year before, in 1960.

All In My Mind was the first and most popular pop hit for R & B singer Maxine Brown from South Carolina.

The Astronaut was a novelty comedy hit for Jose Jimenez, a character that actor Bill Dana created for the Steve Allen Show when he was the head writer. Bill Dana had his own show from 1963 to 1965.

Peanut Butter was listed on the record as 'The Marathons', but it was very confusing because it was actually 'The Vibrations'. It was basically the same tune as The Olympics 1960 hit '(Baby) Hully Gully.'

257

Model Girl was the first solo hit for Johnny Maestro, the lead singer of the Crests, best known for the hits 'Sixteen Candles', 'Step by Step' and others. In 1969 he resurfaced as the lead singer of the Brooklyn Bridge on 'Worst That Could Happen'.

Let Me Belong to You was Brian Hyland's follow up to his biggest hit 'Itsy Bitsy Teenie Weenie Yellow Polka Dot Bikini'. This was his only hit of 1961.

Please Tell Me Why was one of five singles Jackie Wilson released in 1961. 'My Empty Arms' was the only one that reached the top ten.

Frankie and Johnny by Brook Benton was a version of the mid - 19th century traditional folk song. In 1966, Elvis Presley recorded it as the title song of his movie of the same name in which he played Johnny and Donna Douglas played Frankie.

I'm a Fool to Care was the only hit for Joe Barry, who sounded very similar to Fats Domino. This singer/guitarist was born Joe Barrios in Cut Off, Louisiana.

Nag by The Halos was the only hit for this R & B vocal group from New York City, but they provided backing on the hit 'Pretty Little Angel Eyes' by Curtis Lee.

Lovey Dovey was the final top 40 hit for Buddy Knox, a singer from Happy, Texas best known for his 1957 number one hit 'Party Doll'.

Once Upon A Time was a hit for one hit wonder R & B group Rohelle & The Candles featuring Johnny Wyatt on lead vocals.

Triangle was a hit for Janie Grant, whose only other notable hit was 'That Greasy Kid Stuff'. This singer/songwriter from Patterson, New Jersey was discovered by Gerry Granahan of 'No Chemise Please' fame.

I Really Love You was a hit for one hit wonder act The Stereos from Steubenville, Ohio. They were an R & B quintet originally called the Buckeyes. George Harrison later did a remake of this song.

Transister Sister was a hit for Freddy 'Boom Boom' Cannon which made reference to some of the top music artists of the day including Presley, Darin, U.S Bonds, Fats, Connie and Orbison. Transister radios were becoming quite popular back then.

The Bilbao Song was an upbeat hit by Andy Williams which featured new lyrics to a song from the 1929 German musical 'Happy End'.

Halfway to Paradise was the first hit by Tony Orlando, nine years before his first hit with the group 'Dawn'. Tony Orlando was discovered by Don

Kirshner. This song was written by Carole King and Gerry Goffin.

(I Wanna) Love My Life Away was the very first hit for Gene Pitney, a singer born in Hartford, Connecticut and raised in Rockville, Connecticut, who had a respectable string of hits which began with this song in early 1961.

Top 16 Albums of 1961

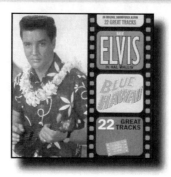

1. Blue Hawaii - Elvis Presley
2. Calcutta - Lawrence Welk
3. Stars On A Summer Night - Various Artists
4. Judy At Carnegie Hall - Judy Garland
5. Camelot - Original Broadway Cast
6. Wonderland By Night - Bert Kaempfert
7. Stereo 35/MM - Enoch Light & His Orchestra
8. Exodus - Soundtrack
9. Something For Everybody - Elvis Presley
10. The Button-Down Mind Strikes Back! - Bob Newhart
11. Carnival! - Original Cast
12. G.I. Blues - Elvis Presley
13. Great Motion Picture Themes - Various Artists
14. Never On Sunday - Soundtrack
15. Goin' Places - Kingston Trio
16. Sound Of Music - Original Cast

Top 16 Country Hits Of 1961

LEROY VAN DYKE

1. Walk On By - Leroy Van Dyke
2. Don't Worry - Marty Robbins
3. Hello Walls - Faron Young
4. Tender Years - George Jones
5. North To Alaska - Johnny Horton
6. Heartbreak U.S.A. - Kitty Wells
7. I Fall To Pieces - Patsy Cline
8. Big Bad John - Jimmy Dean
9. Crazy - Patsy Cline
10. Last Date - Floyd Cramer
11. Are You Lonesome Tonight - Elvis Presley
12. Under The Influence Of Love - Buck Owens
13. I Dreamed Of Hill-Billy Heaven - Tex Ritter
14. The Blizzard - Jim Reeves
15. You're The Reason - Bobby Edwards
16. Right Or Wrong - Wanda Jackson

1. Ernie K. Doe - Mother-In-Law
2. Shep And The Limelites - Daddy's Home
3. Jorgen Ingmann - Apache
4. Chris Kenner - I Like It Like That
5. Capris - There's A Moon Out Tonight
6. Rosie & The Originals - Angel Baby
7. Troy Shondell - This Time
8. Bob Moore - Mexico
9. Curtis Lee - Pretty Little Angel Eyes
10. Buzz Clifford - Baby Sittin' Boogie
11. Jive Five - My True Story
12. Kokomo - Asia Minor
13. Cathy Jean & The Roommates -Please Love Me Forever
14. Jarmels - A Little Bit Of Soap
15. Ramrods - Ghost Riders In The Sky
16. Dreamlovers - When We Get Married

16 Great 'Lost 45's' From 1961

1. Rama Lama Ding Dong - The Edsels
2. Tonight I Fell In Love - The Tokens
3. Girl of My Best Friend - Ral Donner
4. I Just Don't Understand - Ann- Margret
5. You Can Have Her - Roy Hamilton
6. Angel on My Shoulder - Shelby Flint
7. You're The Reason - Bobby Edwards
8. Little Devil - Neil Sedaka
9. Good Time Baby - Bobby Rydell
10. Bumble Boogie - B. Bumble & The Stingers
11. My Kind of Girl - Matt Monroe
12. C'est Si Bon - Conway Twitty
13. Baby Blue - Echoes
14. Johnny Willow - Fred Darien
15. Sacred - Castells
16. Once In A While - The Chimes

1. Hit The Road Jack - Ray Charles
2. Please Mr. Postman - Marvelettes
3. Shop Around - The Miracles
4. The Boll Weevil Song - Brook Benton
5. Stand By Me - Ben E. King
6. Ya Ya - Lee Dorsey
7. Every Beat Of My Heart - Gladys Knight & The Pips
8. Spanish Harlem - Ben E. King
9. Unchain My Heart - Ray Charles
10. Gee Whiz - Carla Thomas
11. Gypsy Woman - Impressions
12. Look In My Eyes - Chantels
13. Please Stay - Drifters
14. It's Gonna Work Out Fine -Ike & Tina Turner
15. Revenge - Brook Benton
16. I Count The Tears - Drifters

1. The Lion Sleeps Tonight - Tokens
2. Blue Moon - Marcels
3. Pony Time - Chubby Checker
4. Quarter To Three - Gary U.S. Bonds
5. Let's Twist Again - Chubby Checker
6. Bristol Stomp - Dovells
7. I Like It Like That - Chris Kenner
8. Who Put The Bomp -Barry Mann
9. Runaround Sue - Dion
10. The Fly - Chubby Checker
11. Baby Sittin' Boogie - Buzz Clifford
12. Let The Four Winds Blow - Fats Domino
13. Rama Lama Ding Dong - Edsels
14. Barbara Ann – Regents
15. Heart & Soul - Jan & Dean
16. Tonight I Fell In Love - Tokens

60's DEAD MUSIC STARS (AND HOW OLD THEY WOULD BE, HAD THEY LIVED as of the end of 2009)

60's Music Artist	Birthdate	Age had they lived
Louis Armstrong	8/4/01	108
Brook Benton	9/19/31	78
Sonny Bono	2/16/35	74
James Brown	5/3/28	81
Johnny Burnette	3/25/34	75
Johnny Cash	2/26/32	77
Ray Charles	9/23/30	79
Patsy Cline	9/8/32	77
Nat King Cole	3/17/17	92
Sam Cooke	1/2/31	78
Bobby Darin	5/14/36	73
Mama Cass Elliot	9/19/41	68
Percy Faith	4/7/08	101
Marvin Gaye	4/2/39	70
Maurice Gibb	12/22/49	60
George Harrison	2/24/43	66
Jimi Hendrix	11/27/42	67
Johnny Horton	4/30/25	84
Burl Ives	6/14/09	100
Bert Kaempfert	10/16/23	86
John Lennon	10/9/40	69
Dean Martin	6/17/17	92
Roger Miller	1/2/36	73
Keith Moon	8/23/47	62
Jim Morrison	12/8/43	66
Rick Nelson	5/8/40	69
Roy Orbison	4/23/36	73
Wilson Pickett	3/18/41	68
Gene Pitney	2/17/41	68
Elvis Presley	1/8/35	74
Lou Rawls	12/1/35	74
Otis Redding	9/9/41	68
Jim Reeves	8/20/24	85
Charlie Rich	12/14/32	77
Marty Robbins	9/26/25	83
Del Shannon	12/30/34	75
Frank Sinatra	12/12/15	94
Dusty Springfield	4/16/39	70
Conway Twitty	9/1/33	76
Dinah Washington	8/29/24	85
Mary Wells	5/13/43	66
Carl Wilson	12/21/46	63
Dennis Wilson	12/4/44	65
Jackie Wilson	6/9/34	75
Frank Zappa	12/21/40	69

♫ This singer had two major hits inspired by movies in the year he was killed by a drunk driver!

♫ This number one Elvis Presley hit was originally a hit in 1927!

♫ This hit was the shortest number one hit single of the rock era!

♫ This hit was written by the Big Bopper and became a number one hit a year after he was killed in a plane crash!

♫ This number one hit returned to the charts two years later to top the charts again!

♫ Hoagy Carmichael wrote this song 30 years before it became a number one hit for Ray Charles!

FIND OUT THAT...and MUCH MORE...INSIDE...1960!

1. **Theme From 'A Summer Place'** by Percy Faith was not only the number one hit of the year, but also the top instrumental of the entire 60's decade. This hit was from the movie which starred Sandra Dee, Troy Donahue, Dorothy McGuire and Richard Egan. Toronto born Percy Faith learned to play the violin when he was seven years old. He died in 1976, the same year he released a disco version of 'A Summer Place'.

2. **Are You Lonesome Tonight** was one of Elvis Presley's biggest hits. This song was a hit originally back in 1927 for Vaughn Duleath and in 1950 for Al Jolson.

3. **It's Now or Never** by Elvis Presley was recorded at the same session as 'Are You Lonesome Tonight'. According to the Guinness Book Of World Records, it was Elvis Presley's biggest selling single with sales topping 20 million. The song was based on 'O Solo Mio', an Italian song written in 1901.

4. **Cathy's Clown** was the Everly Brothers first hit on the new label, Warner Brothers. It also became their biggest selling hit. The brothers from Brownie, Kentucky wrote this multi-week number one hit.

5. **Stuck on You** was Elvis Presley's first new recording since he was discharged from the army on March 5th. RCA racked up over one million advance orders of the record, which was the highest advance of any single to date.

6. **Save The Last Dance For Me** was a number one hit for The Drifters in the same year lead singer Ben E. King embarked on a solo career. This song

was written by Doc Pomus and Mort Shuman, who wrote over a dozen hits for Elvis Presley. This classic hit was produced by the legendary Jerry Leiber and Mike Stoller.

7. **The Twist** by Chubby Checker reached number one in 1960 and again in 1962 when there were several 'Twist' hits on the charts. The song was written and originally recorded by Hank Ballard.

8. **Running Bear** was a number one hit for Johnny Preston almost a year after its writer and producer J.P. Richardson, a .k a. The Big Bopper was killed in a plane crash with Buddy Holly and Ritchie Valens. The Big Bopper and Country singer George Jones supplied the 'oom pah pah' Indian chant in the background as Johnny Preston sang about the Indian brave 'Running Bear'.

9. **El Paso** by Marty Robbins was the first number one hit of the 60's and the longest song to go to number one up until that date. Marty Robbins wrote this song about the city he was fascinated with, even as a child growing up in a state that borders El Paso; - Arizona.

10. **I'm Sorry** was Brenda Lee's biggest hit of all and was cut at the tail end of a recording session, with just five minutes of recording time left. It was one of the first sessions in Nashville to use strings.

11. **Stay** by Maurice Williams and The Zodiacs, which became the shortest number one single of the Rock era, was a huge multi-week number one hit. The song later became a hit for the Four Seasons and in the 70's for Jackson Browne. Maurice Williams previously fronted the Gladiolas and wrote and originally recorded 'Little Darlin' which became a million seller for The Diamonds.

12. **Everybody's Somebody's Fool** was the first number one hit for Connie Francis, one of the most successful female vocalists of the early 60's along with Brenda Lee. This song was written by Neil Sedaka's songwriting partner Howard Greenfield who also co-wrote 'Stupid Cupid' and 'Where the Boys Are'.

13. **Itsy Bitsy Teenie Weenie Yellow Polka Dot Bikini** was the first and biggest hit for a then-16 year old high school student by the name of Brian Hyland. The song was a true story co-written by Paul Vance about his two year old daughter running around in her polka dot bikini. With co-writer Lee Pockriss, it was recorded and went to number one…but just barely.

14. **Alley Oop** was a number one hit for the Hollywood Argyles, inspired by the caveman comic strip of the same name. The song was co-produced by group member Gary Paxton, who was previously 'Flip' of the duo Skip and Flip of 'It Was I' and 'Cherry Pie' fame. This song was written by Dallas Frazier who later wrote hits like 'Mohair Sam' for Charlie Rich and 'Elvira' for the Oak Ridge Boys.

15. **Teen Angel** by Mark Dinning was one of the first teen tragedy songs of the 60's. Others that followed in the early 60's included 'Tell Laura I Love Her' by Ray Peterson, 'Last Kiss' by J. Frank Wilson and 'Ebony Eyes' by the Everly Brothers.

16. **Georgia on My Mind** was Ray Charles' first number one hit. It was a song from 1930 co-written by Hoagy Carmichael. It is now the official song for the state of Georgia.

17. **My Heart Has a Mind Of Its Own** by Connie Francis was written by Howard Greenfield and Jack Keller, who wrote several of her biggest hits. This hit replaced 'The Twist' by Chubby Checker in the number one position.

18. **Why** was a number one hit for Frankie Avalon, who was not only a singer, but an actor as well. While 'Why' was riding the charts, Frankie was off on location in Texas filming the movie 'The Alamo' with John Wayne.

19. **I Want to Be Wanted** by Brenda Lee was a song that originated in Italy where it was included in the original production of 'Never On Sunday'. This was Brenda Lee's second number one hit of 1960.

20. **Mr. Custer** by Larry Verne was a novelty hit about a soldier's plea to Mr. Custer that he didn't want to fight in the battle that was fought at Little Big Horn on June 25, 1876. It was Larry Verne's only hit.

21. **Only The Lonely** was Roy Orbison's first major hit. He was born in Vernon, Texas on April 23rd 1936 and died of a heart attack on December 6, 1988, while he was on the charts as a member of the Traveling Wilburys.

22. **Walk Don't Run** by the Ventures was one of the classic guitar instrumentals of the rock era. This hit fell just short of reaching number one. The Ventures released a new version of this tune in 1964 and it reached the top ten again.

23. **Puppy Love** was Paul Anka's first hit of the 60's. The song was inspired by his on tour affair with Annette Funicello who recorded his song 'Train of Love' the same year. Donny Osmond had a big hit with this song in 1972.

24. **Last Date** was the first and biggest hit for pianist Floyd Cramer, one of Nashville's most sought after session players.

25. **Handy Man** was the first of only two big hits Jimmy Jones charted, both in 1960. In the late 70's James Taylor had a slowed-down hit version of this song.

26. **Greenfields** was a soft, folk-pop song by the Brothers Four who were fraternity brothers at the University of Washington. The song was written in 1956 by Terry Gilkyson and the Easy Riders.

27. **He'll Have to Go** was the biggest hit for Jim Reeves, and a number one song for 14 weeks on the Country charts in 1960. He had aspirations of a professional baseball career which was cut short because of an ankle injury. Jim Reeves died in a plane crash in the summer of 1964 at the age of 39.

28. **Poetry in Motion** was the first of a string of hits for Johnny Tillotson, whose other hits included 'It Keeps Right On A-Hurtin', 'Heartaches By The Number' and 'Talk Back Trembling Lips'.

29. **Chain Gang** was one of 29 top 40 hits Sam Cooke achieved from 1957 to 1965. He was born Samuel Cook, but added the 'e' to his last name because he thought it added a touch of class. He was one of seven children of Annie Mae and the Reverend Charles Cook, a Baptist Minister.

30. **Wild One** was Bobby Rydell's biggest hit and his first of the 60's. Philadelphia's Bobby Rydell also appeared in the film 'Bye Bye Birdie'. The 'B' side of 'Wild One' was 'Little Bitty Girl', which was also a hit.

31. **Sixteen Reasons** was a hit for Connie Stevens at the time she was starring as Cricket Blake on TV's 'Hawaiian Eye'. She appeared in several movies and was married to Eddie Fisher. She also accompanied Edd Byrnes of '77 Sunset Strip' fame on the million selling 'Kookie, Kookie Lend Me Your Comb'.

32. **Sink the Bismarck** was one of three major hits for Johnny Horton, a Country singer born in Los Angeles and raised in Tyler, Texas. He was married to Billie Jean Jones, the widow of Hank Williams. This song was inspired by the movie starring Kenneth Moore, which is based on the sinking of the German battleship in World War 2.

33. **A Thousand Stars** was a big hit for Kathy Young and The Innocents and was recorded when she was only 14 years old. This song was originally recorded as an R & B hit in 1954.

34. **Where or When** was Dion's final top ten hit with the Belmonts. He began his solo career with 'Lonely Teenager' later that same year. 'Where or When' was a Rodgers & Hart composition from the 1937 musical 'Babes In Arms'.

35. **Way Down Yonder in New Orleans** by Freddy Cannon was originally a jazz song written in 1922. He got the nickname 'Boom Boom' from the big bass drum-sound on his records.

36. **You Talk Too Much** was the only hit for New Orleans' singer/pianist Joe Jones. He later produced hits for the Dixie Cups, including their number one hit 'Chapel of Love.'

37. **North to Alaska** was the third and final major hit for Johnny Horton, who was killed by a drunk driver a month after this song peaked on the charts. He was 35 years old when he died on November 5th, 1960. This was the title song from the movie starring John Wayne. It was a number one Country hit for 5 weeks in 1960.

38. **Good Timin'** was the second of two million sellers for Jimmy Jones in a five month span. He would never have any top 40 hits after his exclusive two from 1960.

39. **Volare** by Bobby Rydell was a faster-paced, hipper version of Domenico Modugno's 'Nel Blu Dipinto Di Blu', a multi-week number one hit in 1958.

40. **Sweet Nothin's** was the very first hit for Little Miss Dynamite, Brenda Lee. This song was written by Ronnie Self, who also wrote her next hit 'I'm Sorry', which reached number one. Brenda Lee received a Lifetime Achievement Grammy Award in February 2009.

41. **What in the World's Come Over You** was a top ten hit for Jack Scott, a Canadian from Windsor, Ontario. Two of his four singles in 1960 (his final year in the top forty), reached the top ten.

42. **Night** was a classic piece revived by the charismatic Jackie Wilson from his heyday. In 1960 alone, he charted seven top forty hits.

43. **Because They're Young** was the final hit by 'twangy' guitar instrumentalist Duane Eddy to reach the top ten. It was the title song of the movie which starred Tuesday Weld, James Darren and Dick Clark.

44. **Burning Bridges** was the final top ten hit for Jack Scott. The vocal group 'The Chantones' provided the backing on all of his hits.

45. **Go Jimmy Go** was a bright and bouncy hit for Jimmy Clanton, who also starred in the 1958 Rock and Roll movie 'Go Johnny Go', produced by Alan Freed.

46. **New Orleans** was the first of a string of 'party' hits for Gary U.S. Bonds. Gary was Jacksonville, Florida born Gary Anderson.

47. **He'll Have to Stay** by Jeanne Black was the 'answer' song to 'He'll Have to Go' by Jim Reeves. This was Jeanne Black's only pop hit.

48. **A Million to One** was the only hit for New Jersey's Jimmy Charles, an R & B singer who won the Apollo Amateur contest in 1958. Donny Osmond had a hit with this song in 1973.

49. **Devil or Angel** was Bobby Vee's first top 40 hit. It was originally an R & B hit for the Clovers in 1956.

272

50. **Sailor (Your Home Is the Sea)** was one of the surprise hits of 1960 from a one name, one hit wonder from Vienna, Austria known as Lolita. This hit by Lolita Ditta reached the top 5 in the fall of 1960.

51. **Mule Skinner Blues** was the Fendermen's only hit and it was taken from the original Jimmy Rodgers songbook, written in 1931. The Fendermen were a duo from Wisconsin who formed while attending University together.

52. **Paper Roses** was a hit for Anita Bryant two years after she was 2nd runner-up in the Miss America competition. She later became known for her strong opposition to homosexuality and for being the spokesperson for the Florida Citrus Commission in television commercials. 'Paper Roses' was an equally big hit for Marie Osmond in 1973.

53. **Baby (You've got What It Takes)** was the first of two top ten hits which Brook Benton and Dinah Washington recorded together. This hit was number one on the R & B charts for an incredible 10 weeks.

54. **It's Time to Cry** was a top ten hit for Paul Anka at the very beginning of 1960, and was one of dozens he also composed.

55. **Beyond the Sea** was Bobby Darin's follow up to his biggest hit of all time, 'Mack The Knife'. This very similar style hit was taken from the 1945 French song 'La Mer' and introduced to North American audiences by Benny Goodman in 1948.

56. **Walkin' to New Orleans** was the final official top ten hit by Fats Domino, the legendary singer/songwriter/pianist from New Orleans. He was the winner of the Grammy Hall Of Fame Award and Lifetime Achievement Award in 1987.

57. **Mission Bell** was the only major hit for Donnie Brooks, who was born John Faircloth in Dallas, Texas and raised in Ventura, California. He used several different names before settling on Donnie Brooks, including Dick Bush, Johnny Faire and Johnny Jordan. He died in 2007 at age 71.

58. **Image of a Girl** was a hit by the one hit wonder group The Safaris from Los Angeles, California. They are not to be confused with the group 'Surfaris', known for their hit 'Wipeout'.

59. **Swingin' School** was one of six top 20 hits for Bobby Rydell in 1960, his second year on the charts. This song was from the movie 'Because they're Young'.

60. **Let's Go, Let's Go, Let's Go** was the biggest hit for Hank Ballard and The Midnighters, although 'Finger Poppin' Time' was a close second. Ballard wrote and recorded 'The Twist' before Chubby Checker made a career out of it. Hank Ballard also charted 'The Twist' in 1960, but Checker brought it to number one.

61. **The Old Lamplighter** was a top ten hit for the family act The Browns, led by Jim Ed Brown. This song was originally a hit in 1946 for Sammy Kaye's orchestra.

62. **He Will Break Your Heart** was the first official top ten hit for 'the Ice Man', Jerry Butler. This was a hit again in 1975 when Tony Orlando & Dawn brought it to number one as 'He Don't Love You (Like I Do).'

63. **Finger Poppin' Time** was a top ten Grammy nominated hit for Hank Ballard & the Midnighters from Detroit, Michigan. Ballard was inducted into the Rock And Roll Hall Of Fame in 1990. He died at age 74 in 2003.

64. **Let It Be Me** was a beautiful ballad by The Everly Brothers backed by the Archie Bleyer Orchestra. Originally a French song, a version with English lyrics was introduced by Jill Corey in 1957. Four years later, Jerry Butler and Betty Everett brought it to the top ten again.

65. **Lonely Blue Boy** was Conway Twitty's final top ten hit on the Pop charts. He became a Country music superstar after his Pop music career ended. 'Lonely Blue Boy' was originally recorded as 'Danny' by Elvis Presley in the movie 'King Creole'.

66. **Let the Little Girl Dance** was the only notable hit for R & B singer Billy Bland from Wilmington, North Carolina. He was in the studio when Titus Turner was singing this song and Billy wanted to show him how to sing it. The demonstration was recorded by producer Henry Glover, who released it as a single.

67. **Tell Laura I Love Her** was the first of two top ten hits for Ray Peterson in 1960. This was a teen tragedy song co-written by Jeff Barry, who later went on to co-write hits which included 'Leader Of The Pack', 'Chapel Of Love' 'Then He Kissed Me', 'Sugar Sugar' and many others. Ray Peterson died of cancer in 2005 at age 69.

68. **Let's Think about Living** by Country singer Bob Luman, was a hit the same year he was drafted into the U.S. Army. The song was his comment about the 'death song' fad of 1960. He died of pneumonia in 1987 at the age of 41.

69. **Love you So** was an almost hypnotic hit for Ron Holden, an R & B singer from Seattle, Washington. It was his only top 40 hit.

70. **Kiddio** was a top ten hit in the summer of 1960 for Brook Benton. The song was originally featured in the 1957 film 'Mister Rock And Roll' starring Alan Freed, when Teddy Randazzo sang it. The 'B' side of this single 'The Same One' was also a hit.

71. **Cradle of Love** was Johnny Preston's follow up to his biggest hit 'Running Bear'. He was discovered by J.P.Richardson, a.k.a. The Big Bopper, who wrote his first hit.

72. **Footsteps** was a top ten hit for singer/actor Steve Lawrence, who also recorded many hits with his wife Eydie Gorme. One of Steve's most memorable acting roles was portraying blackmailed manager Maury Sline with John Belushi in the 1980 film 'The Blues Brothers'.

73. **Among My Souvenirs** by Connie Francis was a top ten hit in 1960. Back in 1928, there were four top 20 hit versions of this song.

74. **You're Sixteen** was the biggest hit for Johnny Burnette in the same year as his debut with 'Dreamin'. His older brother Dorsey Burnette was also popular in the early 60's. Johnny Burnette died in the summer of 1964 at the age of 30 as a result of a boating accident on Clear Lake in California.

75. **Please Help Me I'm Falling** by Hank Locklin was number one on the Country charts for an incredible 14 weeks in 1960. Up until his death at 91 in March of 2009, he was the oldest living member of the Grand Ole Opry.

76. **When Will I Be Loved** was an Everly Brothers original written by Phil Everly. 15 years later, in 1975, Linda Ronstadt revived the song and her version was even bigger on the charts than the Everlys' original.

77. **A Rockin' Good Way (To Mess Around and Fall In Love)** was the second top ten duet in 1960 for Brook Benton and Dinah Washington. Washington died 3 years later of an overdose of pills and alcohol at the age of 39. She was married seven times in her short life.

78. **Dreamin'** was Johnny Burnette's debut hit. The Johnny Mann singers provided backing vocals on his 5 hits from 1960 to '61.

79. **Many Tears Ago** by Connie Francis was popular during her most successful year on the pop charts when she had six top 20 hits including two number ones, 'Everybody's Somebody's Fool' and 'My Heart Has A Mind Of Its Own'.

80. **So Sad (To Watch Good Love Go Bad)** was the Everly Brothers' fourth top ten hit of 1960, their first year on the Warner Brothers label. This was a double-sided hit single which had a remake of Little Richard's 'Lucille' on the 'B' side.

81. **Harbor Lights** was the final top ten hit for the legendary 50's vocal group, the Platters. This song was a remake of a hit which had 5 top ten versions on the charts back in 1950.

82. **Pretty Blue Eyes** by Steve Lawrence, was co-written by Teddy Randazzo who also co-wrote two of the biggest hits for Little Anthony & The Imperials, 'Hurt So Bad' and 'Goin' Out Of My Head'. Randazzo also starred in the rock films 'Rock, Rock, Rock' and 'Mr. Rock And Roll'.

83. **My Home Town** by Paul Anka may have been referring to where he grew up in Canada's Capitol City of Ottawa, Ontario. In 1960, Anka also wrote hits for both Annette Funicello and Connie Francis.

84. **Wonderful World** by Sam Cooke surprisingly did not reach the top ten, despite its popularity. This timeless song was written by Sam Cooke, Lou Adler and Herb Alpert. It was a hit in the mid-sixties by Herman's Hermits and in the 70's by James Taylor with Simon and Garfunkel.

85. **Stairway to Heaven** by Neil Sedaka was his first hit of the 60's and his follow up to 1959's 'Oh Carol', a song he wrote for Carole King. This was one of several 60's hits he wrote with Howard Greenfield. The only similarity this song has with the Led Zeppelin hit of the same name is the title.

86. **Mama** by Connie Francis was an Italian song written in 1941, with English lyrics added in 1946. The 'B' side of this single, 'Teddy', written by Paul Anka, reached the top 20.

87. **Alone At Last** by Jackie Wilson was actually based on Tchaikovsky's 'Piano Concerto in B flat'. It was Jackie's second top 10 hit of 1960 and one of five top 20 hits he charted that year.

88. **Theme From the Apartment** was the instrumental theme by Ferrante And Teicher of the Billy Wilder film which starred Jack Lemmon and Shirley MacLaine.

89. **Cherry Pie** was a hit for Skip and Flip. Flip was Gary Paxton, who formed the Hollywood Argyles of 'Alley Oop' fame and then he started his record label Garpax, which 'Monster Mash' was recorded on.

90. **Blue Angel** was Roy Orbison's follow up to his first top ten hit 'Only the Lonely'. Roy Orbison once said in an interview that all of his biggest hits were written in 30 to 40 minutes.

91. **The Village of St. Bernadette** was a hit for easy listening music star Andy Williams, who had a string of middle-of-the-road hits during the 50's and 60's and several popular Christmas albums during that era. Andy Williams also had his own variety show from 1962 - 1967 and again from 1969 - 1971.

92. **Yogi** was a hit for one wonder trio the Ivy Three, who formed while attending College. The song was inspired by the Yogi Bear cartoon character from television.

93. **Happy Go Lucky Me** was a fun hit, complete with crazy laughter for singer/songwriter Paul Evans, best known for his hit 'Seven Little Girls Sittin' In The Backseat' from 1959. Paul Evans wrote 'When' for the Kalin Twins and 'Roses Are Red (My Love) for Bobby Vinton.

94. **Forever** by the Little Dippers, were actually the uncredited Anita Kerr Singers. They sang backup on dozens of major hits in the 60's by Roy Orbison, Brenda Lee, Pat Boone, Jim Reeves and many others.

95. **White Silver Sands** was an instrumental hit by Bill Black's Combo. Bass guitarist Bill Black was a very successful session player on many recordings, including the early hits of Elvis Presley. Sadly, Bill Black died of a brain tumor shortly before his 40th birthday.

96. **I Love the Way You Love** was one of only two top hits achieved by Marv Johnson, both in 1960. This R & B singer/songwriter/pianist was born in Detroit and discovered by Motown founder Berry Gordy Jr. He died in 1993 at the age of 54 after collapsing on stage at a concert in South Carolina.

97. **That's All You Gotta Do** by Brenda Lee was written by a then-unknown singer/actor/guitarist Jerry Reed who had top ten hits of his own over ten years later with 'Amos Moses' and 'When You're Hot, You're Hot'.

98. **You Got What It Takes** by Marv Johnson was co-written by Motown boss Berry Gordy Jr. Marv worked in sales and promotion for Motown during the 70's. A faster-paced 'You Got What It Takes' was revived by the Dave Clark Five in 1967.

99. **In My Little Corner Of The World** was Anita Bryant's follow up to her biggest hit 'Paper Roses' and her only other hit to reach the top ten. In 1958, at the age of 18 she was Miss Oklahoma.

100. **Sleep** was a hit for Little Willie John, an R & B singer who was convicted of manslaughter in 1966 and died in prison in 1968 as a result of an apparent heart attack. Little Willie John also had two hits in 1956, 'Fever' which was made famous by Peggy Lee and 'Talk To Me, Talk To Me' which was covered in 1963 by Sunny & The Sunglows.

101. **Lonely Teenager** was Dion's first hit without the Belmonts. They formed in 1958 and had seven top 40 hits before parting ways in 1960. Dion was inducted into the Rock And Roll Hall of Fame In 1989.

102. **Pineapple Princess** was Annette Funicello's final top 40 hit. She was best known as the most popular member of The Mouseketeers beginning in the late 50's.

103. **Step By Step** by the Crests featured Johnny Maestro on lead vocals. This was their second biggest hit next to 'Sixteen Candles' from the year before.

277

104. **The Hucklebuck** was another dance hit for the 'Twist' King, Chubby Checker. This song was actually written in 1949 and was a top ten hit for both Frank Sinatra and Tommy Dorsey.

105. **Sway** was a popular hit for Philadelphia's Bobby Rydell in his most successful year on the pop charts, 1960. This song was a remake of a song Dean Martin had a hit with in 1954. The flip side , 'Groovy Tonight' was also a hit.

106. **Perfidia** was the Ventures' follow up to their signature hit instrumental 'Walk Don't Run', also from 1960. 'Perfidia' was a remake of a tune which charted five different versions in 1941.

107. **Young Emotions** didn't quite reach the top 10 for Rick Nelson in 1960 when he failed to chart any songs in the top 10. The previous year, 1959, he charted four and the following year in 1961 he charted two.

108. **(You Were Made For)All My Love/A Woman, A Lover, A Friend** was a double sided hit single for Jackie Wilson, who died at the age of 49 in 1984 after having a stroke nine years earlier in 1975.

109. **Down by the Station** was a hit for the Four Preps, a group that formed while at Hollywood High School. They had bigger hits with '26 Miles (Santa Catalina)' and 'Big Man' during the late 50's. Group member Glen Larson later became a successful TV Producer. He went on to produce, write and create TV's 'Battlestar Galactica' and 'Knight Rider'.

110. **Tracy's Theme** was the only instrumental hit for Spencer Ross, who is actually conductor/arranger Robert Mersey. This hit came from the TV drama special 'The Philadelphia Story' from late 1959.

111. **O Dio Mio** was a top ten hit for Annette Funicello three years before she began her movie career in the Beach Party movies with Frankie Avalon.

112. **Don't Be Cruel** was an instrumental hit for Bill Black's Combo. Bass guitar session player Bill Black played on the original recording by Elvis Presley back in 1956.

113. **Summer's Gone** was another hit for singer/songwriter teen idol Paul Anka in 1960. He had many hits from 1957 to 1962, but had a dry spell of no top 40 hits from 1963 through 1968.His next number one hit came in 1974 with '(You're) Having My Baby'.

114. **My Girl Josephine** was a hit for the legendary singer/pianist from New Orleans, Fats Domino. Domino co-wrote most of his own hits with composer Dave Bartholomew.

115. **Feel So Fine** was the third and final hit for Johnny Preston, who charted all of his hits in 1960. This song was originally a hit on the R & B charts in 1955 by Shirley and Lee.

116. **Lady Luck** was a moderate hit by Lloyd Price who had 3 big hits the year before with 'Stagger Lee', 'Personality' and 'I'm Gonna Get Married'. He failed to chart any hits in the top 20 after 1960.

117. **Doggin' Around** was another hit for Jackie Wilson in 1960. In 2004, 20 years after his death, Rolling Stone Magazine ranked him #68 on their list of the 100 Greatest Music Artists of all Time.

118. **Sandy** was the only hit for Cincinnati-born Larry Hall. He died at the age of 57 in September of 1997.

119. **Beatnik Fly** was a hit for Johnny and The Hurricanes, a Rock And Roll Instrumental group from Toledo, Ohio. Leader Johnny Pociak was the saxophone player. This was the fourth and final top hit for Johnny and The Hurricanes, whose previous hits, including 'Red River Rock' were all popular in 1959.

120. **Three Nights a Week** was a top 20 hit for Fats Domino, born Antoine Domino on February 26, 1928. His first hit was titled 'The Fat Man'. His final hit to reach the top 20 was 'Let the Four Winds Blow' in 1961.

121. **Over the Rainbow** by the pop vocal group the Demensions, was a remake of the classic song from 1939's 'The Wizard Of Oz' sung by Judy Garland.

122. **Look for a Star** was a hit for both Gary Miles and Gary Mills, two different singers with very similar names. The song was from the movie 'Circus of Horrors' which starred Donald Pleasance.

123. **Midnite Special** was a 1960 hit for singer/songwriter Paul Evans. It was originally an R & B hit in 1948. It was a hit later by Johnny Rivers and was also recorded by C.C.R. as an album cut.

124. **The Same One** was a hit for Brook Benton, whose real name was Benjamin Franklin Peay. He died at the age of 56 in 1988 as a result of complications from spinal meningitis.

125. **This Magic Moment** by the Drifters featured Ben E. King on lead vocals. This song was later made popular in 1969 by Jay & The Americans when it became even more successful.

126. **You Mean Everything to Me/Run Samson Run** was a double sided hit single for Neil Sedaka. It was popular between his 1960 hits 'Stairway to Heaven' and 'Calendar Girl'.

127. **Smokie - part 2** was the first hit for Bill Black's Combo from their most successful year on the charts. Previous to 1960, he played bass on many of the hits of Elvis Presley and other well known music artists.

128. **Lonely Weekends** was the first hit for Charlie Rich. His style on this hit was closer to Elvis Presley's than the Country style he was later associated with. The Gene Lowry Chorus backed him up on this up tempo hit.

129. **Rockin' Little Angel** was a rockabilly hit for Kentucky born Ray Smith. He later moved to Canada and committed suicide in 1979 at the age of 45.

130. **Fame and Fortune** was the moderately successful 'B' side to Elvis Presley's month long number one hit 'Stuck on You'. Both songs were recorded 15 days after Elvis Presley's Army discharge.

131. **Diamonds and Pearls** was the only hit for the Paradons, an R & B group from Bakersfield, California.

132. **Won't You Come Home Bill Bailey** by Bobby Darin was originally a hit in 1902 for Arthur Collins. The 'B' side of this single was 'I'll Be There' which became a hit for Gerry & the Pacemakers four years later.

133. **First Name Initial** was recorded by Annette Funicello when she was only 16 years old. The former Mouseketeer and Beach Party movie star was diagnosed with muscular sclerosis in 1987.

134. **Trouble in Paradise** was the final top 20 hit for the Crests, featuring Johnny Maestro, who resurfaced in the late 60's as the voice of the Brooklyn Bridge.

135. **Artificial Flowers** was a hit for Bobby Darin the year he married Actress Sandra Dee. This song was from the musical 'Tenderloin' starring Eileen Rodgers.

136. **(You've Got To) Move Two Mountains** was the third and final top 20 hit in 1960 for Marv Johnson in his exclusive year in the top 20.

137. **Money (That's What I Want)** by Barrett Strong, was one of the very first hits for Motown. The Beatles later recorded this song. Barrett Strong later went on to write many Motown hits with Norman Whitfield, including many of the hits of the Temptations.

138. **(There was a) Tall Oak Tree** featured the deep, rich voice of Dorsey Burnette, the brother of Johnny Burnette. Like Johnny, Dorsey also died too soon. He died of a heart attack in 1979 at the age of 46.

280

139. **Another Sleepless Night** by Jimmy Clanton was one of three hits he recorded which were written by Neil Sedaka. Jimmy was born in Baton Rouge, Louisiana and had 7 top 40 hits from 1958's 'Just a Dream' to 1962's 'Venus In Blue Jeans'.

140. **Like Strangers** was the 6th single released by the Everly Brothers in 1960. Their biggest was 'Cathy's Clown', their first on their new label 'Warner Brothers'.

141. **I'll Save the Last Dance for You** was Damita Jo's answer song to the Drifters' 'Save the Last Dance for Me'. The following year, she had a hit with 'I'll Be There', the answer song to Ben E. King's 'Stand by me'.

142. **The Madison** was a hit for Al Brown's Tunetoppers, featuring Cookie Brown. This was their only hit during the rock era.

143. **Hello Young Lovers** was one of the few non-originals by Paul Anka. This song was from the musical 'The King and I', starring Yul Brynner.

144. **Shimmy Shimmy Ko-Ko Bop** was a hit for Little Anthony & The Imperials. They were inducted into the Rock And Roll Hall of Fame in 2009.

145. **Pennies from Heaven** by The Skyliners, featuring Jimmy Beaumont on lead vocals was originally a number one hit in 1936 by Bing Crosby.

146. **Fools Rush In** by Brook Benton was a remake of a Glenn Miller hit from 1940. Rick Nelson revived it again in 1963 and brought it to the top 20.

147. **Lucky Devil** was a hit for Carl Dobkins Jr., whose only other top 40 hit was 'My Heart Is An Open Book', a top 5 hit in 1959. 'Junior' was added to his name when he started singing at age 16.

148. **Hot Rod Lincoln** was a hit by both Johnny Bond and Charlie Ryan in 1960. The first time the song was a hit was in 1951 by Tiny Hill. It became a top ten hit in 1972 by Commander Cody & His Lost Planet Airmen.

149. **Big Iron** was Marty Robbins' follow up to his number one hit 'El Paso' from earlier in 1960. This song was top 5 on the Country charts.

150. **A Fool in Love** was the very first charted top 40 hit for Ike and Tina Turner. They were inducted into the Rock and Roll Hall of Fame in 1991. Their rocky marriage was chronicled in the film 'What's Love Got to Do With It'. Tina went on to have a very successful solo career. Ike Turner died in 2008.

151. **Mountain Of Love** by Mississippi-born and Memphis raised singer Harold Dorman, was the original version of a song Johnny Rivers made famous in 1964. This was Harold Dorman's only hit. He died in 1988 at the age of 62.

152. **Clap Your Hands** was a goodtime, party hit for Canadian group the Beau Marks.

153. **Let's Have a Party** was a hit for Country/rockabilly singer/songwriter/guitarist Wanda Jackson. She toured with Elvis Presley from 1956 to 1957, and this song was introduced by him as 'Party' in his film 'Loving You'. Gene Vincent's Blue Caps provided the backing on this hit.

154. **When You Wish upon A Star** was a hit for Dion And The Belmonts. It was inspired by the version from the Disney animated film 'Pinocchio. It was a number one hit for Glenn Miller in 1940.

155. **Clementine** by Bobby Darin, was written back in 1884 as 'My Darling Clementine'. The 60's cartoon character 'Huckleberry Hound' would sing this song frequently on the popular TV cartoon back then.

156. **Angela Jones** was the only hit for Nashville born Johnny Ferguson, who worked as a Radio DJ in the late 50's. This song was written by John D. Loudermilk, who wrote many hits of the 60's, including all four hits by Sue Thompson.

157. **Barbara** was a moderate hit for another group known as the Temptations. This group was a white quartet from Flushing, New York. Motown's Temptations didn't have their first hit until four years later in 1964.

158. **Bonnie Came Back** was a hit for Duane Eddy, the master of the 'twangy' guitar. This instrumental was the traditional Scottish tune 'My Bonnie Lies over the Ocean'.

159. **Ooh Poo Pah Doo Part 2** was the only top 40 hit for New Orleans R & B singer/drummer/pianist Jessie Hill, formerly of the group Huey 'Piano' Smith in the late 50's.

160. **Tonight's The Night** was the Shirelles very first hit. This girl group from Passiac, New Jersey followed this hit with 'Will You Love Me Tomorrow', the first number one hit written by Carole King and Gerry Goffin.

More Hits of 1960

I Really Don't Want to Know was the final hit for Tommy Edwards. This song was originally a hit for Les Paul and Mary Ford in 1954. Elvis Presley recorded it in the 70's.

Mr. Lucky by composer/arranger/conductor Henry Mancini was the theme of the TV series which starred John Vivyan

To Each His Own was one of the last hits for the Platters during their

282

heyday. There were three #1 versions of this song in 1946.

T.L.C.(Tender Love and Care) by Jimmie Rodgers was his last hit for a period of six years, when he would return with 'Child Of Clay' in 1967.

Am I That Easy to Forget was a hit for singer/actress Debbie Reynolds. This song by the mother of actress Carrie Fisher, was popular the year after she divorced Eddie Fisher. This song was later a hit for Engelbert Humperdinck.

Shortnin' Bread was the only hit for Paul Chaplain, a singer from Webster, Massachusetts. This was a traditional song that was written in the early 1900's.

Peter Gunn by Duane Eddy was the theme of the TV series which starred Craig Stevens. This instrumental was composed by Henry Mancini, who wrote dozens of movie themes back then.

Top 16 Albums of 1960

1. The Sound Of Music - Original Cast
2. The Button-Down Mind Of Bob Newhart - Bob Newhart
3. G. I. Blues - Elvis Presley
4. Persuasive Percussion - Enoch Light/Terry Snyder & All Stars
5. Sold Out - Kingston Trio
6. String Along - Kingston Trio
7. Nice 'N Easy - Frank Sinatra
8. Theme From A Summer Place - Billy Vaughn
9. The Lord's Prayer - Mormon Tabernacle Choir
10. Mr. Lucky - Henry Mancini
11. Heavenly - Johnny Mathis
12. Here We Go Again - Kingston Trio
13. 60 Years Of Music America Loves Best - Various Artists
14. Elvis Is Back - Elvis Presley
15. For The First Time - Mario Lanza
16. Bongos - Los Admiradores

Top 16 Country Hits of 1960

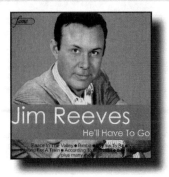

1. He'll Have To Go - Jim Reeves
2. Please Help Me I'm Falling - Hank Locklin
3. Alabam - Cowboy Copas
4. Wings Of A Dove - Ferlin Husky
5. Above And Beyond - Buck Owens
6. Big Iron - Marty Robbins
7. Cathy's Clown - Everly Brothers
8. Let's Think About Livin' - Bob Luman
9. Another - Roy Drusky
10. Each Moment Spent With You - Ernest Ashworth
11. Sink The Bismarck - Johnny Horton
12. Stuck On You - Elvis Presley
13. Scarlet Ribbons - The Browns
14. Hot Rod Lincoln - Charlie Ryan
15. He'll Have To Stay - Jeanne Black
16. Honky Tonk Girl - Loretta Lynn

Top 16 One Hit Wonders Of 1960

1. Maurice Williams & The Zodiacs - Stay
2. Mark Dinning - Teen Angel
3. Hollywood Argyles - Alley Oop
4. Larry Verne - Mr. Custer
5. Joe Jones - You Talk Too Much
6. Fendermen - Mule Skinner Blues
7. Billy Bland - Let The Little Girl Dance
8. Lolita - Sailor
9. Ron Holden - Love You So
10. Bob Luman - Let's Think About Livin'
11. Larry Hall - Sandy
12. Paradons - Diamonds And Pearls
13. Gary Miles - Look For A Star
14. Safaris - Image Of A Girl
15. Al Brown's Tunetopper's - The Madison
16. Ivy Three - Yogi

16 Great 'Lost' 45's from 1960

1. Look For A Star - Gary Miles
2. (There Was A) Tall Oak Tree - Dorsey Burnette
3. Lonely Weekends - Charlie Rich
4. Sandy - Larry Hall
5. Sleep - Little Willie John
6. (You've Got To) Move Two Mountains - Marv Johnson
7. Rockin' Little Angel - Ray Smith
8. The Madison - Al Brown's Tunetoppers
9. Step By Step - The Crests
10. Lucky Devil - Carl Dobkins Jr.
11. Happy Go Lucky Me - Paul Evans
12. Stairway To Heaven - Neil Sedaka
13. Cradle Of Love - Johnny Preston
14. Run Samson Run - Neil Sedaka
15. Shortnin' Bread - Paul Chaplain
16. The Angels Listened In - The Crests

287

The Top 16 R & B/Soul Hits of 1960

1. Save The Last Dance For Me - The Drifters
2. Chain Gang - Sam Cooke
3. You Talk Too Much - Joe Jones
4. Night - Jackie Wilson
5. Baby (You've Got What It Takes) - Brook Benton & Dinah Washington
6. Walkin' To New Orleans - Fats Domino
7. He Will Break Your Heart - Jerry Butler
8. Kiddio - Brook Benton
9. A Rockin' Good Way - Brook Benton & Dinah Washington
10. Alone At Last - Jackie Wilson
11. Wonderful World - Sam Cooke
12. You Got What It Takes - Marv Johnson
13. Doggin' Around - Jackie Wilson
14. Money (That's What I Want) - Barrett Strong
15. Fools Rush In - Brook Benton
16. A Fool In Love - Ike & Tina Turner

The Top 16 Dance/Party Hits of 1960

1. The Twist - Chubby Checker
2. Alley Oop - Hollywood Argyles
3. Itsy Bitsy Teenie Weenie…Bikini - Brian Hyland
4. Go Jimmy Go - Jimmy Clanton
5. New Orleans - Gary U.S. Bonds
6. Let's Go Let's Go Let's Go - Hank Ballard & The Midnighters
7. Finger Poppin' Time - Hank Ballard & The Midnighters
8. Let The Little Girl Dance - Billy Bland
9. You're 16 - Johnny Burnette
10. A Rockin' Good Way - Brook Benton & Dinah Washington
11. Yogi - Ivy Three
12. Wonderful World - Sam Cooke
13. The Hucklebuck - Chubby Checker
14. Money (That's What I Want) - Barrett Strong
15. Shimmy Shimmy Ko-Ko-Bop - Little Anthony & The Imperials
16. Sway - Bobby Rydell

About the author

Ted Yates is an on air radio broadcaster with over 35 years behind the microphone. Most of his radio years have also been spent programming the music and writing radio features and specials, as well as creating music countdowns. Ted is an expert on the hits of the 60's and his love for the decade began when they were new hits during his childhood years.

Ted has interviewed over a hundred well known celebrities including 60's music artists Ringo Starr, Paul Anka, Bobby Vinton, Peter Noone of Herman's Hermits, Mark Volman of The Turtles, Bruce Johnston of The Beach Boys, Del Shannon, Gary Lewis, Bobby Vee, Martha Reeves and many more!

Ted's hobby is music, music and music and now he wants to share his vast knowledge with you in one incredible book about the hits of the 60's and the fascinating facts you'll find both interesting and sometimes surprising!

About the Accompanying CD

The attached CD includes interviews by author Ted Yates with:

Paul Anka, Bobby Vee, Bruce Johnston, Del Shannon, Bobby Vinton, Burton Cummings, Denny Doherty, Bo Diddley, Gary Lewis, Jay Siegel, Otis Williams, Pat Boone, Johnny Mathis, Petter Noone, Reg Presley, and Ringo Starr.